Introduction to Political Economy

Introduction to Political Economy
Sixth Edition

Charles Sackrey, Geoffrey Schneider,
and Janet Knoedler

with contributions by Hans Jensen

ISBN 978-1-878585-93-6

Economic Affairs Bureau publishes *Dollars & Sense*, a bimonthly magazine. *Dollars & Sense* explains the workings of the U.S. and international economies and provides progressive perspectives on current economic affairs. It is edited and produced by a collective of economists, journalists, and activists who are committed to social justice and economic democracy.

Economic Affairs Bureau also publishes the following classroom books: *Real World Macro, Real World Micro, Current Economic Issues, Real World Globalization, Real World Banking and Finance, The Environment in Crisis, Striking a Balance: Work, Family, Life, Grassroots Journalism, Real World Latin America, Real World Labor, The Economic Crisis Reader, Real World Latin America,* and *Unlevel Playing Fields: Understanding Wage Inequality and Discrimination.*

For more information, contact:

Dollars & Sense
29 Winter Street
Boston, MA 02108
(617) 447-2177
www.dollarsandsense.org

Cover design by David Gerratt
Back Cover illustration by James Schneider
Design and production by Kate Davies and Chris Sturr

Printed by Lightning Source Printing (lightningsource.com).

Printed in U.S.A.

Table of Contents

Preface to the Sixth Edition

We have written this book to introduce our readers to what we are calling "political economy." We want to distinguish this kind of economics from the "mainstream" of economics that dominates instruction in contemporary capitalist societies. If you are taking an economics course at almost any U.S. university or college, your teacher has almost certainly assigned you a textbook from what we call the economic mainstream. In the most general terms, how are these two traditions, political economy and mainstream economics, different from each other? We can begin an answer with a passage from one of the very few contemporary textbooks that gives attention to them both.

> Political economy…is more concerned [than mainstream economics] with the relationships of the economic system and its institutions to the rest of society and social development. It is sensitive to the influence of non-economic factors such as political and social institutions, morality, and ideology in determining economic events. It thus has a *much broader focus* than [mainstream] economics. (Riddell, Shackelford, Stamos and Schneider, 2009, emphasis added)

A bit of historical background will help to make sense of this passage. What we are calling "political economy" was first fully developed in the work of Adam Smith, whose 1776 book, *The Wealth of Nations*, contained a fabulously rich combination of theoretical analysis, historical setting, and copious detail. Smith took into account anything and everything that caught his attention, and to read *The Wealth of Nations* is to discover the broad outlines, and countless details, of British life in the late 18th century. For most of the next century, people studying the economy, among the most prominent of whom were Karl Marx and Thorstein Veblen, followed Smith's lead. They produced broadly cast arguments in which there were no predictable boundaries limiting the kinds of knowledge taken into account. While Marx and Veblen, and other such political economists, clearly focused attention on economic activity—how people produced their livelihood and how they divided it up—they roamed far and wide in looking for ideas and information that would help them to explain what they saw.

However, after the middle of the 19th century, more and more social scientists adopted a version of the "scientific method," borrowed from physical scientists such as physicists, chemists, and biologists. Successes in these scientific fields starting in the 16th century had enticed social theorists into taking a scientific approach to their studies, and this was certainly true of economists. By the 20th century, and especially after 1950, economics increasingly came to be expressed in the terms of mathematics and statistics. Presently, the economics profession is dominated, as are the graduate schools that produce professional economists, by economists who exclude from their analyses most of those things that are not readily measurable or appropriate for quantitative model building.

As the discipline has been narrowed, it has pushed to the margin alternative schools of economics, especially political economy. Political economists who, as Riddell, Shackelford, Stamos, and Schneider put it, are "sensitive to the influence of non-economic factors such as political and social institutions, morality, and ideology in determining economic events," have gradually found their work shunned by the major economics journals, often because it is considered to be "non-economic." From our view, the most unfortunate consequence of this trend is that the ideas of writers like Marx and Veblen, and others who extended their work, are rarely studied by graduate students in economics. Correspondingly, when they become professors they teach these important ideas less frequently.

To try to bridge this gap, we have written this book. In this sixth edition, we have done a major revision of much of the book in order to take account of key economic events in the world during the two years that have passed since the previous edition. Most especially, we have made more current those parts of the book that concern the international economic crisis that was just on the horizon when we published our last edition, the continuing effects of globalization on economic activity everywhere, and the growing threat of climate change. We think this new information, important in its own terms, will also attest to the continuing value of the ideas of the writers whose ideas we review and assess.

In our initial chapter, we provide our readers a more detailed look at political economy by comparing its essential ideas and concepts to those of the economic mainstream. We follow this first chapter with three on the central writers in the political economy tradition, Smith, Marx, and Veblen, whose ideas, as we shall see, provide the structural frame for the rest of the book. In Chapter 5, we take up the ideas of John Maynard Keynes, whose work in the 1930s on the booms and busts of modern capitalist societies revolutionized the way economists understand capitalism and the measures necessary to keep it from collapsing. Keynes, who actually straddled the fence between political economy and mainstream theorizing, shared with political economists the practice of casting an exceedingly broad net for useful facts and ideas in his work. Though he had little use for Marx's writings, he often indirectly legitimated political economy by using his grand and eloquent voice to criticize mainstream economists for the narrowness of their studies.

We follow the first five chapters, ones that focus mostly on systems of thought, with four that analyze the impact of these ideas on our own world. In Chapter 6 we describe and analyze social classes in U.S. capitalism, in part because they are a central aspect of all political economy analyses of capitalism. We also discuss social classes because they are crucial to how capitalism shapes our lives, and, as we shall see, because they are virtually ignored by mainstream economics. We then turn in Chapter 7 to the theory of "social balance," developed by John Kenneth Galbraith to describe how corporations cajole and bamboozle us into buying goods and services we don't need, while environmental pollution spreads wider and deeper, and the public sector—the infrastructure—is in a continuing decline. Chapter 8 shows how Marx's ideas were extended to current times in the theory of "monopoly capital" advanced in the 1960s by Paul Baran and Paul Sweezy. These two economists used Marx's key idea of "surplus value" to try to understand what they ultimately called "the irrational system" of U.S. capitalism.

In Chapter 9 we describe the modern welfare state in Sweden, which has been shaped by political economists in that country for over a century. To study the Swedish economy is to catch a glimpse of life in a society where the public understanding of capitalism, how it works, and how it should work, has been influenced more by ideas from political economy than by those from the economic mainstream. In the final chapter, we discuss another exemplary case study of these ideas put into action in the form of the Mondragón Cooperative Corporation (MCC), the world's largest conglomeration of cooperative-run businesses, located in Spain's Basque Country. MCC is notable for several things, most especially that it is a huge and expanding global firm owned completely by it workers, and for its commitment to maintaining an alternative economic model in the age of globalized capitalism.

The sequence of chapters we have chosen here has proven helpful to us in teaching the book to undergraduates, yet we suggest that others use the sequence that makes the most sense for their own courses. In order to encourage readers to go through the book in various kinds of ways, we have written each chapter to work mostly independently of the others. A consequence of this independence is that our readers will find some repetition as they go along. However, we have tried to limit this repetition to information or concepts that can bear a second going over. If our readers are assigned this book alongside a typical mainstream textbook, they can judge for themselves which approach, or which combination of approaches, works best to help them understand the economic world in which most will spend a lifetime trying to making a living.

Acknowledgements

We have a number of thanks to pass on. First are to those colleagues who read earlier drafts of these chapters and gave us good reasons to rewrite parts of each. These helpful critics are: Teresa Amott, Dennis Baumwoll, John Boylan, Lou Casimir, Steve Cohn, Tom Kinnaman, John Kirkland, Catherine O'Connor, Cadwell Ray, Eric Ruckh, Paul Susman, and Amy Wolaver. Ellen Campbell helped to write and to edit the essay on the modern Swedish economy, and a special thanks is due to Hans E. Jensen, professor emeritus at the University of Tennessee, who wrote the essay that formed the basis for our chapter on Adam Smith. Laurie Dougherty provided us with a fine editing of the first edition, and Terry Allen gave us excellent production and design assistance with past editions.

Finally, we want to extend our appreciation to the editors at *Dollars & Sense*, the publishers of the book. Alejandro Reuss provided valuable comments on this and previous editions. For this edition, we were especially fortunate to have as the principal editor Chris Sturr, who worked with us from day one as we went through the revisions. Chris is also a political economist, and in countless ways he helped us better to express what we were trying to say. He was knowledgeable and straightforward enough on several occasions to let us know where our interpretations of historical events, or of the ideas we were describing, were either wrong or misleading. No writer could ask for better help from an editor. Thanks, Chris!

1

The Political Economy Challenge to Mainstream Economics

Discussions of contemporary capitalism have long been dominated by one line of thinking, which we will define below as the "mainstream" of economics. This mainstream has either ignored, or labored to discount, alternative ways of thinking about the economy, such as those that we described in our preface and that fill up this book. A major consequence of the mainstream refusal to take up alternative ways of seeing the economy is that most students taking economics courses in the United States today will not hear about them. We hope that this chapter will provide a good argument for our readers to push ahead to see what mainstream economists have been hiding from them.

WHAT IS MAINSTREAM ECONOMICS?

Like all areas of social inquiry the mainstream school of economics constitutes a broad spectrum of often-conflicting ideas. Thus, when we refer to "mainstream economists," we are necessarily lumping them into a single category that is an obvious distortion, much like that of any such categorization. Our critique in this chapter refers mostly—but not exclusively—to economic models that (1) are narrowly conceived, (2) are quantitative and expressed in complicated mathematical terms, and (3) depend upon certain restrictive assumptions about how people behave, always have behaved, and always will behave. Without question, there are mainstream economists who engage in lively debates on virtually all of the topics we take up in this chapter. Many of them move beyond the strict confines of models and assumptions to examine institutional aspects of the economy. And many empirically investigate people's actual behavior, instead of assuming that they all behave in the same, predictable way.

Why, then, do we focus on those mainstream economists who most narrowly conceive the subject? There are two parts to our answer. The first is that this subset of economists dominates contemporary economics and exercises its dominance through its almost exclusive control over graduate training in economics and the most prestigious economics journals. It is also the subset that has produced all but a few of the Nobel Prize winners in economics. The second reason for our focus is that, of all schools of economic thought we know about, this one is *least* likely to produce results useful to the public. Therefore, a genuinely interesting irony underlies what we write about in this chapter: the very "best" economists, in the view of this dominating subset, produce some of the least useful kinds of economics. We recognize that this is a substantial conclusion, and we hope that reading this and the following chapters will lead our readers to consider it at least as reasonable.

A central part of our argument is that there is a critical distinction between *all* versions of mainstream economics and what we call political economy. This distinction is a matter of methodology, or "method of analysis." Mainstream economists are trained to limit the scope of their analyses— that is to limit the breadth of knowledge they bring to bear on an issue— much more than so than do political economists. In choosing a relatively narrow focus, almost all mainstream economists have gradually and systematically excluded from their studies the political economy point of view. The political economy critique presented here is both a general critique of the mainstream methodology, and a more specific critique of the subset of mainstream economics that is most narrow in its approach.

THE DIFFERENCE BETWEEN THE MAINSTREAM AND ALTERNATIVES

Let's consider the following example that demonstrates the wide chasm between mainstream economics and Marxist economics, a principal kind of political economy. How does each view the production of business profits in capitalism? A mainstream economist might put it like this:

Profits are the payoff to private individuals for "entrepreneurship," for having saved, or borrowed, funds to invest in productive inputs, for having the foresight to know what goods or services to produce with these inputs and the talent to manage how the inputs are used and the goods marketed. Profit-making is the central vehicle by which capitalism is energized because: (1) by investing the funds, producing the goods, and making the profits, the enterprising capitalist gives jobs to people who are not capitalists themselves and who need those jobs in order to live; (2) the capitalist will make the highest profits only by producing goods and services most demanded by consumers; and (3) it is the competitive quest for profits that gives capitalism its extraordinary dynamism and proven ability to drive from the field all competing economic systems.

On the other hand, in the Marxist view, profit is looked upon in this different sort of way:

Over the past 400 years, through its drive to accumulate profits, the capitalist class—by pillage (such as the enclosure movements), murder (wars against and systematic impoverishment of Third World nations), and domination (of workers, consumers, and the political process)—has come to own the resources, factories, and other capital equipment needed to produce goods and services needed by all. Prior to the emergence of capitalism, most people were peasants who owned enough agricultural tools to produce a livelihood. Further, aside from land owned by great landowners like the church and the crown, most land was owned in common. However, gradually they were stripped of these goods, and in order to live they necessarily became wage-workers for capitalists. At their jobs, workers must produce a value greater than their wage, and this excess is called surplus value. This value, created by labor, is seized by the owner and becomes the owner's profits. Competitive pressures generate the dynamic energy of the system and force capitalists to treat their workers as *things*, commodities to be bought and sold like steel ingots or sheets of plywood. Such pressures also shape many capitalists into predators working against the best interests of the larger society.

It is almost as if two different species of beings were talking about two different worlds. How can such great divisions of opinion exist between economists when they take a look at something as central to capitalism as the profits that fuel it?

POLITICAL ECONOMY: A GENERAL DESCRIPTION

To describe political economy, in the way that we use the term (and there other schools of thought within the mainstream framework that describe it differently), we will repeat the one we used in the Preface:

Political economy...is more concerned [than mainstream economics] with the relationships of the economic system and its institutions to the rest of society and social development. It is sensitive to the influence of non-economic factors such as political and social institutions, morality, and ideology in determining economic events. It thus has a *much broader focus* than [mainstream] economics. (Riddell, Shackelford, and Stamos 1998, emphasis added)

Among those who now work in this political economy tradition, as we have described it, there is a variety of differing, often competing, notions about how capitalism works and which way it is heading. Even though there are important distinctions among them, we are able to talk in the same breath about differing schools of thought in political economy because they agree on the following critical points:

1. Although most mainstream economists claim that they are doing "economic science," their work all too often fails to explain and predict actual events in the real world—an essential test of any scientific work.
2. A principal reason for this inability to explain real events is the restrictive assumption of "economic man" in mainstream economics, along with a parallel assumption that human beings by nature have unlimited wants for consumer goods.
3. Mainstream models are typically not presented in the historical context that shapes all human events. Furthermore, most mainstream economists have not studied the history of economic ideas, and thus are unaware that the principal assumptions of their analyses have been challenged by political economists for over two centuries.
4. Mainstream economists typically presume a separation between economic activity and political power.
5. Graduate economic programs are largely confined to mainstream instruction, and a particularly narrow version of that school of thought.

ECONOMICS: THE SCIENCE THAT IS NOT SCIENTIFIC

The debate about methodology between the mainstream and political economists has been going on for a long time. The history of this dispute starts at least as early as the fifteenth and sixteenth century in Europe, when essentially religious explanations of the universe gradually gave way to scientific ones, and with stupendous effects on the world. Columbus' voyage to the New World, Galileo's telescope, Harvey's findings about blood circulation, and Newton's discovery of certain laws of gravity—along with many similarly astounding discoveries in the seventeenth and eighteenth centuries—made inevitable the declining influence of non-scientific explanations of the world. This scientific assault on alternative explanations of human beings and their universe continued, and of course, continues now.

The horrific conditions for many workers crowding into European cities since the early eighteenth century led to the development of a new practical science, public health. The public health movement led governments to promote the habits of healthier living and, especially, to construct systems to protect water systems from sewage. This movement was complemented greatly by the discoveries in the nineteenth century of Louis Pasteur and others unveiling the role of invisible bacteria in the spread of disease. Together, public health and biological science led to a dramatic increase in the life span in industrializing nations after the late nineteenth century. The average life expectancy in the United States in 1776 was about 35 years; it was about 50 years in 1900; and by the year 2010, it had reached about 78 years. Research done by the Museum of Natural History shows that, "From 1900 to 1990 we have gained about 25 years of life expectancy; nearly equal to what had been obtained in the preceding 5000 years of human history!"

The success of physical scientists in describing the world and improving the quality and length of life in industrialized countries led others to imitate their work. Economists in particular tried to design regular, law-like models for social phenomena. It is true that in the case of the two most influential economists of the eighteenth and nineteenth centuries, Adam Smith and Karl Marx, the former wrote without mathematics, and Marx confined his quantitative analysis to a few simple algebraic notations. However, by the late nineteenth century most economists had adopted some version of the "scientific method" as their approach and, in doing so, marshaled the economics profession toward mathematics and statistics.

Also during the nineteenth century, economists borrowed the idea of "equilibrium" from physics. In doing so, economists made an extraordinary leap of faith about their ability to study and predict human activity. When social theorists use the idea of equilibrium in model building, they are implying that patterns of human life in a fundamental way are analogous to, say, the equilibrating balance of forces in our solar system that keeps Mars from ramming us head on. That is, this idea presumes that the economy is typically *stable*, and when buffeted, will always return to stability on its own. A critical implication here is that, if the economy is assumed to be stable and self-correcting, it is better to allow it to function on its own, without extensive government interference. Equilibrating systems, whether among the planets or in people's activity, suggested to Adam Smith and to many economists after him, that they were "natural," and this meant they were "God's work." Smith also believed that individuals possessed a natural self-interest that would lead to "the best of all possible worlds," an idea whose modern embodiment we will take up in detail later on.

Alfred Marshall, an influential British economist writing in the late nineteenth century, was particularly important to the shift from imprecise economic language to the precision of quantitative models that incorporated the idea of equilibrium. Though Marshall warned that "economics cannot be compared with the exact physical sciences," he still believed that economics was specially "advantaged" over the other social sciences. He argued:

> [A] person's motives . . . can be approximately measured by the sum of money, which he will just give up in order to secure a desired satisfaction; or again by the sum which is just required to induce him to undergo a certain fatigue. (Quoted in Riddell, Shackelford, and Stamos 1998, 8)

This means that the prices we pay for products, the amount we invest to try to make profits, and the wage that will induce us to go to work, are all *numbers*, that is *quantities* that can be manipulated by mathematics and analyzed by economists. Marshall and most of his contemporaries thought that the focus of economists should be the prices that emerge in what he called "the ordinary business of life." This meant, for example, learning how self-interested individuals established prices for products, labor (wages), and money (interest rates) in competitive markets.

Marshall and his contemporaries recognized the aggregate economy as cyclical; however, they also thought it was actually formed by all the individual markets added together, and essentially behaved no differently than would a single one of them. Competitive markets were thought to work with equilibrating precision, and in the hands of Marshall supply and demand, acting as "two blades of the same pair of scissors," were the prime determinants of market price.

Complementing Marshall's system, and developing along with it, was the work of economists who saw markets as driven by "marginal" decisions made by producers, consumers, and workers, that is decisions about whether to produce an additional unit of production, to purchase an additional item of consumption, or to work an additional unit of labor time. In this theoretical world, capitalists made decisions by projecting the revenue and cost—thus also the profit—of the next marginal unit to be produced; and consumers behaved in terms of the marginal satisfaction anticipated from a product measured against its marginal cost. Some practitioners of this sort of analysis, who were called "marginalists," even imagined a system of mathematical notations incorporating the marginal decisions of all economic actors into one giant quantitative model.

The marginalists, in focusing a microscope on the margin of economic actions, were especially important in prompting economists to think narrowly, an ironic consequence of their desire to explain everything with a single giant model. Their method implied the fateful idea that the institutional structure of capitalism outside individual markets, such as its system of social classes and the distribution of income and power, was not within the scope of economics. Marginal analysis also implied an extremely limited role for government. If the system was the outcome of a limitless number of individual marginal decisions made in self-regulating markets, then the thick fist of the government could not be expected to solve any economic problem.

In 1879, Marshall published the prototype for the modern economics textbook, which he called *Industry and Trade*. By 1890, he was calling his book *Principles of Economics*, and in this version, the geometric models of supply and demand that all principles students must now learn appeared as footnotes. Though Marshall kept the diagrams in his footnotes, economists who followed with their own principles texts gradually moved the diagrams from the footnotes up to the text where they came to dominate. Thus began the joyful birth, or sad decline, depending on your point of view, of twentieth-century economics.

Further leading to quantification of economics was the theorizing of the British economist, John Maynard Keynes. In his revolutionizing book *The General Theory of Employment, Interest, and Money* Keynes used geometry, mathematics, and compelling and elegant prose to revolutionize the way that modern economists think about the business cycle. Keynes' work gradually won over most economists in the capitalist world. He preferred a dense prose to mathematics or geometry as a way to express his economic theories, and he differed crucially from almost all his predecessors by arguing that capitalism was not a self-equilibrating system. Nevertheless, Keynes' followers constructed diagrams and formulae to carry his theories forward, and these "macroeconomic" models, like the market analysis of Alfred Marshall and the marginalists, successfully lured more and more economists into the encapsulating and often suffocating web of a geometric world.

In 1948, Paul Samuelson of MIT, using his own two-volume mathematical expression of mainstream economics as a model, wrote the first widely used economics textbook. He combined Marshallian analysis, by then called "microeconomics," and Keynesian macroeconomics and called his book *Economics*. This title was, of course, greatly misleading given all the many kinds of economic analysis, most especially political economy, that he simply ignored. Samuelson, in updating his book over the years, gradually added considerable non-quantitative materials, but the geometric models and other quantitative materials that make up the theoretical core of mainstream economics remained central. Samuelson's amalgamation of microeconomics and macroeconomics has come to be called "neoclassical" economics, and within the economics profession, this term is the common way to describe mainstream economics.

Is this mainstream amalgamation actually doing *science*? To the critique that they have left too many crucial aspects of social life out of their models, mainstream economists typically respond with something like this: "Our assumptions might be unrealistic, and our models might be narrowly conceived, but they work better to predict economic behavior than the theories of our competitors." That is, the proof of models is how well they work.

Well, then, how well *do* they work? A good way to answer this key question is to compare the predictions made by economists to those made by *real* scientists. Consider the example of physicists. It is beyond dispute that they know some things, such as the laws of gravity, more or less for sure. Similarly, while medical doctors may differ on particular diagnoses, they know countless things with a high degree of certainty, such as specific physiological dimensions of, and limitations of, the human body. On the basis of highly predictable outcomes, physicists, medical doctors, and other real scientists have enabled human beings to live longer and utterly to transform their natural habitat. All these outcomes stem from a scientific method whereby scientists all over the world test hypotheses over and over again until there is wide-spread agreement about this or that aspect of the physical world, or in the case of medical scientists, this or that aspect of the human body.

Yet, and this is the point, there is nothing similar in the annals of economics, and there can never be a set of principles, models, theories, conclusions, or predictions comparable to those in the physical sciences on which economists base their methods of inquiry. We are not questioning whether mainstream economists work diligently and honestly, as real scientists do. Nonetheless, economists don't know with any degree of certainty what is going to happen in the next instance with respect to much of *anything*. And that is why they always disagree about virtually *everything*. To make the point, we've constructed below a list of central questions about how the capitalist economy operates. As you study economics, no matter what version of it, you will discover that *there is not now, nor has there ever been*, widespread agreement on the answers to these questions among people calling themselves economists:

- How should we measure the unemployment rate, and what will it be next month?
- Will the economy expand and grow over the next month, or over the next year?
- What will happen to total output if the government increases or reduces personal income taxes?
- How do you measure inflation, and how does it affect various people?
- What has caused capitalism to dominate its rivals? Is it economic freedom? Is it greed? Is it imperialism? Is it brilliant entrepreneurship? Is it the surplus value taken from the hands of workers and used to enrich capitalists and allow them to buy more machines, raw materials, labor-power and political influence?
- Why are people rich or poor in capitalism? Luck? Greed? Connections? Hard work and perseverance?
- Does free-market capitalism generate the kind of competition that forces firms to operate in society's long-run interest, or do firms, unregulated, run roughshod over workers, small rivals, consumers, and needy politicians, and promote environmental degradation?
- Is economic power distinct from political power; and if they are not distinct, how are they meshed? How do they affect wages, profits, laws regulating the economy, interest rates, prices, exports, and imports?
- Is a growth in GDP a good thing, or a bad thing?
- Is the Federal Reserve System a "neutral monitor" of monetary policy, or primarily concerned with protecting the interests of wealthy bondholders?
- Is a certain amount of unemployment a good thing for capitalism?
- Does capitalism "provide economic freedom directly [and] also promote political freedom" (Milton Friedman, 1963)? Or is advocating capitalism "like the elephant running through the chicken yard, yelling, 'Everyone for himself!'" (Lester Pearson, past Prime Minister of Canada, 1963)?

If you were to choose at random any professional economist in the world and ask that person any question on the list above, *there is no way to know in advance what his or her answer will be.* If this were true, for example, of the science of physics, who among us would be brave enough to stroll across a bridge or fly in an airplane?

ECONOMIC MAN IN MAINSTREAM THEORIZING

In the view of political economists, the unrealistic treatment of how people behave in capitalist societies is a critical flaw in mainstream economics. The essential assumption of neoclassical economics is that people are utterly selfish, pleasure-maximizing automatons who respond in predictable ways to all stimuli. This theoretical creature is called "economic man," or sometimes "rational man," and this man is not the kind of human being the rest of us would ever know or want to be.

On this point of human behavior and mainstream models, we can usefully turn to John Kenneth Galbraith, one of the most famous modern American political economists, and about whom there is a chapter in this book. Galbraith, a long-time critic of mainstream economics, wrote that the idea of economic man forms part of a rigid system of thought. According to him, this system:

> ...requires that the ultimately valid propositions of economics be essentially given, like the structure of neutrons, protons, atoms and molecules. Once fully discovered they are known forever. Unchanging also, it is held, is human motivation in a competitive market economy. Such fixed and permanent truths allow economists to view their subject as a science... From this closed intellectual exercise, which is fascinating to its participants, intruders and critics are excluded often by their own choice, as being technically unqualified. And, a more significant matter, so is the reality of economic life, which, alas, is not, in its varied disorder, suitable for mathematical replication. (Galbraith 1987, 284-5)

Along with Galbraith, we do not contest the idea that most human beings will try to serve their own long-term interests as well as they can. It is reasonable to assume that in capitalist societies, most of us will seek rewards from the marketplace, whatever our role in it. Yet this readily-observable fact can not help us to know, simply by looking at another human being, what he or she will do in the market *at the next moment.* It is the central practice of real scientists to experiment with the objects of their study until, in their labs, they come to know with some confidence what consistently will happen to Y if they change X? This is not what mainstream economists do because their subject is human behavior, something we have never been able to predict with the kind of confidence that makes real science possible. Therefore, while the scientists are doing science, economists are, as John Maynard Keynes argued, engaging in an exercise in logic based on assumptions that are adopted because they can be quantified, not because they are true or even sensible.

We want to make our point carefully here, so repetition is in order. We recognize that there are broad patterns of behavior in capitalist markets that are predictable. In fact, almost all of us order our individual worlds in terms of these patterns of behavior. However, to go from *broadly predictable* patterns of behavior to the assumption that all of us, all the time, have the knowledge, time, and inclination to maximize economic gains, carries us from reasonable observation to basing economic models on a badly distorted mirror of real human activity. For example, in order to predict consumer behavior, neoclassical models usually assume that all people have perfect information about all of the goods that they might want to buy, they know all of the prices and qualities involved, they know how much satisfaction they will receive from each product if they buy it, and they are completely rational and self-centered. These assumptions imply that when we shop we are not influenced by store displays or impulses that might interfere with the rational calculation of which good will bring the greatest satisfaction to us per dollar we spend. The assumptions also deny that some of us might actually buy more expensive or slightly lower-quality goods because they are produced under better environmental and labor conditions; that is, they ignore the idea that people might value justice, and not just pleasure. The mainstream view of how human beings shop in modern capitalist cultures is, to put the best light on it, quixotic.

There is a further problem here. In mainstream economics, economic man has also long been the idea of "man with unlimited wants." William Rohlf reveals this central assumption in his mainstream introductory text. As he argues:

> The fundamental problem facing individuals and societies alike is the fact that our wants exceed our capacity for satisfying those wants. (Rohlf 1998, 4.)

What is wrong with this statement? Notably, it is outside history: it is constructed for the sake of analysis rather than inferred from what human beings have actually done. As such, Rohlf bases the economic analysis that follows in his book on a "made-up" human being. Thorstein Veblen, whose ideas we will take up in a later chapter, recognized the failure of this model to explain the complicated ways in which people's desires are actually shaped. Veblen saw economic man as central to what he called "the hedonistic approach" to economics, his description of the central tradition in his own day. By using the term "hedonistic," Veblen meant that humans are looked upon as simple "pleasure machines," looking only to maximize their own happiness. In 1919, Veblen wrote that he saw actual human beings as "products of...hereditary traits and past experience cumulatively wrought out under a given body of traditions, eventualities, and material circumstances." (Veblen 1919)

What, then, do we think human beings actually are, for the purposes of studying their economic behavior? For an answer from political economy, we extend these comments from Veblen with some evidence from history.

ECONOMIC MAN AND HUMAN HISTORY

One of the most renowned economists of the twentieth century, Joseph Schumpeter, proclaimed that:

> What distinguishes the "scientific" economist from all other people who think, talk, and write about economic topics is a command of techniques that we class under three heads: history, statistics, and theory...Of these fundamental fields, economic history—which issues into and includes present-day facts—is by far the most important...If starting my work in economics afresh, I were told that I could study only one of these three but could have my choice, it would be economic history that I should choose. (Schumpeter 1954, 12)

History was an essential part of economic analysis, according to Schumpeter, for three reasons. First, a grounding in economic history allows the analyst to understand present economic activity as a key element in the evolutionary changes inherent to social life, and that today is but a single point in the life process; and all that makes up society will be different tomorrow. Second, historical analysis incorporates important institutional "data" that are often excluded from mainstream economic analysis. Finally, Schumpeter argued that those who fail to examine the historical record are likely to commit "fundamental errors" of analysis.

One of the more fundamental errors of mainstream economics has been to insist that the "hedonistic" tendencies of human beings were present from the dawn of time. In fact, the dominant role of these habits has developed in the relatively short era of world history since the rise of capitalism, mostly by those living after 1500 A.D. in Western Europe and North America. Adam Smith, by observing people in his own time, concluded that human beings "naturally" (which, to him, meant innately and God-given) made exchanges based on self-interested behavior. He subsequently decided that the "propensity to truck, barter and exchange"—to offer a good or service to someone else only in exchange for an equally valued good, service, or the equivalent in money—must also be a natural instinct. Moreover, Smith argued that the self-interested trader would only trade to become better off, due to the profit motive. Hence, transactions between humans in the capitalist age came to be seen as exchanges between two flinty-eyed, rationally-calculating, self-interested beings who were always looking to profit on any deal. Though Smith, in other writing, had argued that people were often motivated by other kinds of sentiment, his followers developed the model of human behavior that we have now, one that leaves little room for other human inclinations such as altruism, sentimentality, or a concern for justice.

Was self-interested exchange a "natural" tendency of humans? When Smith wrote in 1776, he was ignorant of, or ignored, the writings of those historians of the ancient world who had described a very different system of exchange in the economies of Greece and Rome. In these civilizations, exchange most often took the form of elaborate systems of reciprocity or redistribution. Ancient Babylon and Egypt both operated systems of redistribution whereby most of the produce of the nation was collected, recorded, and then placed in centralized storehouses. In lean times (to which these primarily agricultural civilizations were especially susceptible), the stored produce was not sold to the highest bidder, but redistributed to all of the citizens, be they peasant, weaver, or potter, according to their needs. These economies were organized along the lines of gigantic households, in which all members of the society were expected to make their contribution to the household and in turn to share in the nation's produce. The Biblical story of Joseph describes just such a redistributive system as well as the rationale for the redistribution based on collective capacities and collective needs, rather than individualistic exchange. Recall that the brothers of Joseph, after selling him into slavery years before, came to Egypt in hopes of asking for some of the stored grains so that they could survive the famine in their native land of Canaan. Joseph, in his capacity as manager of the Pharaoh's stores of grains, gave generously to his brothers, despite their mistreatment of him so many years earlier.

Other exchange often took place for honorific or social purposes, rather than for economic gain. Another Biblical example describes the honorific exchange between King Solomon of Israel and King Hiram of Tyre. Hiram offered Solomon all the cedar and fir trees that he needed for the temple he planned to build, and in exchange Solomon offered him wheat and oil. This was not economic exchange but an exchange of tributes. (1 Kings, 5) Economic historian Karl Polanyi described many such systems of reciprocity—for example, giving gifts of fruit to kin and receiving in return gifts of fish—which existed in pre-capitalist societies. Polanyi argued that this was not barter and trade, but rather a socially organized system of reciprocity, based on sharing with the rest of the community. To sum up, in *The Great Transformation*, Polanyi argued:

> [A]ll economic systems known to us up to the end of feudalism in Western Europe were organized either on the principles of reciprocity or redistribution, or householding, or some combination of the three....In this framework, the orderly production and distribution of goods was secured through a great variety of individual motives...Among these motives gain was not prominent. (Polanyi 1944, 55)

The obvious implication of Polanyi's point is that the mainstream argument—that self-interest and the instinct to barter and trade is a *natural* trait of human beings—is at odds with historical evidence. The most we can say is that self-interested behavior came to be rewarded in pecuniary terms during the short span of human history that has elapsed since the rise of capitalism, and that five hundred years of capitalism have probably reinforced self-interested behavior in ways that make it difficult to suppress. But the latter is a very different proposition than to argue that self-interest is inherent in human behavior. And, in some societies even thought most economic activity is carried out by private firms—such as in Sweden—public policy is nevertheless based upon such human motivation as generosity and reciprocity, rather than on the assumption that all people are greedy in all their transactions. Furthermore, as Adam Smith and others have argued, even those individuals who normally engaged in self-interested behavior often act selflessly on behalf of friends, family and the community.

Space does not allow us to tell the stories of how the first markets emerged and then became the ubiquitous markets of economic theory, or how the human yearning to be productive and creative came to be twisted into a labor-leisure tradeoff in modern economics. Suffice it to say that a careful study of history is an essential part of economic analysis and, to borrow an idea from philosopher George Santayana, we might say that economists who ignore history are doomed grievously to misinterpret it. Whether using the lessons of history in formulating present-day policies to make a better future, or testing the theories of modern economics against all of the learning of historians, history is indeed an essential part of the study of economics.

THE MYTHICAL SEPARATION IN THE MAINSTREAM BETWEEN ECONOMICS AND POLITICAL POWER

In addition to concluding that mainstream economics has peopled its models with creatures existing in a historical, psychological, and cultural vacuum, political economists are also highly critical of the mainstream presumption that economics is distinct from politics or power. As a typical example from one economic principles text (an example picked at random from a shelf of them), consider the following statement:

> How did the very wealthy get that way? Of the 400 people on the *Forbes* magazine list of the richest people in America (with an average wealth of about $500 million each), about one-fourth got rich through inheritance. The other three-fourths, such as Bill Gates of Microsoft, got rich through working, starting their own businesses, inventing new products, and so on. (Stockman 1999, 425)

In this excerpt and throughout his book, Stockman avoids mention of government, the legal system, or any other institutions related to political power that might have played a role in helping the Fortune 400 amass their wealth. In fact, wealth accumulates in any society, either from inheritance or some other way, *because the laws allow it to happen.* For instance, as recently as 1959 the highest federal marginal tax rate was *91%* for all personal income over $200,000! Since then, the laws have been changed, and in 2010 the highest marginal rate—for a couple's income over $373,000—was 35%. In other words, in 2010 the Fortune 400 are accumulating their wealth faster than in 1959 partly because lawmakers changed the laws on their behalf. By comparison, Sweden's welfare state provides all citizens, among other benefits, health care and schooling, and to pay for these benefits Swedes pay over *half* their income in the form of taxes. In the United States, the average tax rate is about 30%, meaning that we have a very different set of rules regarding how much wealth and income individuals keep for themselves and how much will be used for broader, social purposes.

Journalists Donald Bartlett and James Steele (in *America: Who Really Pays the Taxes?*, 1994) demonstrated the extent to which U.S. corporations are subsidized by governments through low or even nonexistent, taxes, and by direct subsidy payments. They discovered innumerable examples of this practice, such as government subsidies totaling over $100 million a year to McDonald's, M&M/Mars, and other companies marketing their goods abroad. In 1999, *Time* magazine updated this research and concluded that in 1997 corporations received almost $200 *billion* in subsidies from state, local, and federal agencies. This huge flow of government payments exemplifies the power of corporations to shape political decisions in their favor, a power that is denied to virtually all citizens except the very wealthy. When did *you* last impose your economic interests on a U.S. Senator or the President, as the owners of large corporations do on a regular basis?

Corporations are able to impose their agendas in this way partly because through their lobbyists they channel enormous sums of money to politicians. One effect of these payments in the past several decades has been lax enforcement of anti-monopoly laws by the anti-trust division of the U.S. Justice Department. Presidents Ronald Reagan, George Bush, Bill Clinton, George W. Bush, and Barack Obama, who in succession directed anti-trust policy, encouraged the marriage of mammoth corporations, such as the $170 billion merger between Exxon and one of its major rivals, Mobil Oil, and the one between Time/Warner and America Online, which created a $350 billion behemoth. Mergers of this order are sold to the public on the grounds that only giant conglomerates can provide the high-quality, low-priced goods for which we are supposed to clamor. Yet, mergers can as often as not mean less competition, higher prices, and a growing challenge to democratic rights in areas where they operate. The social consequences of allowing mergers and other forms of deregulation were exemplified most dramatically by the financial crisis of 2007-2010 where a long, successful lobbying effort led to the deregulation of certain activities of financial firms, and that led to the crisis and eventual deep recession.

Our point here is important if we are to distinguish adequately between mainstream economics and political economy. To the former, political power is most often considered part of the background institutional structure which is, as they put it, "taken as a given" and thus is left to political "scientists" or others to worry about. It is this determination to ignore the political consequences of concentrated economic power in capitalism that allows conservative mainstream economists such as Milton Friedman to argue that capitalism always "promotes political freedom." For their part, political economists see capitalism as *intrinsically political*: the capitalist workplace often is a rigid hierarchy of control, and the allegedly "neutral" government acts disproportionately—as even reasonably alert children now know—in the service of the rich and powerful.

Karl Marx suggested that the government in modern capitalist countries is "the executive committee of the capitalist class," that is, of the rich and the powerful. As you will likely discover in an economics principles course, income inequality is now greater in the United States than in any other advanced capitalist society, and it has consistently been among the most unequal for over two centuries. This is the case because our laws allow it. The political economist might explain why Bill Gates is worth $90 *billion*, while at the same time over *forty million* people in the United States do not have health insurance, in this way: powerful people and corporations have consistently led efforts in the United States to deny adequate health care to all citizens, while they have spent lavishly to ensure that lawmakers make rules of the capitalist game that allow individuals to accumulate vast fortunes. This political economy view is quite a different explanation from the theory of income distribution that Stockman suggests—the idea that most people get what they earn primarily through hard work and creativity.

THE SPREAD OF MAINSTREAM ECONOMICS AND ITS PROBLEMS WITH REALITY

Despite the many serious limitations of mainstream economics, it has maintained its dominance over economic thinking in the U.S., both off and on the campus. It's a cat with considerably more than nine lives, but the "Great Recession" of 2007-2010 proved once again that this body of quasi-scientific ideology cannot adequately explain the real world.

As we noted earlier, MIT economist Paul Samuelson fused Marshallian microeconomics with the macroeconomics of John Maynard Keynes to construct what he and others called a "neoclassical synthesis." He used this foundation to publish the first edition of a textbook called, simply, *Economics*, one that set the stage for the eventual dominance of mainstream economics over all its heterodox competitors. Its basic template also became the one used for almost all economic principles texts thereafter. The mind-numbing narrowness of this synthesis was surpassed only by the arrogance of its title, *Economics*, implying that everything that might legitimately be said about the subject was *inside the book*. In the first and later editions of the text Samuelson mentioned heterodox ideas rarely, and when he did it was usually in order to demean them (as we shall see).

Other influential textbook writers adopted a similar approach, ignoring or caricaturing heterodox ideas. For example, among the most popular principles texts through the 1960-1980 period was *Economics: Principles, Problems, Decisions*, by Edwin Mansfield, an expert on efficiency who consulted for such firms as Exxon and Mobil. As an example of Mansfield's dismissal of the relevance of heterodox economics, his 1974 version had 717 pages, and only four of them were dedicated to alternative ideas, with most of the language used as an opportunity to dismiss Marx. Mansfield later expanded to intermediate economics textbooks, and altogether he sold "several million copies [that were] adopted at over 1,000 U.S. colleges and universities, and were translated and widely used abroad." (University of Pennsylvania, *Almanac*, November 25, 1997) This flight from alternative economic ideas in textbooks imposed on students, and especially the flight from the ideas of Marx, occurred during the Cold War starting in the late 1940s and continuing until the late 1980s. It was likely safer to dismiss his ideas as those of the evil parent of communism than to see him, like much of the rest of the world, as a powerful social theorist and historian.

By 1980, Samuelson, responding to the kind of radical political economy that had begun to emerge in then turbulent 1960s, sank to banal sarcasm in his treatment of ideas outside his neoclassical synthesis. Of the 829 pages of that year's edition, sixteen were allocated to the "evolution of economic doctrines." He had this to say about the ideas of John Kenneth Galbraith, one of the most important heterodox economists of the 20th century:

> Galbraith's "criticism" cannot itself kill. But, it acts like a virus, softening the way for more deadly critiques by the New Left and its professional radical economists.

This comment was made two decades after Galbraith had written *The Affluent Society* (1958), where he argued prophetically that by championing "free" markets and limited government, mainstream economists were an important cause of the "social imbalance," by which we overwhelm our society with too many consumer goods and too few public ones. Samuelson also added a twelve-page appendix summarizing his view of the principal ideas in the thousands of pages of Marx's books, pamphlets, letters, and speeches. In the conclusion, he wrote that, "The use of Marxian categories did all too often addle the wits of those hoping to understand the realistic laws of motion of Western Economic Systems." Without question, these are the words of someone who, for all his cleverness, was badly misled by the idea that he was doing science, where economic laws are the equivalent of those in physics.

The flood of neoclassical texts that followed Samuelson's 1948 book cemented the overwhelming dominance of the mainstream version of economics in U.S. higher education. There were alternatives that came along, and there were many more textbooks in the specialized fields that included, or were based on, heterodox ideas. But the mainstream won the textbook war due to its control of graduate programs and economics departments, rather than the usefulness of its ideas. In the early 2000s the most popular mainstream principles textbook was *Essentials of Economics* by N. Gregory Mankiw. Its 2004 edition has 600 pages, mentions Marx on two of them, and completely ignores virtually every other heterodox luminary in the history of Western economic thought. Exemplifying the underlying market-worship in Mankiw's book, an all-pervasive prejudice that he clearly does not recognize, he writes that, "Although some of the arguments [for foreign trade restrictions] have some merit in some cases, *economists* believe that free trade is usually the better policy" (emphasis supplied). Heterodox economists have long documented the many negative effects of free trade, including the practice of international firms to seek out the cheapest possible wages no matter the effect on domestic and foreign labor markets, to ignore environmental regulations in countries that can't control them, and often to add dramatically to income inequality. Mankiw's combination of arrogance and ignorance is clear in his claim that to be an "economist" one must believe in free trade.

It is impossible to know for sure, but a reasonable guess is that well over 90% of all economic students in the United States are currently grilled in the mainstream of economics, and alternative views, at best, are tacked on along the way. The fact that the overwhelming majority of economics students in the United States will have learned about demand elasticity but not about Marx, Veblen, Galbraith, or the sharp criticism of quantitative economics made by Keynes, is brainwashing, no matter how you look at it.

THE FREE MARKET IDEOLOGY AND THE REAL WORLD

Because so much of mainstream economics is dream work, rather than plausible arguments based on what people actually do, its theories and models are bound at times to fail quite miserably. One of the most dramatic examples was the failure of mainstream economists to foresee the financial meltdown that began in 2005 and led to the deep recession beginning in 2007. Though there were many causes for this crisis, it began with the collapse of the U.S. financial markets, and that occurred in large part because of lack of adequate regulation of the financial industry.

As early as 1994, members of Congress and later some federal regulators called for stricter rules to deal with the huge growth in very complex financial instruments, especially those known as derivatives. In 1998, one such regulator, Brooksley Born, vigorously pressed for rules to regulate the derivatives market, but she met with stiff resistance from Robert Rubin, the Treasury Secretary, and Alan Greenspan, head of the Federal Reserve System (known as "the Fed"). Both were adamant that a federally regulated financial system could not possibly compete with the outcomes that they were certain would come from free markets. In holding this view, they were, of course, marching arm-in-arm with the majority of mainstream economists for whom deregulation is a crucial element in the path to free market utopia. In fact, two such economists, Myron Scholes and Robert Merton, won the 1997 Nobel Prize for Economic Science for creating a mathematical model for evaluating derivatives. Ironically, a principal reason given for awarding Scholes and Merton the prize was that their model had, "generated new types of financial instruments and facilitated more efficient risk management in society."

We will focus on the major player in this battle over regulation, Alan Greenspan, because he was an economist with mainstream, pro-market biases, and his role in this crisis was pivotal. His actions also provide cautionary evidence of what can happen when people with these ideas in their heads get real political power. As background experience to become head of the Fed, and thus the presumed neutral arbitrator of U.S. economic policy, Greenspan had been a financial consultant for thirty years before he joined the Fed. He was also a long-time fan of Ayn Rand, a defender of individualism and free market capitalism, and he has described himself as a "libertarian Republican." Along this libertarian way, he was an advisor to Richard Nixon, and was a corporate director for such giants as Aluminum Company of America (Alcoa); Automatic Data Processing, Inc.; Capital Cities/ABC, Inc.; J.P. Morgan & Co., Inc.; Mobil Corporation; and The Pittston Company.

This bundle of experiences apparently strengthened Greenspan's view that government regulation was to be resisted at all costs, and there is ample evidence that he was among the most important foes, if not *the most* important foe, of regulation of the financial markets during his time at the Fed. Key details of his role in the matter are supplied in an article entitled, "What Went Wrong," written by Anthony Faiola, Ellen Nakashima and Jill Drew (*Washington Post*, Oct. 15, 2008). They argue that while derivatives did not

THE POLITICAL ECONOMY CHALLENGE 21

trigger the collapse, their "proliferation, and uncertainty about their real values, accelerated the collapse of the [huge investment firms] and magnified the panic that has since crippled the global financial system." These writers suggest strongly that no one worked harder than Greenspan to keep derivatives from being regulated. In one 1998 meeting with Brooksley Born, when she said her agency was under attack for pushing for regulations of derivatives, Greenspan responded to her sharply and said, "Regulation of derivatives transactions that are privately negotiated by professionals is unnecessary. Regulation that serves no useful purpose hinders the efficiency of markets to enlarge standards of living." Arthur Levitt, who was head of the Securities and Exchange Commission and frequently met with Greenspan to discuss regulating derivatives said that, "The Fed was really adamantly opposed to any form of regulation whatsoever."

Ten years after dressing down Born, after the financial crisis had begun, Greenspan appeared in congressional hearings led by Henry Waxman, a Democrat from California. Here is how that exchange is reported by David Leonhardt in the *New York Times*, Oct. 23, 2008.

> Greenspan admitted fault in opposing regulation of derivatives and acknowledged that financial institutions didn't protect shareholders and investments as well as he expected. [Waxman asked him] "In other words, you found that your view of the world, your ideology, was not right, it was not working." "Absolutely, precisely," Greenspan replied. "You know, that's precisely the reason I was shocked, because I have been going for 40 years or more with very considerable evidence that it was working exceptionally well."

Things had, indeed, been going well for Alan Greenspan from 1968 to 1987 while he was consulting for investment firms and helping to direct huge capitalist firms. The good times continued for him during his years running the Fed, from 1987 to 2006. During that period, the economy mostly expanded, and though the truth of the matter is not known or knowable, Greenspan was given a good deal of the credit for that expansion. Corporations enjoyed growing profits and shared Greenspan's affection for deregulation; politicians found it easier to be elected with a growing economy; and the media had already started mixing up celebrity gossip with other news, and they became central to making Greenspan an economic hero. None of this cheering crowd, however, took a look at other things that were happening. And none of this crowd heeded the warnings of Marx, Veblen, Keynes, and Galbraith that market speculation regularly results in economic crises.

In fact, during Greenspan's tenure at the Fed real wages for workers remained virtually the same while the income of the corporate elite and other rich people skyrocketed. In those two decades, one of the two greatest *upward* redistributions of income occurred; as one consequence, the ratio of CEO salaries to the average wage of their workers went from about 40:1 to about 500:1. The stagnation of wages at the bottom which prompted greater and greater consumer indebtedness, and the increasingly rampant speculation at the top during the era of deregulation, created the environment for a financial crisis that many heterodox economists (and almost no mainstream economists) saw coming. The great "Maestro," as Bob Woodward called Greenspan in his adoring book of that title, was a key player in establishing the inequality and unregulated environment that brought us all down into a recession that badly threatened the welfare of much of the population of the world.

All this raises an interesting question: has any of this real-world experience, that seems to make a mockery of much of mainstream economics, with its rational actors, equilibrating markets, and championing of the unregulated free market, diminished its parishioners' faith in their way of doing things? Probably not.

Patricia Cohen, who took a look at the matter, summarizes her conclusion with the title of an article, "Ivory Tower Unswayed by Crashing Economy?" in the *New York Times*, March 5, 2009. She writes this essential summary of her argument:

> [In the wake of the financial collapse] prominent economics professors say their academic discipline isn't shifting nearly as much as some people might think. Free market theory, mathematical models and hostility to government regulation still reign in most economics departments at colleges and universities around the country. True, some new approaches have been explored in recent years, particularly by behavioral economists who argue that human psychology is a crucial element in economic decision making. But the belief that people make rational economic decisions and the market automatically adjusts to respond to them still prevails.

She quotes James K. Galbraith, a leading heterodox economist, as saying, "I don't detect any change at all." He described the profession as "like an ostrich with its head in the sand.... It's business as usual. ... I'm not conscious that there is a fundamental re-examination going on in journals."

These ostriches, to use James Galbraith's metaphor, are not likely to be pushed aside by graduate students with different ideas, at least not for a long while. Robert Shiller, a Yale economist, told Cohen that graduate students who stray too far from the dominant theory and methods seriously reduce their chances of getting an academic job. He concludes: "I fear that there will not be much change in basic paradigms... The basic curriculum will not change."

Cohen also reports, "In addition to Berkeley and the University of Texas, professors at a number of departments including those at the University of Chicago, Harvard, Yale and Stanford, say they are unaware of any plans to reassess their curriculums and reading lists, or to rethink the way introductory courses are organized." Dani Rodrick, a Harvard economist, told her, "The problem wasn't with the economics but with the economists... We have fixated on one of the possible hundreds of models and elevated that above the others."

Fixated, indeed, is the right word, and the word becomes "catastrophic" when an economist like Alan Greenspan, fixated on those ideas, maneuvers his way into a position of great power.

WHAT SHOULD ECONOMISTS ACTUALLY DO?

As heterodox economists, we suggest a way of doing economics—a basic methodology—that recognizes the political economy approach from the mainstream one in the following four different ways:

1. We believe that human nature is pliable and conditional, rather than fixed.
2. We make explicit value judgments about the way we think the world ought to be and do not pretend to be objective scientists.
3. A central basis of our analysis is empirical and historical (and thus inconclusive), rather than theoretical models typically aimed at being conclusive.
4. The questions we ask, our method of answering them, and all the other aspects of our investigations, are couched in a language designed for all people who want to build a more reasonable world, rather than symbolic jargon accessible only to the few.

The best way we can demonstrate these basic principles is to turn to the work of those political economists whom we consider among the greatest such practitioners, Adam Smith, Karl Marx, Thorstein Veblen, John Maynard Keynes, John Kenneth Galbraith, and the other voices we draw upon in our survey. They will show us how it's done.

SUGGESTIONS FOR FURTHER READING

Colander, David and A.W. Coates, eds. *The Spread of Economic Ideas.* New York: Cambridge University Press, 1998.

Galbraith, John K. *The Age of Uncertainty.* Boston: Hougton-Mifflin, 1977.

Keynes, John M. *Essays in Biography.* Harcourt-Brace, 1933.

Myrdal, Gunner. *The Political Element in the Development of Economic Theory.* Cambridge: Harvard University Press, 1965.

Polayni, Karl. *The Great Transformation.* New York: Farrar and Rinehart, 1944

Routh, Guy. *The Origin of Economic Ideas.* New York: Vintage Books, 1977.

Veblen, Thorstein. "Why is Economics Not an Evolutionary Science?" in *The Place of Science in Modern Civilization.* New York: Huebsch, 1990.

2
Adam Smith
and the Philosophy of Limited *Laissez-Faire**

I. INTRODUCTION

Adam Smith, one of history's most influential economists and philosophers, lived in Great Britain from 1723 to 1790. His writings on morals and economics have excited controversy ever since he published his two important books, *The Theory of Moral Sentiments* (1759) and *An Inquiry Into the Nature and Causes of the Wealth of Nations* (1776). Economists, in particular, have engaged in heated debates about what Smith "really meant." The late George J. Stigler, a Nobel Prize-winning conservative economist, offered one particular interpretation of Smith's work. At the *Wealth of Nations* Bicentennial Conference at the University of Glasgow in 1976, Stigler began his talk by saying: "I bring you greetings from Adam Smith, who is alive and well and living in Chicago."[1] He was alluding to the extreme "free market" school of economics at the University of Chicago. The picture that Stigler painted of Smith was that of an advocate of competitive capitalism, free trade, and an efficiently working price mechanism—the same ideas promoted by Chicago economists like Milton Friedman and Arnold Harberger. By focusing his at-

*   This chapter is a revised and edited version of an essay written by Hans E. Jensen, Professor Emeritus of Economics at the University of Tennessee, Knoxville. Professor Jensen is a renowned historian of economic thought, who has published articles on the works of Clarence Ayres, Thorstein Veblen, John Maynard Keynes, Alfred Marshall, Karl Marx, John Stuart Mill, Joseph A. Schumpeter, and Adam Smith.

tention narrowly on Book I of *The Wealth of Nations*, especially Chapter VII,[2] Stigler argued that Smith's *magnum opus* was an incontrovertible argument for the efficiency of unregulated markets. That some free enterprisers view it as such a sacred document is indicated by the fact that the Association of Private Enterprise Education bestows its Adam Smith Award on worthy workers in the vineyard of free enterprise economics.

However, others challenge this interpretation of Smith as a radical proponent of unregulated markets. For example, Karl Marx considered Smith one of "the best representatives" of "classical political economy," which Marx understood as "that economy which ... has investigated the real relations of production in bourgeois society, in contradistinction to vulgar economy, which deals with appearances only ... and ... seeks plausible explanations of the most obtrusive phenomena."[3] Thus Marx implied that Smith had written *The Wealth of Nations* from a *holistic* point of view,[4] intimating that Smith dealt with the whole economic system and with the interrelations of its constituent parts. Similarly, Horst C. Recktenwald argues that *The Wealth of Nations* must be viewed "comprehensively as an integrated *whole*" focusing on the entire, dynamic macroeconomy.[5] Thus, rather than narrowly focusing on markets and prices, as many mainstream economists do, Smith was indeed a true political economist interested in constructing a comprehensive picture of the economy within society. The inaccurate picture of Smith results from the fact that mainstream economists usually select a narrow cross section of Smith's writings as the key part of his contribution to economics—generally the passages that focus on the efficiency of markets. This obscures the breadth of Smith's ideas as well as his skepticism about the motives and behaviors of business owners.

Smith's purpose in engaging in this holistic analysis was to show how public happiness could be enhanced. He considered this to be an extremely important, and necessary, task because his contemporary society was not "happy" in as much as the "far greater part of ... [its] members ... [were] poor and miserable."[6] Smith was clearly very much concerned with the welfare of all citizens.

As we will see below, Smith crafted a powerful argument in favor of limited *laissez-faire* in the context of a critique of the mercantilist economic policies that dominated his era, the late eighteenth century in Britain. Whether these ideas apply to the contemporary world will be left to the reader to judge. Furthermore, it will become clear that Smith had deep reservations about the behavior of the wealthy elites of his day, who often seemed to profit at the expense of the public thanks to political connections and rigged markets. It will again be left to the reader to determine how Smith would feel about the concentration of economic and political power today. In addition, to emphasize how misleading the "Chicago view" of Smith's work is, this chapter will demonstrate that Smith considered the alleviation of poverty to be the central priority of an economic system, and he supported public measures such as building infrastructure and providing education that would improve the functioning of the market system. These ideas suggest that Smith was a far more subtle and complex thinker than he is often made out to be, and that he was very much a political economist (as we defined it in the previous chapter) with a broad understanding of the institutional foundations of a market economy.

To substantiate these claims, the chapter will endeavor to indicate what Smith really *said* in his works, rather than what we or others claim he really meant. Inasmuch as he is not around to tell us what he meant, one can do no better than ascertain what Smith said—in the hope that his writings might reflect what he meant. As Samuel Hollander observed, textual interpretation is no easy matter.[7] For this reason, we try to avoid assertions about what Smith said, using direct quotations as far as practicable. We begin our inquiry by reporting on what Smith said about his concerns and objectives as a practitioner of political economics.

II. SMITH'S OBJECTIVES

Smith said that he wrote *The Wealth of Nations* in order to explain how rampant poverty among the "labouring poor" could be eliminated from this "great body of the people." He observed that poverty has to be measured by the rate of "mortality ... among the children of the common people." He noted that "half of mankind die before 5 years of age. But this is the case only with the meaner and poorer sort, whose children are neglected and exposed to many hardships from the inclemencies of the weather and other dangers."[9] Smith's "sympathies went," therefore, "wholly to the [poverty-stricken] labourer" and his family.[10] As his first biographer put it, *The Wealth of Nations* served Smith as an outlet for his "ruling passion, of contributing to the happiness and the improvement of society" through the elimination of working-class poverty.[11] Hence he declared it to be his objective to identify those processes that must be encouraged in order to bring forth a "well-governed society, [in which] ... universal opulence extends itself to the lowest ranks of the people."[12] In this state of affairs, so "great a quantity of every thing is produced that there is enough both to gratify the slothful and oppressive profusion of the great, and at the same time abundantly to supply the wants of the artisan, [the labourer], and the peasant."[13] In this latter quotation, we can see Smith's antagonism towards the rich and powerful of his era, as well as his emphasis on raising the standard of living of the working class.

As we shall see, Adam Smith attempts to identify the economic institutions and policies that would best enable his society, eighteenth-century England, to achieve economic growth and alleviate poverty. He argued that economic growth came from greater productivity and innovation, but that only in the right context, with the right incentives and the correct economic policies, would innovation turn into invention and economic growth.

III. SMITH ON GROWTH AND DEVELOPMENT

How did Smith envision that increased wealth of the entire nation would come about? There is only one way: The annual "produce" of the nation must come to bear "a greater ... proportion to the number of those who are to consume it."[14] In other words, economic growth must occur. And the incomes generated by growth must be distributed in such a way that the conditions of the poor improve, even while the "slothful and oppressive" elites maintain their lifestyles. Smith's focus on economic development through growth led him to investigate those forces that contribute to or hinder growth. This he saw as the essence of economics. Hence he defined "Political Oeconomy" as the study of "the nature and causes of the wealth of nations."[15] Here he conceived of wealth both as a stock of income-producing (human and non-human) capital *and* as a stream of real income. Smith was of the opinion that a study of wealth must (a) provide an explanation of the sources and characteristics of the two types of wealth and (b) contain a description of those individuals and institutions that are the recipients of real income. Hence he provided the following extended definition of his discipline: "Political oeconomy ... proposes two distinct objects; first to provide a plentiful revenue or subsistence for the people, or more properly to enable them to provide such a revenue or subsistence for themselves; and secondly, to supply the state or the commonwealth with a revenue sufficient for the public services. It proposes to enrich both the people and the sovereign."[16]

To Smith, the cause of economic growth and development was the "improvement in the productive powers of labour." Furthermore, increases in labor productivity were "the effects of the division of labour."[17] The division of labor results in greater specialization, which enhances efficiency and productivity:

This great increase of the quantity of work, which, in consequence of the division of labour, the same number of people are capable of performing, is owing to three different circumstances; first to the increase of dexterity in every particular workman; second to the saving of the time which is commonly lost in passing from one species of work to another; and lastly, to the invention of a great number of machines which facilitate and abridge labour, and enable one man to do the work of many.[18]

Smith argued that the aspect of specialization that affects labor productivity the most is the substitution of machinery for labor. He pointed out, for example, that when the workers in a pin factory were "accommodated with the necessary machinery," the resultant division of labor and specialization increased each worker's daily output from "twenty" pins to "four thousand eight hundred pins a day." Similarly, in his discussion of the production of a wool coat, Smith pointed out that the introduction of machines was instrumental in molding the specialized skills of the "sorter of the wool, the wool-comber or carder, the dyer, the scribbler, the spinner, the weaver, the fuller, the dresser, with many others,"[19] and in replacing some workers.[20]

In explaining how technology-fueled growth and development might come about, Smith pointed out that this evolutionary process was caused by a unique interaction between invention and innovation. He described each of these activities, which he viewed as being performed by specialized agents, in some detail. In so doing, he argued that inventors provide the hardware that is innovated by "undertakers,"[21] Smith's term for entrepreneurs. Hence we turn first to Smith's discussion of invention.

IV. SMITH ON INVENTION
Exogenous and Endogenous Invention

Smith commenced his inquiry into the nature and processes of invention by observing that we "have not nor cannot have any complete history of the invention of machines, because most of them are at first imperfect, and receive gradual improvements and increase of powers from those who use them." He speculated conjecturally that it "was probably a farmer who made the original plow." Similarly, some "miserable slave who had perhaps been employed for a long time in grinding corn between two stones probably first found out the method of supporting the upper stone by a spindle." Subsequently, a "[millwright] perhaps found out the way of turning the spindle with the hand."[22]

Smith was of the opinion that a similar evolution occurred in manufacturing. Thus he observed that a "great part of the machines made use of in those manufactures in which labour is most subdivided, were originally the inventions of common workmen, who, being each of them employed in some very simple operation, naturally turned their thoughts towards finding out easier and readier methods of performing it."[23] When Smith began his search for the sources of economic growth and development, such work-related, or *endogenous*, inventions were being phased out in favor of inventions that occurred outside, or separate from, the work process. Smith described these *exogenous* inventions in the following manner:

> All the improvements in machinery, however, have by no means been the inventions of those who had occasion to use the machines. Many improvements have been made by the ingenuity of the makers of the machines, when to make them became the business of a peculiar trade; and some by that of those who are called philosophers or men of speculation, whose trade it is, not to do any thing, but to observe every thing; and who, upon that account, are often capable of combining together the powers of the most distant and dissimilar objects.[24]

Thus like Clarence Ayres, a twentieth-century American institutionalist, Smith argued that all inventions "result from the invention of previously existing tools ... and devices so as to form new tools ... and devices."[25] He labeled the person who makes such a combination *exogenously* a "philosopher," usually with a background as a scientist, technologist, or engineer.[26]

As Smith saw it, makers of exogenous inventions were set apart from the rest of society by virtue of their "education" and the "habits" and "customs" that they acquired on the path leading to their emergence as inventive technicians. As these philosopher-technicians specialize, "[e]ach individual becomes more expert in his peculiar branch, more work is done upon the whole, and the quantity of science [and inventions] is considerably increased by it."[27]

The Decline of Endogenous Innovation and the Alienation of Labor

During his lifetime, Smith observed the number of exogenous inventions increasing while endogenous inventions became less frequent. Smith identified two major causes of the substitution of exogenous inventions for endogenous inventions. The former type of inventions rose to prominence because of increased educational opportunities for a growing number of potential inventive technicians. Endogenous inventions dwindled because of a decline of the inventive capabilities of workers. The following (one of his most famous comments) is Smith's description of the latter phenomenon, which he saw as one of the consequences of the increased division of labor that occurred in the wake of growing application of machine technology in manufacturing.

> In the progress of the division of labour, the employment of the far greater part of those who live by labour, that is, of the great body of the people, comes to be confined to a few very simple operations; frequently to one or two. But the understandings of the greater part of men are necessarily formed by their ordinary employments. The man whose whole life is spent in performing a few simple operations, which the effects too are ... always the same ... has no occasion to exert his understanding, or to *exercise his invention in finding out expedients for removing difficulties which never occur.* He naturally loses, therefore, the habits of such exertion, and generally becomes as stupid and ignorant as it is possible for a human creature to become. ... His dexterity at his own peculiar trade seems, in this manner, to be acquired at the expense of his intellectual, social, and martial virtues.[28]

Moreover, "the division of labour, having reduced all trades to very simple operations, affords an opportunity of employing children very young." This, in conjunction with the fact that their "parents can scarce afford to maintain them," means that the youngsters' "education is greatly neglected." As soon "as they are able to work, they must apply to some trade by which they can earn their subsistence" by performing a few simple operations.[29] Hence the minds of the children become just as torpid as those of their parents. When the members of each cohort of children reach maturity and become parents, the same fate will await their offspring and so on to following generations.

One can clearly observe the contradiction Smith sees in specialization and mechanization. On the one hand, specialization is instrumental in the expansion of productivity that will hopefully improve the standard of living of the poor. On the other hand, specialization has some obvious, negative effects on workers and their families—the "alienation" of the worker that, as we will show in the following chapter, Marx would later take up in depth in his analysis of capitalism. Although Smith never entirely resolved this contradiction, as will be discussed in the section on economic policy, he hinted at the possibility that endogenous inventions might be revived as a byproduct of an expansion of public education, which might resurrect the role of the laborer in the manufacturing process.

Smith noted that the environment in which potential inventive philosophers were reared was different from those of working-class youth. The potential inventors were born to families of "some rank and fortune" who were able to provide their offspring with the best education available to their class. Being properly educated, the budding inventors were in a position to acquire and apply the technological knowledge necessary for an exogenous invention, and they found ample opportunity to apply this knowledge: "The understandings of those who are engaged in such employments can seldom grow torpid for want of exercise."[30] Hence Smith believed that a critical mass of inventions would soon come about because "[m]ore heads are occupied in inventing the most proper machinery" than ever before. As a result, "a variety of new machines [has] come to be invented for facilitating and abridging labor." This augured well for the future, Smith thought, because the invention of more machines would spawn even "more … to be invented."[31]

Smith was fully aware, however, that in and by itself, an invention has no economic effect. An invention will be economically effective only if it is applied and used in productive processes, what the economist Joseph Schumpeter called "innovation." This process requires not just inventive workers or technicians or even philosophers of invention, but also entrepreneurs who will risk capital trying to realize the economic promise of an invention.[32] Smith was convinced, however, that if innovation was to flourish, it required an economic order whose institutions encouraged, even impelled, undertakers to innovate. Hence, before we can look more carefully at Smith's analysis of the process of innovation, we first need to consider his pronouncements on economic policy, competition, and incentives.

V. SMITH ON ECONOMIC POLICY

Smith's Critique of Mercantilist Policies

Smith postulated that the past and present were characterized by a "slow progress of opulence," or wealth. He believed that growth was slow due to the stifling of inventions by the unfavorable mercantilist policies of the day.[33]

Under mercantilism, the economy was controlled by the king and a handful of huge, monopolistic trading companies. The term "mercantilism" came from the merchants who founded these great trading companies and from the policies established by monarchs to promote economic growth by aiding the merchants to corner domestic and international markets. According to Smith, the basic fallacy of mercantilism, in which all its mistaken policies were rooted, was the postulate that "wealth consists in money, or in gold and silver."[34] Instead, he argued that "wealth does not consist in money, or in gold and silver; but in what money purchases, and is valuable only for purchasing."[35]

Under mercantilism, the attainment of a so-called favorable balance of trade became the overarching policy doctrine in countries devoid of gold or silver mines. As he put it, "those metals could be brought into a country which had no mines such as the United Kingdom, only by the balance of trade, or by exporting to a greater value than it imported." Mercantilism's "two great engines for enriching the country, therefore, were restraint upon importation, and encouragement to exportation." The former "consisted sometimes in high duties, and sometimes in absolute prohibition." Export, on the other hand, was stimulated sometimes by bounties [subsidies],[36] sometimes by advantageous treaties of commerce with foreign states, and sometimes by the establishment of colonies in distant countries."[37]

According to Smith, this mistaken commercial policy, designed to increase the nation's stock of money rather than its productive power, was only one feature of mercantilism that prevented the economy from increasing the real incomes of the working poor. Smith identified "regulation" of business enterprises as another tool of mercantilist policy that retarded the growth of wealth and well-being.[38]

For one thing, the government had devised regulations that encouraged business people to collude. As much as Smith is made out by his contemporary admirers to celebrate business owners, he was deeply distrustful of their motives. Smith put it thus:

> People of the same trade seldom meet together, even for merriment and diversion, but the conversation ends in a conspiracy against the public, or in some contrivance to raise prices. It is impossible indeed to prevent such meetings, by any law which ... could be executed... But though the law cannot hinder people of the same trade from sometimes assembling together, it ought to do nothing to facilitate such assemblies; much less to render them necessary.[39]

Thus, while Smith was skeptical about the ability of government to prevent such collusion, he certainly did not think the government should be in the business of promoting such combinations. Yet this was precisely what the mercantilist governments had done. They enacted regulations that required all those engaged in the same trade in a particular town to register with the government, thereby facilitating collusion by directly connecting everyone engaged in that trade.[40] Ostensibly, this regulation was issued in order to enable a state to collect taxes from businessmen "to provide for their poor, their sick, their widows and orphans." Smith argued that the majority of a chartered assembly could "enact a by-law with proper penalties, which will limit the competition more durably than any voluntary combination whatever." The chartered assemblies, or trade associations, functioned not only as "enlarged monopolies" in each commodity market, but also as monopsonies in the purchase of labor in local labor markets.[41] According to Smith, employers were "always and everywhere in a ... constant and uniform combination, not to raise the wages of labour above their actual rate.... Masters too sometimes enter into particular combinations to sink the wages of labour even below this rate."[42]

Here we can observe Smith's nascent theory of class conflict, developed and extended significantly by Marx, based on the fundamental premise that the interests of owners are often in opposition to the interests of workers. Smith believed that the inequality generated by an unfair economic system had the potential of erupting into open conflict.

> Wherever there is great property, there is great inequality. For one very rich man, there must be at least five hundred poor, and the affluence of the few supposes the indigence of many. The affluence of the rich excites the indignation of the poor, who are often driven by want and prompted by envy to invade his possessions. It is only under the shelter of the civil magistrate that the owner of that valuable property . . . can sleep a single night in security.[43]

Smith also censured the government for granting individual business owners special privileges, including monopolies on the production and, sometimes, exportation of a particular commodity. He likewise denounced the "statutes of apprenticeship" and the "law of settlements." The former required that no person could work in any trade or craft "unless he had previously served to it an apprenticeship of seven years." The laws of settlements forbade every "poor workman, when thrown out of employment either in one trade or in one place," from seeking "for it in another trade or another place." If he nevertheless should do so, he would suffer prosecution or removal from his new employment.[44] Smith condemned both sets of statutes for two reasons. In the first place, they "restrain[ed], in particular employments, the competition ... [that] might otherwise go into them." Hence the regulations strengthened the power of employers. Second and, in Smith's opinion, of greater importance, the statutes were "real encroachments upon natural liberty."[45]

In Smith's opinion, the regulation of foreign trade and the granting of monopolistic power to business enterprises were intimately connected and intertwined parts of mercantilism. The foreign trade policies were measures designed to accommodate the business community's hunger for money. By granting monopolistic power to enterprises and trade associations, the businessmen could charge exorbitant prices for goods sold at home and abroad. As Smith put it, the "price of monopoly is upon every occasion the highest which can be got."[46]

Smith had no doubt that the real engineers of mercantilism were, in fact, the huge firms that dominated and controlled the economy and the government:

> [T]he monopoly which our manufacturers have obtained against us ... [has] become formidable to the government, and upon many occasions intimidate[s] the legislature. The member of parliament who supports every proposal for strengthening this monopoly, is sure to acquire not only the reputation of understanding trade, but great popularity and influence with an order of men whose numbers and wealth render them of great importance. If he opposes them, on the contrary, and still more if he has authority enough to be able to thwart them, neither the most acknowledged probity, nor the highest rank, nor the greatest public service can protect him from the most infamous abuse and detraction, from personal insults, nor sometimes from real danger, arising from the insolent outrage of furious and disappointed monopolists.[47]

Smith admonished that the "proposal of any new law or regulation of commerce which comes from this order, ought always to be listened to with great precaution ... [because it] comes from an order of men ... who have generally an interest to deceive and even oppress the public, and who accordingly have, upon many occasions, both deceived and oppressed it."[48] Smith was convinced that the mercantilist regulations were instigated by the state at the behest of powerful business interests. "That it was the spirit of monopoly which originally both invented and propagated this doctrine, cannot be doubted"; in other words, the government's economic policies were "always directed ... by the clamorous importunity [or pressure] of partial interests."[49] Smith was therefore of the opinion that the state and its institutions were corrupt because legislators, administrators, and justices were obedient and servile lackeys of actual and would-be monopolists.[50] He thundered: "[we should] break down the exclusive privileges of [firms and] corporations [i.e., trade associations], and repeal the statute of apprenticeship ... and add to this the repeal of the law of settlements"; in short, rescind "all those laws which restrain ... competition." Smith hoped that true (perfect, atomistic) competition between firms in product and labor markets would lead to better products, greater productivity, lower prices, and higher wages. Smith was confident that once the "sovereign [i. e., the government] is completely discharged from ... the duty of superintending the industry [i.e., industriousness] of private people, the obvious and simple system of natural liberty establishes itself on its own accord."[51] Smith was, perhaps, overly optimistic here about the possibility of a system of natural liberty establishing and regulating itself without the oversight of a government safeguarding the welfare of workers and consumers. *Laissez-faire* has seldom operated in the idyllic fashion that Smith hoped it would, a topic taken up in greater detail in the next chapter on Marx.

The Proper Role of Government in Adam Smith's System

It is important to note that Smith did not equate natural liberty with raw *laissez-faire*. He was too much of a humanitarian to fall into that trap. The government had to serve some public functions and to endow the private sector with a human face, to use a term that has been tossed around by some present-day politicians. "According to the system of natural liberty," said Smith, "the sovereign has ... to attend to ... three duties of great importance."[52] He enumerated these as follows:

> [F]irst the duty of protecting the society from the violence and invasion of other independent societies; secondly, the duty of protecting, as far as possible, every member of the society from the injustice and oppression of every other member of it, or the duty of establishing an exact administration of justice; and, thirdly, the duty of erecting and maintaining certain public works and certain public institutions, which it never can be for the interest of any individual, or small number of individuals, to erect and maintain; because the profit could never repay the expence to any individual or small number of individuals, though it may frequently do more than repay it to a great society.[53]

The first of government's functions, to provide for the common defense, is clear enough and rarely contested as a general principle. However, the second and third functions of government are not so clearly understood or readily accepted. As far as justice is concerned, Smith was ready to entrust the government with a monopoly on its administration because in the absence of such a monopoly, "civil society may ... be a Scene of Bloodshed and disorder every man revenging himself at his own hand whenever he fancies himself injured." In other words, society "cannot subsist among those who are at all times ready to hurt and injure one another." As Smith saw it, the government's administration of justice is, therefore, "the main pillar that upholds the whole [social] edifice."[54] How the administration of justice can avoid the problems that plagued mercantilist governments—special interest influence and unequal treatment under the law—is not clear. Regarding public goods, Smith contended that government should provide, maintain and operate certain unprofitable institutions (public goods), which made him an advocate of limited *laissez-faire*. He divided such institutions into "those facilitating the commerce of the society, and those for promoting the instruction of the people."[55]

In the first category, Smith included the construction and "maintenance of the public works which facilitate the commerce of any country, such as good roads, bridges, navigable canals, harbours, etc." He observed that the objective of this kind of public works was "to facilitate commerce in general." Also, the government should establish institutions and provide facilities for the benefit of "particular branches of commerce, which ... require extraordinary protection,"[56] that is, import duties to protect key sectors from foreign competition. Here Smith acknowledges the need for government to insure trade is free and fair in certain markets.[57]

Smith defended his proposal for this first category of public goods, government construction and operation of unprofitable domestic infrastructure institutions, on the grounds that they would enable business firms to spawn welfare-generating economic activities. Hence this particular recommendation is in harmony with his desire to contribute to the emergence of a system of limited *laissez-faire*.[58] However, his defense of import protection might benefit some of the "enlarged monopolies." So why did he take this apparently non-Smithian approach? He gave two reasons. One is a rather sheepish argument to the effect that the "protection of trade ... has always been considered as essential to the defence of the commonwealth, and upon that account, a necessary part of the duty of the executive power."[59] His second justification is more in line with his humanitarian inclinations. "Humanity may ... require," said he, that "natural liberty" and "freedom of trade should be restored only by slow gradations, and with a good deal of reserve and circumspection." If all government restrictions on imports, the various state grants of monopoly power, and the executive's protection of businesses overseas were "taken away all at once," chaos would surely follow. Such an act would "deprive all at once many thousands of our people of their ordinary employment and means of subsistence."[60] The persons who would lose their meager level of living by such a revolutionary change were precisely those laboring poor whose welfare Smith wished to see improved manifold through the adoption by government of his proposed scheme for the institution of limited *laissez-faire*. In other words, Smith recommended a step-by-step dismantling of the institutions of the mercantilist state that so favored monopolies. Neoliberal shock therapy (to use the modern phrase for drastic, free-market reforms) would be too devastating to the fabric of society.

In addition to government provision of infrastructure, Smith advocated a second category of public goods: expansion of public education. If inventions were to occur at a sufficient rate by suitably talented people *and* if the inventions were to be operated by technologically adequate operatives, it would be necessary for society to make much greater investments in human capital than was done under the regime of mercantilism. Thus, Smith hoped to stimulate exogenous invention by "philosophers" and to improve the education of the typical worker enough to spark a renewed increase in endogenous innovation from the workforce. For perhaps the first time in the history of economics, Smith described the importance of investments in *human* capital:

> When any expensive machine is erected, the extraordinary work to be performed by it before it is worn out, it must be expected, will replace the capital laid out upon it, with at least the ordinary profits. A man educated at the expense of much labour and time to any of those employments which require extraordinary dexterity and skill, may be compared to one of those expensive machines. The work which he learns to perform, it must be expected, over and above the usual wages of common labour, will replace to him the whole expense of his education, with at least the ordinary profits of an equally valuable capital.[61]

In Smith's view, therefore, part of the nation's fixed capital consisted of

> the acquired and useful abilities of all the inhabitants or members of the society. The acquisition of such talents, by the maintenance of the acquirer during his education, study, or apprenticeship, always costs a real expence, which is a capital *fixed and realized ... in his person*. Those talents, as they make part of his fortune, so do they likewise of that of the *society* to which he belongs. The improved dexterity of a workman may be considered in the same light as a machine or instrument of trade which facilitates and abridges labour, and which, though it costs a certain expence, repays that expence with a profit.[62]

As with infrastructure, education creates spillover (external) benefits for society as a whole, and should be provided at a higher level than would be supplied by the private sector.

As Smith saw it, the principal form of investment in human capital consists of two intertwined activities or procedures. One consists of public outlays for the production of the social good of education. As explained by Smith in the passages quoted above, the other one involves the expenditures on life-sustaining resources by students during the period in which they are being educated, plus, Smith might have added, their foregone incomes during that period.

Smith recommended that the education of the young be made the responsibility of the government on behalf of society at large. The ignorance and stupidity created by the division of labor and specialization, Smith believed, would continue to be the hallmark of "the labouring poor ... unless government takes some pains to prevent it." Hence "some attention of government is necessary in order to prevent the almost entire corruption and degeneracy of the great body of the people."[63] In view of this, Smith recommended that the "public ... facilitate ... [and] encourage ... even impose upon almost the whole body of the people, the necessity of acquiring those most essential parts of education," which he identified as the ability "to read, write, and account." And, said Smith, the "public can facilitate this acquisition by establishing in every parish or district a little school, where children may be taught" these essentials. As part and parcel of his concept of harnessed *laissez-faire*, Smith opined that the "public can impose upon almost the whole body of the people the necessity of acquiring those most essential parts of education, by obliging every man to undergo an examination or probation in them before he ... be allowed to set up any trade either in a village or town corporate."[64] Thus education of young males[65] had two purposes, according to Smith. In the first place, it was to provide potential innovators with the intellectual acumen and the knowledge and abilities that would be required for the making of innovations. Second, and of equal importance, it was to endow future working-class generations with the ability and know-how that were prerequisites for operating the new productive equipment that would be placed on factory floors by innovators. Moreover, when the operatives become thus educated, improvements of machines in the plants where they work may again emanate from the (endogenous) "inventions of common workmen."[66] This would be an added stimulus to economic growth and development.

The Labor Theory of Value

Smith emphasized education so strongly because of his belief in the labor theory of value. Smith placed human labor at the center of the economy. It is human beings who produce the nation's output and are the only value-generating factor of production. Smith stated this proposition in the opening sentence of the first chapter of *The Wealth of Nations*:

> The annual labour of every nation is the fund which originally supplies it with all the necessaries and conveniences of life which it annually consumes, and which consists always, either in the immediate produce of that labour, or in what is purchased with that produce from other nations.[67]

The labor that Smith had in mind was the "productive" labor of all the participants in the productive process from beginning to finish: inventors, innovators, undertakers, and ordinary workers. The labor of each of these actors in the economic drama "fixes and realizes itself in some particular subject or vendible commodity, which lasts for some time at least after that labour is past. It is, as it were, a certain quantity of labour stocked and stored up to be employed, if necessary, upon some other occasion."[68] Thus Smith developed and employed what may be called a "labor-embodied" theory of production—a commodity's value is determined by the amount of labor it embodies. John Maynard Keynes was almost alone among economists to appreciate this central aspect of Smith's economics. Keynes put it in this way: "I sympathise ... with the ... classical doctrine that everything is *produced* by *labour*.... It is preferable to regard labour, including, of course, the personal services of the entrepreneur and his assistants, as the sole factor of production."[69] As we shall see in the next chapter, Marx disagreed with the notion that the capitalist could be treated as just another laborer, because to Marx capitalists profited from what they forced laborers to do, not from what they worked to produce themselves.

In the terms of his labor-embodied theory of value, Smith argued that the "value of any commodity ... to the person who possesses it, and who means ... to exchange it for other commodities, is equal to the quantity of labour which it enables him to purchase or command. Labour, therefore, is the real measure of the exchangeable value of all commodities."[70] Although Smith switched here to a labor-command theory of value—the value of a commodity is determined by the amount of labor it takes to purchase that commodity—it is clear that labor is the factor that determines exchange value in Smith's system of limited *laissez-faire*. He realized, of course, that money serves as an intermediary in the buying and selling of commodities. Despite the fact that the "real price" of a commodity exists in the labor-containing "quantity of the necessaries and conveniences of life which are given for it; its nominal price, [consists] in the quantity of money" which is actually paid for it. Smith argued that the money price of an article tends to reflect its real price in terms of the quantity of another labor-embodied commodity that it would fetch in the market place. That is, the money prices of articles are "adjusted … by the higgling and bargaining of the market" in such a fashion that these nominal prices become truly representative of the labor-determined ratios at which the commodities exchange.[71] In other words, the prices generated by the forces of supply and demand reflect the value of labor contained within each good. To Smith, labor was the primary factor creating value and determining prices in an economy, and education to increase the productivity of labor was therefore a key public institution in promoting economic growth and the general welfare.

The Invisible Hand and the Consequences of a System of Limited *Laissez-Faire*

Smith concluded his discussion of the role of public institutions in the economy with this reiteration: "The expense of maintaining good roads and communications is, no doubt, beneficial to the whole society, and may, therefore, without any injustice, be defrayed by the general contribution of the whole society" in the form of taxes and other levies for the government's use in financing the erection and maintenance of public works. "The expense of the institutions for education … is likewise, no doubt, beneficial to the whole society, and may, therefore, without injustice, be defrayed by the general contributions of the whole society."[72]

Once Smith's proposed system of limited *laissez-faire* is fully established as a going concern, every "man, as long as he does not violate the laws of justice, is left perfectly free to pursue his own interest in his own way, and to bring both his industry [i.e., industriousness] and capital into competition with those of any other man, or order of men." Thus "competition will immediately" become the sole mechanism for the formation of commodity prices, wages, and other charges. And, the "price of free competition … is the lowest which can be taken." Smith did not view competition as a condition in which a seller, or supplier, passively adjusts his output, or supply, in response to changing price signals emanating from the relevant market, as implied by the supply and demand model of mainstream economics. On the contrary, Smith's concept of competition was one of active rivalry, or "rivalship of competition," as he put it.[73] For example, in manufacturing and commerce, the undertakers are "rivals" who strive to "supplant" each other. They do so by several methods: bids, counter-bids, and "under-selling." This type of "competition … is advantageous to the great body of the people" because of the resultant minimal prices that are generated dynamically in a process of growth.[74] Although each individual undertaker "intends only his own gain," he is led by the "invisible hand [of competition] to promote an end which was no part of his intention." In other words, the driving force of "self-love," or self-interest, is transmuted wondrously into social welfare for the masses.[75]

Morals, Competition and Justice as Regulators of *Laissez-Faire*

To Smith, competition was not always enough to insure that self-interest operated in the best interests of all. Smith also saw the need for a sound moral basis in society. In terms of self-interest, Smith noted that people were not entirely selfish and that they do (and should) care for others. Indeed, Smith began his first famous book, *The Theory of Moral Sentiments*, with the following statement: "How selfish soever man may be supposed, there are evidently some principles in his nature, which interest him in the fortune of others, and render their happiness necessary to him."[76] Smith wrote extensively on the social framework and moral basis necessary to make the market system work. As Jerry Evensky observed in his commentary on ethics and early economic liberalism, "Only in a community of ethical individuals can the invisible hand do its job properly, for it is ethics that keeps the hands of individuals from disabling, and thus distorting the actions of, the invisible hand. In the absence of such an ethical community, competition becomes destructive. In Smith's master metaphor, it is ethics that stands between a beneficent society and the Hobbesian abyss."[77] Similarly, as noted earlier, Smith emphasized that a system of justice is also a requirement for the invisible hand to function appropriately. In other words, Smith argued that it is *only with competition, justice, and moral sentiments that self-interest would operate in such a way as to promote the general welfare of society.*

The degree to which markets today actually operate to promote the general welfare of society is open to debate. For example, in the above passages, Smith seems to assume that markets would *always* be sufficiently competitive to generate low prices, new innovations, and enough competition for labor such that workers would be treated well and paid fairly. Smith hoped that greed, tempered by moral sentiments, competition, and a system of justice, would invariably serve the interests of humanity. As we shall see in the other chapters in this book, Karl Marx and many other political economists disagree with these assumptions about the functioning of a *laissez-faire* system and greed. It is also important to recognize that Smith made his argument for limited *laissez-faire* in the context of a critique of mercantilism, in which the state was used on behalf of special interests. Smith did not consider the possibility of a state working on behalf of its citizens to guide the market system. So while Smith opposed government intervention in the form of *mercantilism*, it is unclear whether he would support modern forms of government intervention in the marketplace. Anti-trust laws to preserve competition, environmental regulations to prevent abuse of the environment, labor laws to protect workers, product safety laws to protect consumers, and the expansion of public investment in the economy are but a few of the areas in which modern governments interfere with the market system. But these laws do not necessarily depart from Smith's beliefs in competition, the centrality of moral sentiments, and the provision of public goods with spillover benefits.

Nevertheless, although he had never observed such a system in practice, Smith believed that a system of natural liberty, or harnessed *laissez-faire* with rivalrous competition, is the proper economic environment for the virtuous entrepreneurial activity of growth-promoting and development-fostering innovation.[78] In fact, Smith thought the market system would be so innovative that economic growth would render any flaws in the market system irrelevant. We now turn to Smith's analysis of innovation, the key to the market system functioning in the manner he hoped.

VI. SMITH ON INNOVATION

Smith believed that, in the unregulated markets of the just society, each profit-seeking undertaker is forced by the ubiquitous invisible hand unintentionally to "render the annual revenue of the society as great as he can."[79] In theory, if undertakers are not as productive as possible, they will be supplanted by rivals. This assumes, of course, that undertakers cannot collude with rivals or rig markets in their favor and thereby profit without being productive, an activity that is rampant under capitalism (as we will see in later chapters on Marx, Veblen, Galbraith, and others). Smith saw three key kinds of activities in which productive undertakers engage. The first of these may be termed *revolutionary* entrepreneurial functions; the second, *imitative* entrepreneurial functions; and the third, *routine* entrepreneurial functions.

The first function is labeled revolutionary because it is the principal institutional instrument by means of which a "great revolution" is brought about in productive processes with the result that "public opulence" is greatly enhanced. The practitioners of the function are especially "daring" undertakers who are eager to take "extraordinary" or "superior risk." They run such risks when they acquire new and untried inventions from the tribe of inventing philosophers. Typically, these inventions consist of "new machines" which promise to serve as efficient instruments "for facilitating and abridging those operations" that are executed by each of the workmen who are in the employ of the brave undertakers.[80] Once an entrepreneur has placed the acquired new innovation in operation, the abridgement of labor manifests itself in the form of "advances ... [in the] division of labour." Consequently, the "quantity of materials which the same number of people can work up, increases in great proportion as labour comes to be more and more subdivided; and as the operations of each workman are gradually reduced to a greater degree of simplicity." When this happens in the shop of a particularly pace-setting undertaker, the marketable output increases and the unit cost of production declines. According to Smith, in the markets characteristic of his day, where firms were very small relative to the size of the market, such an entrepreneur could supply more of his good without increasing perceptibly the total quantity brought to market by all firms, and the market price would not sink.[81] With constant prices, lower unit costs and greater output, the bold undertaker's profits increase substantially.

Capital Accumulation, Investment and Innovation

How does a bold undertaker obtain the means for the innovation of a particular new invention? Smith's answer was: by accumulating capital. Undertakers must save a proportion of the surplus (revenues minus wages) in order to invest in new inventions. Smith emphasized that surpluses originate in profit and that profit is a "deduction from the produce of ... labour."[82] According to Smith:

> In all arts and manufactures the greater part of the workmen stand in need of a master to advance them the materials of their work, and their wages and maintenance till it be completed. He shares in the produce of their labour, or in the value which it adds to the materials upon which it is bestowed; and in this share consists his profit.[83]

Smith considered this extraction of labor-created profit by the undertakers to be fundamental in the entrepreneur economy because it made possible those entrepreneurial savings which he viewed as the first step in the process of innovation. Smith was not concerned, as Marx was, with the fact that the undertakers might have amassed their initial investments in unethical ways, nor did he object, as Marx did, to the undertaker taking some of the laborer's output. Rather, Smith saw the amassing of capital as a positive development. The following is Smith's eulogistic praise of saving and capital accumulation:

> Parsimony, and not industry [i.e., dexterity, skills, and industriousness on the part of the agents of production], is the immediate cause of the increase of capital. Industry, indeed, provides the subject which parsimony accumulates. But whatever industry might acquire, if parsimony did not save and store up, the capital would never be the greater.[84]

Without saving, no new innovations would occur, no "additional quantity of industry" would be put "into motion" and no "additional value [would be given] to the annual produce" of the nation.[85] But in a system of natural liberty, the invisible hand of competition forces profit-seeking, bold undertakers to be parsimonious so that they will have available the wherewithal for innovation when the same unseen hand impels them to be on the prowl for newly invented machines that may "enable one man [on their work force] to do the work of many." In other words, competition ensures that each pace-setting entrepreneur furnishes his workers "with the best machines which he can ... afford to purchase." Hence such an innovator will be able to make "the most proper distribution of employment ... among his workmen" so that they may "produce as great a quantity of work as possible."[86] Competition ensures that all firms save and invest, and that firms produce as efficiently as possible.

The process of revolutionary innovation begins with the act of saving on the part of bold undertakers and ends when they install and operate the new and superior machinery that their savings enable them to acquire from inventors. Thus, Smith conceived of the act of revolutionary innovation in terms of four operations, or processes: (1) capital accumulation (savings); (2) acquisition of inventions through the expenditure of the accumulated capital; (3) installation of the acquired inventions; and (4) start-up of the equipment in question.

These are the innovative activities in which a relatively small number of bold undertakers engage. And they do not do so in a haphazard fashion. On the contrary, they make plans and design projects in order to "regulate and direct all the most important operations of labour, and profit is the end proposed by all those plans and projects." Because of this careful planning of the employment and distribution of labor in the process of innovation and beyond, the pioneering undertakers' expectations of extraordinarily high rates of profit are validated. As each entrepreneur enlarges his scale of operations in a succession of innovations, "not only the number of profits increase, but every subsequent profit is greater than the foregoing."[87]

The Role of Competition and Imitation in Limiting Incomes

In the condition of perfect liberty, and hence rivalrous competition, the relatively small number of bold undertakers in each trade cannot "long enjoy their extraordinary profits without any new rivals. Secrets of this kind ... can seldom be long kept; and the extraordinary profits can last very little longer than they are kept."[88] Once the secrets are out, hordes of *imitating* undertakers copy the innovations of the courageous entrepreneurs. Although "timid undertaker[s]"[89] do not dare to take the risk inherent in innovation, the profits garnered by the pioneers prompt the imitators to engage in what appears to be risk-free replication of the pioneers' innovations. Consequently, there is a substantial increase in production and supply as more and more producers copy innovations and experience increased productivity. The result is that the "quantity brought to market exceeds the effectual demand" and the "market price will sink."

At the same time, the demand for labor is increased by the spur of activities engendered by the imitating undertakers. The result is that wages go up. At the same time, labor productivity increases due to the increase in stock of physical capital as a result of innovation and imitation. A "smaller quantity of labour [can now] produce a greater quantity of work." Higher wages are offset by higher productivity. Thus, although *extraordinary profits* are wiped out because of the fall of the prices of output, the acceptable minimum rate of *ordinary profit* is preserved by the increase of productivity. The undertakers are therefore not tempted to withdraw part of their stock from their firms.[90] In other words, innovation and subsequent imitation increases productivity, reduces goods prices, and increases the demand for labor along with the wage rate. Bold undertakers return to earning a normal rate of profit after the imitators catch up, and the standard of living of the people improves as prices fall. Thus Smith saw competitive capitalism gradually raising the incomes of the workers and limiting incomes of the rich.

The bold undertakers are eager to recapture their lost rates of extraordinary profits, however. Hence they engage in a new round of innovations. They are successful initially in restoring their lost rates of abnormal profit. But once again the rate of profit is soon forced down to a normal level by the imitation of timid undertakers. After an interval, the bold undertakers innovate again. Their success is once more short-lived because of the predictable responses of timid undertakers. Smith viewed this cycle as a phenomenon that would continue to characterize an economic system of limited *laissez-faire*. In the long run, the market "prices of all commodities are [therefore] continually gravitating" toward their "natural price," which is the minimum price that must be paid in order for the undertakers to reap the ordinary rate of profit. It means that the workers are the gainers of technological advancement through innovation and imitation. As Smith put it, the "liberal reward of labour," and the "greatest public prosperity [is] the effect of increasing wealth."[91] To repeat: This increase in the standard of living of workers is caused by the timid undertakers' imitations of the bold entrepreneurs' innovations of those exogenous inventions that were made previously by technologically minded philosophers. Entrepreneurs cannot earn more than a normal profit over the long term, but the standard of living of workers steadily increases as productivity improves and goods prices fall. Smith's depiction of the process of innovation and imitation is laid out in Figure 2.1.

Figure 2.1. Smith's View of Invention and Imitation in Competitive Markets

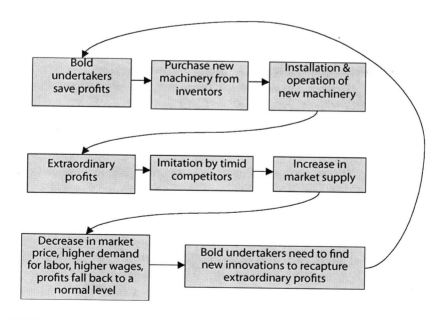

In addition to innovation and imitation, undertakers perform certain *routine* entrepreneurial activities that Smith identified as "inspection and direction" of their enterprises. He observed, however, that in "many great works, almost the whole labour of this kind is committed to some principal clerk."[92] Consequently, the bold and the imitating entrepreneurs can concentrate their attention on the tasks of innovating and imitating, respectively.

VII. CONCLUSION

Smith's system of natural liberty is a mixed economy in which invention, innovation, and imitation in the private sector are supported, promoted, and furthered by institutions ensconced in the public sector. As mentioned above, Smith thought the dynamic interaction of the public and private sectors would result in a process of growth and development in which the members of the working class are the principal beneficiaries. He believed that is so because the institutionalized "invisible hand" of competition directs each profit-seeking undertaker to promote "an end which was no part of his intention," namely, optimal social welfare for all citizens including, for the first time in history, the working classes. "In ease of body and peace of mind, all the different ranks of life are ... upon a level." That is so, Smith reiterated, because all profit-seekers are "led by an invisible hand to make nearly the same distribution of the necessaries of life, which would have been made, had the earth been divided into equal portions among all its inhabitants, and thus without intending it, without knowing it, advance the interest of the society."[94] This was Smith's way of predicting that the institutions of modified *laissez-faire,* especially that of rivalrous competition, would in the long run effect a nearly *equal* distribution of real income. Almost alone among prominent Smith scholars, D. D. Raphael detected this radical position in Smith's work. Raphael put it in this way: Smith's invisible hand guides gain-seeking individuals "to distribute it [i. e., income] more equally, so as to approach *equality.*" And Raphael added: Smith "knows very well that the effect comes about automatically through the interplay of individual interest and the system of exchange. His perception of this truth is one of his great contributions to economic understanding."[95]

As Smith predicted, the limited *laissez-faire* regime adopted to varying degrees in England and other European countries in the 19th century was able to produce impressive rates of economic growth. But it did *not* yield a nearly equal distribution of income, nor did the working class tend to see most of its benefits. A principal reason for this limit in Smith's vision is that, though he saw the giant firms on the horizon of capitalism, he did not anticipate how they would replace his "limited *laissez-faire*" capitalism with a vastly more complex system. His bucolic, beneficent system would become a mammoth network of monopoly firms surrounded by a host of smaller firms that would come and go as the economy rose and fell. The new system would produce entirely different outcomes regarding wages, innovation, prices, income distribution, and the overall effects on all the participants.

Karl Marx, whose ideas we will take up next, began producing his descriptions of the laws of motion of a capitalist system about 75 years after Smith published *The Wealth of Nations*. He had great appreciation for Smith's skill in describing how a market system would work with relatively small firms, with an adequate supply of willing and able labor, and with a neutral government providing only for the national defense, justice, and public works. He also agreed with Smith in general about the labor theory of value.

But Marx, and the other writers to follow in this book, were working to understand the form of capitalism that replaced Smith's economic world. This new kind of economic system led political economists following Smith to produce a broader version of political economy, especially in adding an analysis of how the huge firms—far from being neutral—would shape the government to do their bidding. Marx would go so far as to claim that in capitalist societies, the government generally served on behalf of the business owners. We will now turn to Marx to see why he would reach such a conclusion, as well as the many others that have long captured the attention of students of market capitalism.

3
Karl Marx
and the Contradictions of Capitalism

 Our goal in this chapter is to present a coherent summary of Marx's analysis of economic forces in society and how they shape human lives. We will do that in two parts. The first briefly outlines a theory of historical change that Marx developed with his long-time collaborator, Frederick Engels. In 1845-6, the two wrote a manuscript, *The German Ideology*, that contained their explanation of historical change, called "the materialist conception of history." We will very briefly provide a structural outline of this conception of history with a few examples to help the reader learn the basic terminology of the system.

We will then turn to a more lengthy examination of how Marx applied his theory of historical change to capitalism. This application is spread over thousands of pages of material that Marx and Engels wrote. However, the single most compact presentation is in *Capital*, Volume I, and the second part of this chapter will concentrate attention on the arguments about capitalism in that book. *Capital* is by far Marx's most thorough application of his materialist conception of history: one is actually an example of the other, and by presenting them in sequence we hope to clarify the "Marxian" view of capitalism. Marx's analysis of capitalism is an intricate theoretical structure, buttressed by a huge compendium of historical description, and when studied closely it can be genuinely breathtaking in its breadth and depth.

We also want readers to see the great divide between Marx's analysis of capitalism and that of most current mainstream economists, who tend to look upon capitalism as a "given system," and exhibit little or no profession-al interest in the historical process that gave rise to it. They have ripped eco-nomic analysis from its historical context, ignoring the development and evolution of the capitalist system. As we move the Marxist world, we will see how substantial this difference is between his work and that of main-stream economists.

I. THE MATERIALIST CONCEPTION OF HISTORY

Marx asks a fundamental question confronting all human societies. What must we do to survive? To live, we must mix our intelligence and our energy —our work—with the basic "materials" of the world we find ourselves in: its soil, water, and air. We must work with what's at hand in order to make this today into tomorrow. In 1878, Frederick Engels summarized his and Marx's theory of historical change in the following way:

> The materialist conception of history starts from the principle that produc-tion, and with production the exchange of its products, is the basis of every social order; that in every society that has appeared in history the distribution of the products, and with it the division of society into classes or estates, is determined by what is produced and how it is produced, and how the prod-uct is exchanged. (Engels 1975, 74)

The economic organization of human society, or the "mode of produc-tion" as Marx called it, is therefore the most powerful factors in determining social structure. Notably, the way society is organized to produce necessities —for example, organized into serfs and lords in feudalism, or into owners and workers in capitalist societies—constitutes the "class structure" of soci-ety. Since virtually all production involves many different people, Marx con-centrated on production as a *social* activity and analyzed the class structure created by the organization of production.

Marx's method of analysis is very different from that of Adam Smith, who focused on how *individuals* behaved within a benignly competitive capitalist society. In contrast, Marx sought to understand the forces that cause the economy to change over time. He believed that change resulted from the struggle between opposing, or "dialectical"—what we might think of as "contradictory" or competing—forces inherent in all societies. As an example, one Marx made much of, all economic systems produce hierar-chies of social classes, with a top and a bottom, and endless competition and resentment at every level in between. These class struggles emerge in the form of wars, revolutions, democratic reform, and in other ways, and one can find them grinding away in any history book. That is, social classes are inherently contradictory—inherently opposing—forces in every society.

Marx found that the social activity of production took many different forms throughout history, with stages of social organization corresponding to techniques of production. He noted that European society passed through a number of different modes of production, including primitive communalism, slavery, and feudalism, on its way to capitalism. He concluded that capitalism is simply the latest in a series of modes of production and that it, too, will yield to some other mode of production in the future.[1]

The pattern of ownership of tools and materials generally shapes the system of social classes in a society. The two dominant classes in capitalism are the bourgeoisie and the proletariat. Below, we will discuss their relationship and what generates conflict between them, but for now we can emphasize their different stations with a brief look at how wealth in the United States is divided between them. Throughout modern U.S. history, the richest 10% of the U.S. population has owned the bulk of all stocks and bonds, reaching 90% of all stocks and over 90% of all bonds at the turn of this century, a proportion that is unlikely to change meaningfully in the near future. (Mishel, Bernstein, and Allegretto 2005, 287; Henwood 1997) Since owning the stocks and bonds of companies means owning their "means of production," the wealth-producing capital of the United States is almost all owned by one tenth of the population. In order to make a living, most of the other 90% who work do so either for these richest 10%, their managers, or in the non-profit sector of the economy.

Furthermore, from the 1970s through 2010, the U.S. working class experienced a dramatic decline in income relative to that of the owners and top managers for whom they work. For example, in 1965, the average CEO's salary was 44 times the average factory worker's wages, but by the early 2000s it had reached *over 500 to 1*. The changing fortunes of owners and workers in U.S. capitalism are fine examples of what Marx meant by the inherent struggle between workers and capitalists. They also exemplify the inherent contradictions, or dialectical pressures, within U.S. capitalism, because sustained relative declines in income for the majority of a society's population tend to produce political upheaval. The interests of Wall Street rarely coincide with those of Main Street, and the conflicts between them can be powerful.

Marx summarized his idea of inherent class struggle in the following passage from *The Communist Manifesto*, written in 1848:

The history of all hitherto existing society is the history of class struggles. Freeman and slave, patrician and plebeian, lord and serf, guild-master and journeyman, in a word, oppressor and oppressed, stood in constant opposition to one another, carried on an uninterrupted, now hidden, now open fight, a fight that each time ended, either in a revolutionary re-constitution of society at large, or in the common ruin of the contending classes. (Marx and Engels 1998, 34-5)

We will return to this matter of class conflict, but we turn now to another principal argument in Marx's materialist conception of history, the claim that every mode of production fundamentally shapes other aspects of society. In describing this view, C. Wright Mills, a sociologist influential in the 1950s and 1960s, wrote in *The Marxists*:

Political, religious and legal institutions as well as the ideas, the images, the ideologies by means of which men understand the world in which they live, their place within it, and themselves—all these are reflections of the economic basis of society. (Mills 1962, 82)

The extent to which political institutions in capitalist countries reflect the needs of the capitalist class can hardly be lost on any person living in the United States today, where it seems that government at every level is for sale to the highest capitalist bidder. Less obvious, but also important, is the symbiosis between religion and the emergence of capitalism in Europe. Religious beliefs in hunter-gatherer societies usually emphasize the importance of nature and the role of people within it, and this reflects the importance of the natural environment to survival in that mode of production. Marx was struck by how convenient to the emergence of capitalism had been the teachings of the early Protestant denominations. These new denominations, which developed after Martin Luther's 16th-century revolt against Catholicism, stressed that one should accept one's lot in life and that all would be better in the hereafter. Such a belief, of course, made people more willing to accept the dislocations and deprivations so many experienced in early capitalism. In one of his more memorable phrases, Marx described religion as the "opiate of the masses" because he believed that workers in early capitalist societies had, quite understandably, adopted religious beliefs as the only hope in an inexorably grim world.

Marx also argued that what he called the "cash nexus" of capitalism would eventually demean and devalue all that it pulled under its spreading wings.

In 1846, in *On the Jewish Question*, he noted that money could transform all things, until money itself was all that was important in life:

> Money abases all the gods of mankind and changes them into commodities. Money is the universal and self-sufficient value of all things. It has, therefore, deprived the whole world, both the human world and nature, of their own proper value. Money is the alienated essence of man's work and existence; this essence dominates him and he worships it. (Marx and Engels 1978, 50)

In Marxist language, alienation derives primarily from a process called "commodification." Everything—flesh and blood, inanimate objects, music, poetry, *everything*—is ultimately "for sale" in the capitalist marketplace. We all know countless examples of commodification. Each Christmas, to suggest an obvious one, most of us in Christian countries celebrate the birth of Jesus with an avaricious, competitive, often depressing orgy of consumption of mostly unnecessary products. What was once a simple affair of gift giving to exemplify Christian charity has become in advanced capitalism a gruesome distortion of the original idea. Capitalism, as we all know, incessantly works on all of us to buy things we don't need. However, what Veblen called "the sales effort" is unleashed with a special fury at Christmastime. By the time it is over, a substantial minority of us need anti-depressants as an antidote to the lack of Christmas joy that millions of advertisements told us the gifts, the cards, and the Christmas tree would bring.

Creative output of all kinds is also systematically commodified in capitalist societies, co-opted and transformed by pop culture or the advertising industry. For example, in the 1980s, Paul McCartney of the Beatles tried to buy from a record company the rights to many of the popular songs that he wrote with John Lennon. However, McCartney was outbid by another pop icon, Michael Jackson, who then proceeded to sell the rights to some of these songs to advertising firms. The Beatles song "Revolution," written in response to the political turmoil of the 1960s, was put in the service of selling sneakers. Some Beatles fans might call this sacrilege, but to a Marxist this kind of commodification is the predictable outcome for cultural products in capitalism. "Public" radio stations that increasingly depend upon corporate funds to stay alive, the "Tostitos" Fiesta Bowl, and the Nike swoosh on the uniforms of athletes and coaches at all levels of sports around the world exemplify the way in which things that were not once part of the cash nexus have become commodities.

For Marx, the most costly form of commodification occurs when capitalists buy labor-power in labor markets. This commodity, labor-power, is—as we shall describe in detail later—the irreplaceable aspect of capitalist production, because without hired laborers to produce the output capitalism cannot exist. Even in this age of high technology, labor costs still make up roughly two-thirds of the costs of production for firms, indicating how essential labor remains in the production process. When a capitalist buys labor-power, however, he or she must treat that labor-power like any other input; it must be bought as cheaply as possible and drained of its last ounce of usefulness for profit-making. The fact that labor-power is brought to the market by a human being is, of course, a problem. Human beings, unlike sheets of plywood and computer chips, have imagination, wishes, plans, and dreams, perhaps even to challenge the boss! While imagination and dreams and independence of mind can make for productive workers, such traits can also be problematic for many capitalists trying to maximize profits. Who wants an imaginative dreamer—someone who thinks for himself or herself—on the assembly line, or as a secretary, or in the mind-numbing jobs in retail sales and custodial work that are the fastest growing niches in the economy?

Because workers are interested in many things other than their jobs and, in fact, many workers hate their jobs, capitalists face the complicated problem of focusing their employees' attention on the work at hand. The modern capitalist workplace, particularly in the United States, is usually a dictatorship, where all the rules are made by the bosses and followed by all workers who want to keep their jobs. Capitalists want ordered work from conforming, non-complaining bearers of crucial labor-power. They want a "thing," rather than a human being. This is the commodification of labor—a linchpin of Marxist analysis.

Globalization, a major social transformation now engulfing everybody, everywhere, provides a good example of the materialist conception of history, particularly its dialectical and contradictory nature. Globalization is the ultimate expression of the unregulated market system, as capitalism expands inexorably in search of new markets and cheap, desperate labor. Marx described this search for desperate labor-power in his often-flamboyant style by suggesting that "[t]he worshipful capitalists will never want for fresh exploitable flesh and blood, and will let the dead bury their dead." (Marx and Engels 1978, 215) For capitalists, globalization can be immensely profitable as they search the globe for the cheapest labor and resources to minimize their costs of production. Capitalists can also increase the scale of both production and profits by adding customers from the furthest reaches of the world.

However, capitalists are not the only actors. As often as not, their behavior produces countervailing responses and unintended consequences. In recent decades, one important consequence of globalization has been the decline of the real wages of the working class in the United States. U.S. laborers cannot easily maintain their own wage levels when capitalists put them in competition with low-wage workers in developing countries all over the globe making as little as $.25 an hour. Yet, as Marx saw clearly, low wages in capitalism would mean that the system could produce more than could be sold, resulting in an international crisis of "underconsumption." Such underconsumption was an element in the crisis that started in 2007, when the collapse of the housing market undermined the ability of the typical family to buy goods. Furthermore, the increasing inequality generated by globalization tends to destabilize the political institutions of developing societies. Many workers in such societies will not, without limit, accept low wages and rotten working conditions without rising up in resistance. In the Marxian view, this new set of conflicts generated by globalization, this new dialectal situation, will generate new societies, which we now can only imagine vaguely. Such new societies emerge continually in human history and come into being as a result of the inevitable class struggle inherent to them all.

To sum up this brief summary of Marx's theory of history: He believed that in order to survive, people must construct economic systems—modes of production—and that in all societies these modes heavily shape the way people behave. Capitalism, now the dominant mode of production in the world, is no exception to this rule, and we have looked at a few of the ways this system shapes our lives. Marx argued that capitalism is a system of social classes that are in conflict and that the cash nexus of capitalism will in the end make commodities of almost all things and people.

How, then, does capitalism actually work? How does it make us into what we are, and especially into commodities? We have only hinted at the answer to this question, and now we turn our attention to the broader and deeper answer developed in *Capital*.

II. MARX'S CRITIQUE OF THE CAPITALIST MODE OF PRODUCTION

After Marx and Engels developed their materialist conception of history, sporadically between 1845 and 1857, Marx began work on a longer project to describe and explain the "laws of motion" of capitalism. The overall structure of that explanation had been presented compactly in the first part of *The Communist Manifesto*, but its dozen or so pages gave only a fleeting glance at the complete story. The expanded version was published in 1867 in the first volume of what was to be a multi-volume project, and Marx gave it the title *Capital: A Critique of Political Economy*. The book was first published in German, and later editions in French (1872) and English (1886) made his critique available to most parts of the industrialized world. Marx was emphatic that the purpose of this book, and of all his analysis, was not just "to understand the world, but to change it."

Das Kapital.

Kritik der politischen Oekonomie.

Von

Karl Marx.

Erster Band.
Buch I: Der Produktionsprocess des Kapitals.

Das Recht der Uebersetzung wird vorbehalten.

Hamburg
Verlag von Otto Meissner.
1867.
New-York: L. W. Schmidt, 24 Barclay-Street.

Cover of the original 1867 (German) edition

The first volume of *Capital* was the only one published during Marx's life. Volumes II and III were prepared by Engels from Marx's notes, and Volume IV, more a massive compendium of economic ideas than an extension of his critique, was edited by a German Marxist, Karl Kautsky, between 1905 and 1910. We will focus almost entirely on Volume I because in it, Marx presents his most fundamental arguments about capitalism, especially the relationship between the owners/managers of capital and wage earners who work for them. By focusing on *Capital*, we do not want to leave the impression that it is a compact statement of all that Marx wrote, for his other voluminous writings have been highly influential in modern thought, particularly in the social sciences and the humanities. Nonetheless, as an argument about how the production system of capitalism came to be, how it functions, and the crucial implications of those functions, *Capital* works well on its own. Its central ideas are quite easy to understand when placed in a modern context, using the experiences common to people who live in capitalist culture. It is our purpose here to take up the major themes in Marx's critique of capitalism in precisely that kind of context. We will begin our analysis by elaborating on the principal players we alluded to above, as Marx dramatically did in his own writings.

Players on the Capitalist Field, I: Owners/Managers
Marx argued that most people engaged in economic activity in the capitalist mode of production would fall into one of two major groups. First, there are the capitalists and their managers, or what Marx called the "bourgeoisie." Their identifying trait is that they own or manage the capital equipment of society, the buildings, furniture, materials, and everything else needed to

produce commodities (goods and services for sale). Like the classical econo-mists before him, such as Adam Smith and David Ricardo, and mainstream economists in our time, Marx believed capitalists have the single goal of ac-cumulating and maximizing profits from their investments in machines, materials, and labor-power. And, like those before him, he had a high regard for the power of this capitalist accumulation process to accomplish gigantic tasks. As early as 1848, in the *Communist Manifesto*, Marx wrote:

> [The capitalist class] during its rule of barely one hundred years, has created more massive and more colossal productive forces than have all preceding generations together. Subjection of nature's forces to man, machinery, appli-cation of chemistry to industry and agriculture, steam navigation, railways, electric telegraphs, clearing of whole continents for cultivating, canalization of rivers, whole populations conjured out of the ground—what earlier cen-tury had even a presentiment that such productive forces slumbered in the lap of social labour? (Marx and Engels 1998, 40-1)

Few in our own capitalist age would disagree with this claim, though oth-ers might use less florid language to make it. Marx says elsewhere in the *Manifesto* that capitalists can be depended upon constantly "to revolutionize the means of production," by which he meant that the owning-managing class will never stop imagining ways to make their production more efficient and therefore less costly. A new technique, a new revolution in the means of production, will give the individual capitalist the power to make extra profits until the inevitable occurs and competitors adopt the same technique, or per-haps even better ones. Less industrial societies will have their "walls battered down by cheap commodities," as Marx put it in the *Manifesto*, for no mode of production can compete with capitalism in its capacity to drive down costs and shape the world after its own image. The globalization of capitalism that is now restructuring the world economy is a process Marx saw with uncanny accuracy in 1848, as reading the *Manifesto* will demonstrate.

For Marx, when the capitalist brings together land, labor, and capital, he or she produces a volatile mix that inevitably produces conflict. This view that struggle preeminently characterizes the capitalist workplace puts him at odds with Adam Smith and most others in the classical school, and with main-stream economists. It is, of course, not lost on mainstream economists that owners often have conflicts with their workers. Yet, anything beyond a per-functory mention of the relationship between labor and capital, or what Marx called the "social relations of production," is left outside the province of mainstream economics. From his different perch, Marx saw market competition as compelling owners to see their workers as two-sided creatures. On the one hand, workers are crucial for production. On the other, they are unpredictable and resistant to change and authority. They are given to slowdowns if not monitored carefully, and, if united, they possess the collective power to demand higher wages and better working conditions. They can even halt production altogether by going on strike. This threat means that workers must be continually controlled, their rebellions promptly squelched.

Marx concluded that this world of hostile workers and hungry competitors would ultimately corrupt even the most saintly capitalist. It doesn't matter whether he or she is a Christian, Muslim, or Jew; is friendly or mean-spirited; is Asian, Latin American, or what you will. Ultimately, the forces of competition can entice the most well-intentioned capitalist to reduce wages when possible, break the law, buy the politicians, adulterate the product, or even close the factory if doing so is necessary to maximize profit. Whereas mainstream economists see competition as the "invisible hand" that gives capitalism great moral authority over other economic systems, Marx saw competition as an unrelenting pressure that threatens to drag all capitalists down to the moral level of the most unscrupulous ones. As an example, Marx emphasized in *Capital* that without laws against child labor, *some* capitalists will hire children if doing so will lower costs, and the advantage thereby gained will force competitors downward into a squalid moral abyss. This imperative to follow the least scrupulous leader produces the assaults of the capitalist class on their customers, on their workers, and on the environment that one can find described daily in any newspaper.

Assessing the great power of competition to shape the actions of capitalists, Marx wrote:

> To the outcry as to the physical and mental degradation, the premature death, the torture of over-work, [capital] answers: Ought these to trouble us since they increase our profits? But looking at things as a whole, all this does not, indeed, depend on the good or ill will of the individual capitalist. Free competition brings out the inherent laws of capitalist production, in the shape of external coercive laws having power over every individual capitalist. (Marx 1967, 257)

Later in *Capital*, Marx vividly exemplified these effects of competition on capitalist morality by quoting a contemporary, T. J. Dunning, who had written:

With adequate profit, capital is very bold. A certain 10% [profit] will ensure its employment anywhere; 20% certain will produce eagerness; 50%, positive audacity; 100% will make it ready to trample on all human laws; 300%, and there is not a crime at which it will scruple, nor a risk it will not run, even to the chance of its owner being hanged. (Marx 1967, 760)

Marx's description of owners differs dramatically from the mainstream version, in which the capitalist stands triumphantly on a pedestal, a heroic risk-taker who has brought together land, labor, and capital. To paraphrase Marx's parody of that version, "Mr. Capital and Mr. Labor combine with Madam Land to produce the best of all possible worlds for them all."

Players on the Capitalist Field, II: The Workers

Estranged Labor. Beginning in his early writings, Marx assigned great importance to the oppression of workers under capitalism. In 1844, Marx wrote a long manuscript that provided a structural overview of his thinking about "economics" at the time. The notes lay undiscovered for almost a century, yet when they were published in English in the 1950s as the *Economic and Philosophic Manuscripts*, they generated great interest among Marxist scholars, who found a modern-sounding and compelling view about how capitalist wage labor limits human freedom.

In particular, the *Manuscripts* contained a section called "Estranged Labor," in which Marx described what, for him, were the fundamental conditions of labor under capitalism and the reasons that he found them so appalling. Marx argued that workers in capitalism are alienated from their work, their fellow employees, and themselves, and this argument became a preeminent theme for him and for all those who followed in his footsteps. According to Marx, workers' alienation stemmed from historical processes starting in 14th-century England that gradually separated (alienated) workers from the land and tools with which they had forged a living as peasants. Eventually their survival depended on being hired as wage laborers. Marx described the terrible consequences of alienation for workers in what has become the most famous passage from "Estranged Labor":

[Labor] is external to the worker, i.e., it does not belong to his essential being;...[I]n his work, therefore, he does not affirm himself but denies himself, does not feel content but unhappy, does not develop freely his physical and mental energy but mortifies his body and ruins his mind. The worker therefore only feels himself outside his work, and in his work feels outside himself. He is at home when he is not working, and when he is working he is not at home. His labor is therefore not voluntary, but coerced; it is forced labor. It is therefore not the satisfaction of a need; it is merely a means to satisfy needs external to it. Its alien character emerges clearly in the fact that as soon as no physical or other compulsion exists, labor is shunned like the plague. External labor, labor in which man alienates himself, is a labor of self-sacrifice, of mortification. Lastly, the external character of labor for the worker appears in the fact that it is not his own, but someone else's, that it does not belong to him, that in it he belongs, not to himself, but to another...it is the loss of the self. (Marx and Engels 1978, 74)

This conclusion that "lost labor" is a "lost self" perhaps says it all, yet does so in a far too general way. Fortunately, soon after writing the *Manuscripts*, Marx entered into his long collaboration with Frederick Engels, and they turned out thousands of pages in the form of essays, books, newspaper articles, and letters about capitalism. An ongoing burden of these pages was to explain to workers the nature of the system that oppressed them and to urge them to rise up against it. What follows are the key ingredients of this explanation.

Divided labor. In *Capital*, Marx had a good deal to say about the causes of estranged labor, and his analysis was more in the language of classical economics and less in the philosophical language of his earlier writing. In three key chapters of the book (13-15), Marx outlined the evolution of what 19th-century economists called the "division of labor" (what we now call "specialization"). Marx saw that a central reason for the estrangement of factory labor was the fact that it was profitable for owners to break tasks down into smaller individual units of work. As production was reduced to repetitive, mindless tasks, workers suffered physical injuries and mental frustration. Marx quoted from a French economist of the time to describe the grim consequences:

> To subdivide a man is to execute him, if he deserves the sentence, to assassinate him if he does not.... The subdivision of labor is the assassination of a people. (Marx 1967, 363)

The words are a bit different here than in the Manuscripts of 1844, but the argument is the same: *the capitalist mode of production, by necessarily and sys-*

tematically dividing labor to the greatest extent possible, denies most working people the opportunity to do the kind of creative work that Marx thought was essential to their humanity.[2]

Controlled labor. How do capitalists force workers to do jobs that are so physically and spiritually deadening? With the development of manufacturing (used in this context to mean, "production by hand") in 17th- and 18th-century England, and with the industrialization that followed, production moved from homes to factories. Small farmers and cottage industry producers had never had much control over the prices paid them by large merchants, but industrial workers had even less control over all parts of their work. Because factory workers toiled for owners rather than for their own immediate benefit, the owners monitored their efforts carefully. Indeed, industrial production created the need for a new kind of worker—managers and supervisors—to keep other workers doing increasingly alienating work. The division of labor, Marx put it, gradually separated "the hand from the brain" in capitalist workshops by generating ever more tasks demanding simple, repetitive motions but not much knowledge or control of the whole production process. This knowledge, originally held by workers, was transferred to managers. Marx often compared the factory system to the way military officers keep the ranks in order. As he put it in *Capital*, when production begins:

> ...[the capitalist] hands over the work of direct and constant supervision of the individual workmen, and groups of workmen, to a special kind of wage-laborer. An industrial army of workmen, under the command of a capitalist, requires, like a real army, officers (managers), and sergeants (foremen, over-lookers), who, while the work is being done, command in the name of the capitalist. (Marx 1967, 332)

To Marx, the increasing complexity of production in capitalist systems demanded ever more complex and sophisticated ways to keep workers performing jobs they typically do only in order to pay their bills.

What people involved in capitalist firms want from the experience varies with their relationship to the firm: do they own, manage, or supervise the work, or do they do it themselves for wages? The owners want brisk, timely, committed work, done as quickly as quality standards will allow. They want workers to show up on time, to stay as long as they are supposed to, and longer if possible, and to perform flawlessly, efficiently, and without complaint. Workers, though, compelled to make a living, would prefer a friendly, flexible environment, over which they have some measure of control. Thus, workers keep their noses to the grindstone only when forced to do so by managers, supervisors, electronic monitors, spies, or whatever else the owners can use to compel them to greater productivity.

In brief, then, the major players on the capitalist field are capitalists hustling for profits and workers hustling for a wage or salary. We have described the two main classes in the way that Marx chose to describe them, "in relation to each other." By this he meant that the term "capitalist" refers to someone who hires "wage laborers," that neither can exist without the other. Their relationship to each other produces the central dramatic action of the capitalist mode of production. Like all good dramatic action, this one is a waxing and waning struggle, and, in this case, what is being fought over is what Marx called "surplus value."

Surplus value. For Marx, the origin of profit in capitalism was what he called "surplus value." This is a very different explanation of profit than that offered by mainstream economists. To appreciate the difference, consider the following (quite typical) version from a popular mainstream principles textbook:

> Profit can be looked at as the reward you get for taking a chance for society, and winning. If you hire some factors of production and make something the people want, and if you do it efficiently, you will be rewarded. Your profit is your reward. But if you guess wrong you get no reward. You lose. Your loss is your "punishment" for using society's resources in ways the society didn't want its resources to be used. (Bowden and Bowden 1995, 63)

Let's look at Marx's alternative tale about how profits emerge in capitalism. Marx defined "surplus value" simply as the difference between the value of what a worker produces and what he or she is paid. Capitalists take this as profit, although it comes from the labor of the workers. In his analysis, Marx adopted what he calls "socially necessary labor time" as his standard of value for products exchanged in the market. The exchange value of a good or service is determined by the average number of hours of labor time that went into its production. In other words, Marx advanced one version of the general argument that the value of goods is determined by the labor that goes into them. The issue of what gave products their value had been debated by social theorists before Marx, and Adam Smith and David Ricardo were only the most prominent among the many who had earlier put forward this kind of "labor theory of value."

Marx's own version of this theory was much more closely argued, and he used the first several chapters of *Capital* to work out its internal consistencies and logical implications. In these chapters, Marx assumed that value, as he defined it, would in the long run determine (more or less) market prices. In Volume III of *Capital* Marx attempted to prove that the labor theory of value could be used as a basis for determining market prices. However, many critics have not been persuaded, and the debate continues. Fortunately for us, the framework Marx established about value is useful in analyzing capitalism, and this is true whether value determines prices, as Marx argued, or not. In the example below, we will work with the market prices of labor, materials, capital equipment, and products, rather than their embodied "socially necessary labor time." And, as we shall see, doing so does no harm to the analysis.

FREDERICK ENGELS, 1868

The idea of surplus value is easy to understand for anyone who has worked for wages or for a salary. Take for example, a young woman, a recent graduate from college who is offered $26,000 dollars a year to work for a capitalist company. What can we surmise about this transaction? The former student will likely be taking such a job because she is making an important transition in life and will soon pay the bills heretofore paid by her parents. She will probably have surveyed the possibilities and taken the best job available, given all her needs. What we know for certain is that the owner will be looking for one thing from the work of the student, and that thing is profit. In a nutshell, then, our new worker will be expected to produce something over $26,000 of new value. She will also be using equipment and materials in her work, and the owner must of course pay for these, too. But, in our example, such costs are assumed as already paid, and we are focusing solely on the new value added by our ex-student. She knows the rules, too, we can be sure. She knows that if she does not produce an amount of value greater than the $26,000 that she's paid, she will unceremoniously be ushered out the door.

None of this would be news to anyone raised in a capitalist society, though mainstream economists choose to look at it differently. Of course, they know that workers are hired to make profits for a firm, yet they typically avoid analyzing the historical processes that created that distribution of income and power. However, Marx was centrally concerned with the way this distribution came to be and how it shaped profit-making, once established. To answer these questions, Marx developed a detailed historical description of how the land and tools necessary for production were stripped from peasants and artisans, forcing them to work for wages in order to survive. Under capitalism, when the entrepreneur and the worker arrive at the workplace to seek their fortunes, the principal rule that emerged from this historical (rather than natural or divine) process is that the worker must labor to produce surplus value for the entrepreneur.

Marx explained the ways in which capitalists extracted surplus value from workers in his analysis of the working day. In this discussion, to which we now turn, he probed a number of interesting questions that mainstream economists long ago stopped asking.

The Working Day

At the beginning of his great historical essay called "The Working Day" (chapter 10 of *Capital*), Marx broke down the day into two parts, creating a very simple model but one with complex implications. He asked the reader to look at the day of the typical employee as comprised of two parts, as follows:

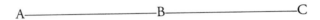

A————————————B————————————C

The first of these parts, A—B is the part of the day it takes for the worker to produce enough output to pay for his or her wage. We can more clearly exemplify this if we continue to use the example we began earlier with our recent graduate making $26,000 a year. We have chosen that apparently random number on purpose because it allows us to draw a simple example to make the point. Such an annual salary would come to $500 a week, or $100 a day. This means that, on average, each day this worker must add extra value to the firm's output of more than $100 in order to justify continued employment.

To extend the example, let's assume that this employee adds value to the firm's output of $160 a day or, assuming the typical eight-hour day, $20 an hour. Already, we can see that the employee is making surplus value (profit) for the owner, because the $160 of added value is more than the $100 daily salary. As we take one step further into this analysis, we move away from the de-politicized firm of the mainstream and into the world seen in Marxist terms. That step is simply to say this: if the employee is adding $20 per hour of value she will have produced enough value to pay for her wage during the first five hours of the day. Given the eight-hour workday in our example, that means for the last three hours our ex-student will be producing *surplus* value for the capitalist, the only reason why she was given the job in the first place. Marx called the first five hours of this day "necessary labor" and the remaining three hours "surplus labor" to differentiate the part of the day the worker was working for the wage, and the part of the day spent toiling to produce the owner's profits.

Marx focused the whole center section of *Capital*, several hundred pages, on these last three hours, or the B—C part of the day. He did so because this is the part that provides the capitalist surplus value, the quest for which is the distinguishing trait of capitalism. Marx did not, in his theorizing anyway, pass judgment on the process of creating and maximizing surplus value in capitalism. As we have already learned, the capitalist is only doing what is necessary to survive, and the worker is doing the same thing. The nature of the working day, in Marx's view, is a way to look at the experience of most people who live in capitalist culture, because most of them do work to produce surplus value for someone else. What did Marx make of this particular configuration of the day? The answer is "just about everything," and here we will take up the most important things.

Extending the working day. To begin with, we can ask ourselves a simple question: what are the ways the owner of a firm can increase the B—C part of the day? One immediate way would be simply to extend the length of the working day. Marx called surplus value generated this way "absolute surplus value," to distinguish it from "relative surplus value," which we will take up soon. If our recent graduate worked ten hours a day, rather than eight, this would generate roughly another $40 of surplus value for the firm. The rub, of course, is that it is illegal for the owner to do that in most modern capitalist countries without paying a premium for "over-time" hours. Marx describes the political realities of the length of the working day this way:

> But when the transaction was concluded, [the worker] discovered that he was no "free agent," that the period of time for which he is *free* to sell his labor-power is the period of time for which he is *forced* to sell it, that in fact the vampire will not let go "while there remains a single muscle, sinew or drop of blood to be exploited." For "protection" against the serpent of their agonies, the workers have to put their heads together and, as a class, compel the passing of a law, an all-powerful social barrier by which they can be prevented from selling themselves and their families into slavery and death by voluntary contract with capital. In the place of the pompous catalogue of the 'inalienable rights of man' there steps the modest Magna

Carta of the legally limited working day, which at last makes clear "when the time which the worker sells is ended, and when his own begins." (Marx 1967, 416, emphasis added)

Some of the more compelling periods of U.S. and British history, and of that of all capitalist societies, describe the battle waged over the length of the working day. When Marx was writing *Capital* in the 1860s, British laborers were engaged in protracted and often bloody battles with owners over the conditions of work in virtually every industry.

The most intense, and often quite violent, elements of the struggle between capital and labor in the United States occurred roughly between 1865 and 1920. For a vivid portrayal of this struggle, see the late Howard Zinn's powerful book, *A People's History of the United States*, Chapters 10-15. Marx saw the battle over the length of the working day as an inevitable outcome of the capitalist mode of production, and focusing on the B—C part of the day made it obvious why this was the case. Both parties, owner and worker, have diametrically opposed needs: the former has strong incentives to keep the worker on the job as long as possible, while the latter will typically strongly prefer to make the workday shorter.

Laws concerning the workday, along with a tangled forest of others that have sprung from the same soil, exist in all advanced capitalist countries. The unending political battles in the United States for the past sixty years over workplace safety, social security, unemployment compensation, minimum wages, welfare, trade, monetary and fiscal policy—to name only a suggestive list of issues—attest to this fact.

Once the length of the working day is fixed, the essential nature of the "contested terrain," as economist Richard Edwards described the workplace, does not change. Surplus value remains the goal of owners, while high wages and good (if not easy) working conditions are the goals of workers. What's a poor owner to do? Consider again the working day, A——B——C. If "A——C" is limited by law to represent eight hours in total, and the owner wants the part of the day in which the workers produce surplus value, B——C, to be as long as possible, what are ways to expand that part of the day? The answer must be to restructure work so that the laborer pays for the wage earlier in the day; or, in terms of the diagram, to restructure work so that "B moves to the left." Marx called profits made by such changes *relative* surplus value, and distinguished them from greater profits made simply by lengthening the working day.

Technological displacement of workers. Market competition and the hunger for surplus value always force owners to replace their workers with machines when it is profitable do to so. Making workers more productive with better, faster machines means that they pay for their wage earlier in the day. Marx took up the issue of machinery at great length in Chapter 15 of *Capital.* Although his argument concerns British industrial capitalism in the 19th century, his point remains relevant. He says this:

> [A] machine immediately becomes a competitor of the workman himself. The self-expansion of capital by means of machinery is thenceforward directly proportional to the number of the workpeople, whose means of livelihood have been destroyed by that machinery. The whole system of capitalist production is based on the fact that the workman sells his labor-power as a commodity. Division of labor specializes this labor-power, by reducing it to skill in handling a particular tool. So soon as the handling of this tool becomes the work of a machine, then ... the workman becomes unsaleable....That portion of the working-class thus by machinery rendered superfluous, either goes to the wall in the unequal contest of the [other outmoded industries] or else floods all the more easily accessible branches of industry, swamps the labor market, and sinks the price of labor-power ... (Marx 1967, 405-6)

Of course, this is the natural process by which technological unemployment occurs in capitalism. As an example from our own capitalist world, assume a capitalist firm that can make 1,000 units of a commodity at an average price of $1.00, with a process that uses one machine and 100 workers. Then, a supplier drops by with news about a new machine which will allow the owner to produce the same 1,000 units but with only 50 workers and at a cost of $.80 per unit. Will the capitalist fire 50 of his workers? Almost certainly, though he or she might first of all use the threat of the machine as a way to speed up the work and increase productivity that way.

In the two preceding chapters, 13 and 14, Marx had demonstrated, as he had in *The Communist Manifesto*, a genuine appreciation for the ability of the bourgeoisie to develop technology rapidly enough to transform the world with a previously unprecedented breadth and speed. He remained committed to the idea that machines could, in a mode of production designed for "free men," deliver people from the drudgery that has been the lot of most of them throughout human history. Yet, with the emergence of a system whose central dynamic is the production of surplus value, the machine becomes the agent of the worker's displacement, it promotes the exploitation of women and children, and, most horribly, it crushes workers between its moving wheels. Selected quotations from Chapter 15 will make his point. On the moral imperatives of capitalism and the machines, Marx wrote:

> In so far as machinery dispenses with muscular power, it becomes a means of employing laborers of slight muscular strength....The labor of women and children was, therefore, the first thing sought for by the capitalist who used machinery. (Marx 1967, 372)

and:

> [M]achinery sweeps away every moral and natural restriction on the length of the working day. Hence, too, the economic paradox, that the most powerful instrument for shortening labor-time, becomes the most unfailing means for placing every moment of the laborer's time and that of his family, at the disposal of the capitalist for the purpose of expanding the value of his capital. (Marx 1967, 385)

Concerning dangers of the factory, Marx had this to say:

> [In the factory] every organ of sense is injured in an equal degree by artificial elevation of the temperature, by the dust laden atmosphere, by the deafening noise, not to mention danger to life and limb among the thickly crowded machinery, which, with the regularity of the seasons, issues its list of the killed and wounded in the industrial battle. (Marx 1967, 401)

On this last point, Marx was, as we have said, writing about industrial capital rather than U.S. capitalism today (with its 70% of the workforce in the services industries), but we should not presume his comments about safety are outdated. For example, the U.S. Bureau of Labor Statistics reported that in 2005 more than 5,000 workers were killed on the job in U.S. private companies, and 4.2 million workers experienced non-fatal injuries or illnesses. That is, the mechanized capitalist workplace remains a threat to life and limb. For those workers who remain on the job, and ambulatory, what else can the owner do to get them to pay for their wage earlier in the day?

Cutting wages. Let's assume that the student from our earlier example is toiling away for $26,000 a year in a capitalist firm with one hundred workers, and then the owner decides to cut wages for all of them. Doing so would increase surplus value by moving the "B" part of the work day to the left, if we assume productivity doesn't change, because at a lower wage workers will provide enough extra value to pay for their wage earlier in the day. Will the workers accept these wage cuts like good soldiers? It depends, of course, and Marx made it clear he believed this battle over wages, like that over all the other conditions of work, would wax and wane.

As an excellent example of this ongoing struggle between capital and labor over wages, for about 25 years after World War II, real wages for American workers (that is, wages after accounting for inflation) rose regularly. This was because of steadily rising productivity and because, with roughly one-third of the workforce unionized, including virtually all wage-earners in the big industries, labor unions had genuine collective power at the workplace and on the national political scene. However, for several reasons, including declining employment in the manufacturing sector, globalization, and the intentional strategies of major capitalists to reduce the rate of unionization, labor's power relative to bosses began to decline in the early 1970s. Since then, the rate of unionization has fallen dramatically: in 2010 less than 10% of the labor force was unionized. Now real wages for an hour's work are lower for most workers than they were in 1970. The current generation of "bottom line" employers is no more cold-blooded than their counterparts from, say, 20 years, or 120 years ago. The difference is that the weakened political power of workers allows the cold-bloodedness, ever lurking in capitalism, to prevail where it could not in the 1950s when unions were powerful. To put it another way, if we ask when employers try to lower the wages of their employees, the answer comes quickly to any of us: whenever they can get away with it.

Speeding up the workplace. Consider again our student and her 99 fellow workers in the hypothetical capitalist firm. Let's say that this company provides consulting services to other firms.[3] Maybe fifty of its workers use computers to keep information flowing through the office, or to keep tabs on costs; maybe the other fifty are outside the office consulting, drumming up customers, or hanging out when they can get away with it. How could the owner speed up the work of these hundred employees? Or, formulaically, how can he or she make them more productive and, by doing so, enlarge the B—C part of the workday? The owner could monitor the work of those fifty on the computers, rank them according to their speed, and publicize the rankings. Or, the owner might devise ways to speed up the efforts of the outside workers by increasing the number of contacts they must make, or by transferring to them some of the computer work usually done in the office. When, we ask again, will the owners/managers speed up the work of employees? The answer, again, is: whenever they can get away with it. Further, given the nature of work in most capitalist firms, we can also predict when workers will not do the work their bosses want them to: whenever they can get away with it.

Moving the production somewhere else. Another method by which owners try to enlarge the B—C part of the day is to seek out lower wages somewhere else. Most of the shoes worn by Americans used to be made in mills in New England, produced by family-owned firms that dominated local economies but nonetheless provided relatively high wages and a good measure of job security. Gradually, the plants were moved to the southern United States because wages were lower there and, stemming from the same conditions that generate low wages, there was a relative hostility to organized labor. But before long, producers were moving their mills further south to places like the Dominican Republic, where wages were even lower; then, the move was to Taiwan and South Korea. This quest for the lowest wages reached its nadir when the Nike Corporation moved its production to Indonesia, where in the early 1990s, its subcontractors hired young women to make Nike shoes for fourteen cents an hour.

To sum up Marx's arguments about "relative surplus value": he showed that confining the length of the working day to a maximum number of hours did not change the essential dynamic of the capitalist mode of production. It simply mandated that capitalists "intensify labor," to use Marx's term, in order to maximize surplus value. Concretely, this meant cutting wages, speeding up work, replacing workers with machines, and marching around the globe in search of low-wage workers.

The Industrial Reserve Army

In Chapter 25 of *Capital*, Marx theorized about the horrific conditions endured by so much of the working class in Britain. His guides into this territory included dozens of reports of Parliamentary investigations, as well as Frederick Engels, whose book *The Condition of the Working Class in England* (1844) had early on helped draw Marx's attention away from philosophy and toward political economy. In Chapter 25, Marx paid particular attention to the nature of what we call "unemployment" and the reasons that it regularly occurs in capitalism. What distinguishes Marx's treatment from current ones is in part the tone of his writing. Marx called those without jobs in capitalism "the industrial reserve army." His words conjure complex images that present a far richer notion about workers without jobs than the abstract mainstream term "unemployment." Consider the implications of Marx's term. First, he uses a military metaphor, "army," reminding us that those without jobs are foot soldiers in some capitalist's army and, like their counterparts in the real army, utterly at the mercy of the "generals" directing the struggle. More important, however, is the word "reserve," which in Marx's definition carries crucial political and economic implications.

The unemployed in Marx's system are "in reserve" in the sense that capitalists always need a pool of them in order to make surplus value. Consider an economic recession, where production and employment spiral down together, the decline in each bringing about further declines in the other. The first workers to get the axe will typically be the last ones hired back, and they will be those considered the least skilled, least educated, least desirable for whatever reasons. If the contraction is great enough and long enough, an increasing number of those losing jobs will be more educated and experienced.

We all know this, but Marx adds the emphasis that for capitalism to function, these people must take their lumps, if not in silence, at least without posing a political threat. In other words, capitalism *absolutely depends upon* a class of people at the bottom who can be fired without explanation and who also are not able to organize resistance to the system that has tossed them out. Instead of resisting, capitalism demands that these workers graciously blame their lot on themselves, rather than blame a production system that makes their unemployment necessary and predictable. Further, capitalist systems need the reserve army to hold down wages: a pool of unemployed, financially desperate workers reminds those who still have a job that they can easily be replaced if they make demands on their employers. And finally, the reserve army serves the needs of capitalism in times of economic growth. When the economy starts expanding, it won't grow for long unless there are people "in reserve" who can be absorbed back into the system. Naturally, the capitalists' hope is that those in reserve will not have made themselves into a *real* army in the meantime.

Throughout *Capital*, Marx fulminates and rages about the lot of workers in capitalism in between the lines of his dense theoretical arguments. It deeply provoked his moral outrage. Yet in mainstream economics, unemployment is considered either a short-term failure of the system or a long-term failure of hopeless individuals. The relationship between joblessness and the political system is also generally ignored because, as is usual in mainstream economics, politics and questions of power are cavalierly ignored.

Social Classes

The idea of the army of unemployed points to the fact of social classes in capitalism, about which Marx had much to say. One of the more intriguing aspects of life in U.S. society is that those who shape opinions, including many professors, deny the existence of social classes. Instead of concepts such as "working class" or "ruling classes," they have substituted entirely different ideas and metaphors, such as "social status" or the "melting pot." The "American Dream" anchors a mythical understanding of ourselves, and in it any child can make it to the top by trying hard enough. Those who actually have done so are paraded through our media and our history books as proof of typical experiences, though they are not that at all. Research debunks the myth with a crashing finality by showing that the best way to get to the top is to be born to parents already there.

Marx wrote often about social class, both theoretically and through his accounts of key events of his times. However, his theory is quite undeveloped, and he never abandoned what he argued early on in the *Manifesto* that society is ultimately divided into the two great camps of the bourgeoisie and the proletariat. In his system, other classes were fated to extinction. "Petite bourgeoisie" is Marx's term for owners of small firms, intellectuals, and all others who do not hire wage-laborers. He also referred to those truly outside the production system as the "lumpenproletariat," a term very close to the current idea of the "underclass." Marx believed that smaller firms would ultimately fail to compete with big firms and members of the petit bourgeoisie would be "hurled into the proletariat" along with all those intellectuals who did not end up as apologists for capitalism.

Some later thinkers have criticized Marx's division of society into two classes as overly simplistic. A crucial question arises: Who is truly a worker, and who is not? Are supervisors workers? Are medical doctors? How about teachers in public schools, or in private schools? These are important questions, not always answered clearly by Marx's choice to put everyone into two warring groups. Yet, a two-part class system is not as superficial as it might seem. Consider U.S. society, where most of us work for wages or salaries in positions where the following conditions prevail: We do not control what we produce, how it is produced, or how it is priced; we have nothing to say about whether our workplace will be open tomorrow; we must take the wage offered us, even if it is not enough to live on (unless we can easily get another job or are part of a union that will collectively fight for higher pay). And, our labor is "divided" as a matter of course, and it will be sub-divided into ever-smaller tasks as long as it is profitable for owners to do so. If these are the conditions of your job, you are a worker in the Marxian version of the capitalist world. On the other hand, if you do have some control over these matters, you are a capitalist, or a high-ranking official in a capitalist firm; that is, you are in the capitalist class.

Without question, this classification is oversimplified. Owners of small firms typically have much less control over the market in which they operate than do the owners of large, powerful ones. And, there is an obvious difference in the significant control over work held by a carpenter working for a construction company and the gofer who spends all day bringing nails and wood the carpenter needs to the do the job. Marx was aware of these differences, and this complexity of the modern world has led latter-day Marxists to construct variations on Marx's themes, mostly by adding classes that don't fit very neatly into any of his categories. For instance, Pat Walker's *Between Capital and Labor* (1978) describes a "professional managerial class" made up of professionals such as doctors, lawyers, academics, and others who have some control over their working environment but who do not typically hire wage-laborers and earn surplus value. Other scholars have, in this same vein, tried to account for these "in between" classes. In their accounting for professionals, these theorists are not abandoning the Marxist framework but are trying to modernize it so that it remains a viable paradigm in which to think about capitalism.

Implicit in Marx's discussion about social class is the quite limited number of roles that can be played out in modes of production. As an example, presume that a youngster reads captivating books that make him or her want to be a shining knight, or a provincial duchess, or a hardy English yeoman, or a Plains Indian warrior, or a pioneering woman ready to prove herself when pushed up against the rough elements of the weather (not to mention patriarchy), or the fair-minded leader of a workers' council in a democratic socialist country. It is not possible to play these, or any number of other roles, if one resides in modern capitalism, because you can only be an owner, a worker, a government servant, or someone else inhabiting a role shaped by capitalism. And inside your role, you must play it to the hilt to survive: as an owner you must worship the bottom line, and as a worker you must obey the owner. This does not mean, of course, you have no agency—no free will—but as Marx put it so very well:

Men make their own history, but they do not make it just as they please: they do not make it under circumstances chosen by themselves, but under circumstances directly encountered, given and transmitted from the past. The tradition of all the dead generations weighs like a nightmare on the brain of the living. (Marx and Engels 1978, 595)

By placing people in social classes according to "their relationship to the means of production," Marx introduced new language and a larger, more powerful theoretical framework. Discussions of social class continue to ignore Marx at a cost. As one economist, Teresa Amott, put it:

> ... No matter how far from *Capital* the debate [about social class in capitalism] has strayed, Marx's original conceptions continue to define the shape and logic of the argument. In fact, one could argue that the burden of twentieth-century thought on class has been the task of rehabilitation, elaboration, deconstruction, and contestation of Marx's original construction of class, that to criticize Marxist concepts of class, one must stand in the space that Marx cleared. (Amott 1996)

As Amott argues, though Marx did not himself give the same kind of full theoretical treatment to social class as did many other writers, he established the framework for a discussion about social classes in capitalism that continues today. How could there not be social classes in our society when even small children know that the people who own or control the businesses also own houses, cars, food, and clothes that are almost always better than those of the people who work for them?

Other Economic Arguments about Capitalism

Capital is a book of about seven hundred pages, and in it Marx wrote about many aspects of capitalism. We have taken up those arguments that dominate the book and which remain mostly germane, even eye-opening, to readers in our own day. We have ignored some of his arguments because they do not have a great deal to say about our own world. Still other claims Marx made do not merit much explanation in this kind of review, because they are now so commonly accepted. However, we will mention two of the latter kind of argument because they have a particular importance to *Capital*. We will also say a few words about Marx's theory of revolution.

Booms and busts. In mainstream economics, John Maynard Keynes is generally considered to have founded the modern study of the business cycle in the mid-1930s. However, the history of economic thought is now rarely taught in graduate schools, and thus economists usually do not know that others, including Marx, had developed complex and persuasive theories of the business cycle. One problem is that Marx scattered arguments about the instability of capitalism throughout all four volumes of *Capital*, and few readers have taken the time to compile and assess his claims. Marx's arguments are also largely unknown to mainstream economists for ideological reasons, and, as we have pointed out, these economists have gradually come to ignore all that he wrote. Even though mainstream economists are rarely familiar with them, Marx made a series of strikingly modern arguments about the business cycle. One argument from Volume II is this:

> The ultimate reason for all real crises [recessions/depressions] always remains the poverty and restricted consumption of the masses as opposed to the drive of capitalist production to [produce as much as possible]. (Marx 1981, 484)

This idea, called "underconsumption," is central to most modern macroeconomic theories. In the second and third volumes of *Capital*, Marx developed other intriguing theories of the business cycle. In one of them, Marx anticipated the ideas of Keynes in arguing that there is interdependency between the investment and consumption sectors of a capitalist economy. In Volume II, he showed with fine logical consistency that over- or under-production in one of these economic sectors can produce a "realization" crisis, or what we call a recession or depression. It is only because British economists, who with Keynes developed modern macroeconomics, were not reading Marx that they did not see that much of their own work only extended what he had already written about.

The centralization of capital. Marx was the first major social theorist to predict that capitalism would lead to a growing centralization of power in the hands of a few capitalists. By "centralization," Marx meant what we call horizontal, vertical, and conglomerate mergers (firms merging, respectively, with one of their competitors, suppliers, or firms from a completely different industry). In Chapter 25 of *Capital*, Marx explained how the capitalists' need to mechanize production would produce ever more costly machinery and buildings. These expensive new technologies would drive down costs, and smaller firms not able to buy the newest machinery would be driven out of business or gobbled up by the bigger ones. The financial industry, too, would verge toward centralization. Ultimately, both it and these large financial and industrial firms would shape business regulations in capitalist states to allow for more centralization in the future. Marx's arguments on these matters are more interesting for their prescience than as new information. Yet interestingly, Marx tied the centralization of capital to the eventual collapse of capitalism, because he thought that as monopolies grew in power, they would hurl more and more workers, and the owners of small firms, into an increasingly immiserated proletariat. The result, he predicted, would be unrest and then revolution.

The centralization and immiseration that Marx described have clearly been underway in most capitalist societies. Consider the effect of the immense Wal-Mart chain. Its monopolization of retail sales has made it ever more difficult for Main Street merchants to compete with it. Wal-Mart has two principal advantages over its smaller competitors: Its huge stores spread the overhead for each sale over hundreds of thousands of products in the typical store. And, Wal-Mart directly purchases sizeable proportions of the total output of such giants as Procter & Gamble. This gives it the market leverage to buy at volume prices considerably lower than those charged to smaller outlets. Direct purchases such as these immediately wipe out whole strata of small wholesalers and threaten all retailers that compete with the giants. Millions of small business owners, particularly those who are not highly educated or do not have professional skills, have been hurled into jobs with low pay and no control over their work.

The theory of revolution. In one rhetorical outburst in the next-to-last chapter of *Capital*, Marx predicted that capitalism was doomed and that it was but a matter of time before the capitalist "expropriators"—another of his terms for capitalists who extract surplus value—were themselves "expropriated." (715) Marx argued that booms and busts would grow increasingly tumultuous, each one leaving more small firms driven from the field and more workers in ever-greater misery. That tumult would eventually lead to an overthrow of the capitalist class. That this has not happened is a testament to the resilience of capitalism and its great capacity to adapt to technological and political changes. Marx was aware of this adaptability, and in particular, he thought that in democratic capitalist societies workers might restructure the system and make it more "civilized" without overthrowing it. In his view, however, a "reformed" capitalism, with laws providing improved working conditions and less income inequality would still be exploitative and workers would remain alienated. In this sense, efforts to reform capitalism would simply prolong the oppression of the working class. To some degree, this is what happened in the capitalist welfare states in Northern Europe, as we shall see in the chapter on Sweden.

Whether the workers of the world will ultimately "unite" and overthrow their oppressors remains to be seen. Capitalism continues to experience recurring crises that throw hundreds of millions of people out of work and to leave billions of people without enough to live on. Further, financial crises, such as the one that began in 2007, usher forth recessions or depressions and other destabilizing events and slow economic activity the world over. At what level of world unemployment would Marx's prediction about revolutionary upheaval come true? It remains to be seen. In fact, this tipping point might be a smaller level of unemployment if this were to combine with food shortages or other problems that could well result from global climate change.

The Moral Standing of Capitalism

In the last six chapters of *Capital*, Marx took up a fundamental question: where does accumulated capital originate? He answered that it had begun with slavery and imperialism. The substance of his answer is embodied in his idea of what he called "primitive accumulation." In Chapter 31, he provides key historical examples:

> The discovery of gold and silver in America, the extirpation, enslavement and entombment in mines of the aboriginal population, the beginning of the conquest and looting of the East Indies, the turn of Africa into a warren for the commercial hunting of [black people], signalized the rosy dawn of the era of capitalist production. (Marx 1967, 703)

These examples follow two chapters on the enclosure movements, particularly in Britain starting in the sixteenth century and continuing up to Marx's time. Enclosure was a process by which the crown, the land barons, the church, and eventually the capitalists, seized for their own use vast stretches of land long used by peasants and the yeomanry to produce their livelihood. The effect was to drive most of this agricultural work force into the cities as vagabonds or wage laborers.[4] For British peasants whose livelihood was stolen, enclosure was brutality, and its example was a key one that led Marx to argue that capital originated in plunder and violence. Because wealth and power are passed down from generation to generation, this early pillaging remained the foundation of the distribution of wealth and power in Marx's time. Later on in the chapter, Marx hurled forward this verbal thunder:

> If money, according to Augier [a Frenchman writing in 1842] "comes into the world with a congenital blood-stain on one cheek," capital comes dripping from head to foot, from every pore, with blood and dirt. (Marx 1967, 760)

In these last six chapters, Marx made two interconnected claims. The first was that capitalism was born in pillage and murder, and the second was that it is a system of unremitting oppression and violence against working people. Do these claims have any merit as descriptions of modern capitalism? Was U.S. capitalism built on violence and plunder? Does it remain oppressive to the majority of the people who live in it?

The answer, of course, depends on whom you ask. The history of the United States has received countless tellings, offering dramatically different answers to these questions. Were John D. Rockefeller and J.P. Morgan "robber-baron" criminals, as some historians have concluded? Or was their inexorable drive to accumulate profits, and their need constantly to revolutionize the means of production, the forces that brought modern industrial capitalism into being? Or were capitalists both plunderers and revolutionaries, as seems to be Marx's position? For those who adopt the benign meritocratic view of capitalism, its inequalities of opportunity and outcome can be justified with the claim that it has always been an open system in which all who genuinely make the effort can rise to the top. This view is, without question, the dominant one in our times.

Others, though, see things quite differently. They argue that central to modern capitalism are owners and managers who *by definition* live off surplus value produced by someone else; who *must* create mindless tasks for most of their workers; who *must* withhold loyalty to their workers; who *must* fire, or replace, or even harm their workers' health, if doing so will increase their surplus value; and who *must* monitor their workers' efforts to keep them on jobs which many hate.

This is a language of force and oppression, and to a Marxist it is also the language of plunder and pillage. Surplus value, expropriated from the workers only because the capitalists control the productive system, is the means by which these owners build their fortunes, amass their political power, and dominate the capitalist world. And capitalists' quest for surplus value requires them to do damage to everything in their path. Consider tobacco executives who kill their customers for surplus value, or Nike's Phil Knight, who has become a billionaire off workers toiling under wretched conditions, or the countless chemical companies that have dumped toxic materials onto fields where children now play. Consider, and as exemplifying an unending pattern in the history of U.S. capitalism, the marauding executives from Enron, WorldCom, and Arthur Andersen, who in the early 2000s stole from everyone in their path: workers, customers, suppliers, and owners of their stock. Finally, consider the refusal of all these actors to take responsibility for their human and environmental destruction. Are such characters on the modern capitalist stage any different from the "blood-sucking werewolves" of Marx's world? Like everything else, it depends on your point of view.

III. CONCLUSION

Marx was a prodigious writer, and this introduction is meant to urge readers to look into his work for themselves. Whereas we have tried to explain Marx's conception of history, and the basic ideas about capitalism advanced in the first volume of *Capital*, the other works of Marx and Engels contain thoughtful elaborations of their ideas, often in powerful and elegant language.

If one wants to take on *Capital*, or some of Marx's other more demanding texts, the best way to do so is in a college course or a reading group. On the other hand, much of what Marx and Engels wrote is quite accessible, and interested readers can certainly browse and read independently. Our readers should give Marx another chance and not listen to those who claim from the rooftops, "Marx is dead!" Quite frankly, that is a claim that could only be made by someone who has never read his works.

SUGGESTIONS FOR FURTHER READING

In the case of the works of Marx and Engels cited below, there are many publishers of each item. We have thus confined reference information to the initial publishing date of each of them.

Engels. *The Condition of the Working Class in England*, 1845.

Engels. *Socialism: Utopian and Scientific*, 1880.

Marx and Engels. *The Communist Manifesto*, 1848. (The 1998 Verso edition of the Manifesto, subtitled "A Modern Edition," contains a useful introduction by British historian Eric Hobsbawm.)

Marx. *Wage-Labor and Capital*, 1849.

Marx. *Capital*, Vol. 1., 1867.

Marx. *The Civil War in France*, 1871.

Marx. *The Critique of the Gotha Program*, 1875.

About Marx-Engels and their thought:
Brewer, Anthony. *A Guide to Marx's Capital.* London: Cambridge University Press, 1984.

Cohen, G.A. *Karl Marx's Theory of History: A Defence.* Princeton, N.J.: Gerald Allen, 1941.

McClellan, David. Karl Marx: *His Life and Thought.* New York: Harper-Row, 1974.

Applications of Marxist economic theory:
Baran, Paul, and Paul Sweezy. *Monopoly Capital: An Essay on the American Economic and Social Order.* New York: Monthly Review, 1966.

Zinn, Howard. *A People's History of the United States.* New York: Harper Perennial, 2003.

4

Thorstein Veblen and the Predatory Nature of Contemporary Capitalism

INTRODUCTION

Thorstein Veblen is another of the political economists whose theories of the economy diverge significantly from the standard neoclassical (i.e., mainstream) analysis that is offered in standard economics textbooks. Veblen's system of analysis has some similarities to that of Marx. Veblen treats the modern American economy as being dominated by business interests and inherently prone to cyclical crises, rather than resembling the mythical perfectly competitive world created by Adam Smith. Veblen also makes conscious use of learning from the other social sciences in order to analyze the factors that he thought to be most important for understanding the economy—economic and social change.

Before we proceed, let's dismiss one of the common complaints about Veblen: his unique writing style. Critics of Veblen, and even many of his admirers, characterize much of his writing as irony, and many dismiss his work as humorous satire. As one example, a famous passage from Veblen examines the role of habit in human thought processes. In this passage, Veblen observes that the "patriotic spirit" is less the product of individualistic rational choice by citizens of a given country than the result of inculcation of certain feelings of sentiment and loyalty by our peers and national institutions. In other words, according to Veblen, most of us arguably gain a feeling of national pride from living our lives in a particular country or region, but that pride is derived not from a careful comparison of the costs and benefits of living in our own country and a rational assessment of the institutions and government apparatus, but instead from our tendency to be loyal to and fond of our own home country just because we know it best:

> The patriotic spirit, or tie of nationalism, is evidently of the nature of habit. ... More particularly is it a matter of habit...what particular national establishment a given human subject will become attached to on reaching what is called "years of discretion" and so becoming a patriotic citizen. The analogy of the clam may not be convincing, but it may at least serve to suggest what may be the share played by habituation in the matter of national attachment. The young clam, after having passed the free-swimming phase of his life, as well as the period of attachment to the person of a carp or similar fish, drops to the bottom and attaches himself loosely in the place and station in life to which he has been led; and he loyally sticks to his particular patch of oose [sic] and sand through good fortune and evil. It is, under Providence, something of a fortuitous matter where the given clam shall find a resting place for the sole of his feet, but it is also, after all, "his own, his native land" etc. It lies in the nature of a clam to attach himself after this fashion, loosely, to the bottom where he finds a living, and he would not be a "good clam and true" if he failed to do so; but the particular spot for which he forms this attachment is not of the essence of the case. At least, so they say. "It may be, as good men appear to believe or know, that all men of sound, or at least those of average, mind will necessarily be of a patriotic temper." (Veblen 1998, 134-135)

Veblen's writing was often characterized by such subtle sarcasm, but the sarcasm masked cogent and important analysis. To quote his most famous student, Wesley Clair Mitchell, "there [was] always an aura of playfulness about his attitude toward his own work in marked contrast to the deadly seriousness of most economists." (Quoted in Galbraith 1972, v) The humor sometimes employed by Veblen may have softened his message somewhat. As John Kenneth Galbraith put it in his introduction to a 1972 reissue of *The Theory of the Leisure Class*, "That Marx was an enemy whose venom was to be returned in kind, capitalists did not doubt. But not Veblen. The American rich never quite understood what he was about—or what he was doing to them."

As we will see, Veblen coined a number of phrases well-known to us today: phrases such as "conspicuous consumption," and "leisure class," and "captains of industry." These were not mere clever turns of phrase, but rather theoretical concepts as central to his system of analysis as concepts such as self-interest and profit-maximization are to neoclassical analysis. To understand the importance of conspicuous consumption or to see the role played by the captains of industry, we will situate those terms within his system of analysis.

THE ROOTS OF VEBLEN'S UNDERSTANDING OF THE ECONOMY

Veblen was a careful observer of the changes taking place in the United States economy at the beginning of the twentieth century and an innovating economist who specialized in studying economic change. Many of Veblen's views of the economy were conditioned by his father's experience as a farmer in Minnesota contending with the changing economy of the post-Civil War United States. In the early 1870s, Midwestern farmers had taken advantage of new agricultural technologies to improve wheat processing and, in turn, to expand their production. As you learn when you study the operations of competitive markets, a bumper crop causes a rightward shift in the supply curve that tends to lower prices—a good thing for consumers, but not necessarily for farmers. Indeed, lower prices led to falling incomes and economic misfortune for many farmers. Farmers attributed their financial woes to the groups who seemed to be prospering. To quote Joseph Dorfman, biographer of Veblen, farmers reacted with a "wave of bitterness against the business interests...from the country-store trader and banker to the railroad company." (Dorfman 1961, 14) Fellow Minnesotan and chief lecturer for the Grange, Ignatius Donnelly, lamented in 1873: "Could the ordinary man retain his economic independence, or must he become the wage slave of the possessor of great wealth?" (Dorfman 1961, 16)

Midwestern farmers believed themselves to be victimized by several groups of villains: the railroad tycoons who raised their rates and made it costlier for them to ship their produce to the East, the bankers who advanced them loans and then demanded payment even when falling prices destroyed the farmers' profits, the jobbers or wholesalers who bought the farmers' produce at low prices and resold these products at higher prices. To the typical farmer, it appeared that he was doing all the productive work and losing money while the railroads, middlemen, and financiers were profiting at his expense. Yet the decisions of the railroads, middlemen, and financiers, at a remove from the farmers and workers, dictated the economic fortunes of the actual production workers. Below we will explore this distinction between what Veblen called "pecuniary" and "industrial" activities in more depth.

Veblen also examined other conflicts which he thought were central to the pace and direction of economic change. For Veblen, the conflict between scientific or "matter-of-fact" thinking and superstitious or animistic thinking explained the often slow pace of change in our increasingly technological society. According to Veblen, past-binding thinking locked society into habitual ways of thinking and being. Even today we can find examples, ranging from persistent superstitions about Friday the thirteenth, to the persistent gender and racial stereotypes that hinder women and minorities from rising to the top of corporate hierarchies or earning salaries comparable to their white male counterparts. In the same way, we can see the conflict between what Veblen once referred to as "imbecile institutions" (his term for past-binding behavior) and the logic of the machine process, his metaphor for modern production techniques. This conflict, in Veblen's view, could impede technology's path and even alter its beneficent consequences. In one obvious example, the modern school year in the United States still includes a three-month summer break, even though that summer break no longer serves its original purpose—to free children to work on family farms during the busy summer months. As a result, U.S. children attend school on average two fewer months during the year than Japanese children.

VEBLEN'S EVOLUTIONARY ANALYSIS

Veblen, like many early economists, was first trained in philosophy, so he took great pains to examine the philosophical foundations of the received economics of his day. He found that those foundations were outmoded for understanding the kind of economics emerging in the twentieth century. Mainstream economics then and now relied on the philosophical underpinnings of natural law that swept social science thinking in the late eighteenth century. This was the period during which Adam Smith wrote *The Wealth of Nations*. Smith and other early classical economists were influenced by the work of Isaac Newton, and they described the social world in the same terms that physical scientists used to describe the physical world. The physical universe was seen as an immense clock set into motion by a Divine Clockmaker, and the social universe was seen to be similarly well organized and mechanically ordered. Just as the Newtonian laws of physics kept the physical world operating in orderly fashion, the "natural" economic laws of the marketplace would channel the self-interested actions of human beings toward mutually beneficial outcomes for all. The natural order of the social universe was believed to be a system of free markets, with humans free to consume and to work as they pleased, but controlled, if not by the Divine Clockmaker, then by his close counterpart, the "invisible hand." Adam Smith developed this metaphor to describe the impersonal market forces which he and his followers believed regulated the economy, a natural regulator that precluded intervention by earthly (government) regulators.

The Newtonian worldview led economists to see a world that was for the most part fixed and immutable. To quote David Hamilton, these early economists assumed that "the social order of their day was the natural product of sufficient reason and therefore fixed." (Hamilton 1991, 22) Most economic historians agree that Adam Smith's England did in fact resemble the microeconomic model of perfect competition, even though great joint stock companies dominated much of England's international trade. (Heilbroner 1999)[1] Hence Smith could justifiably construct a model of a perfectly competitive economy, where many small producers competed and self-interest alone sufficed to maintain social order and to produce the maximum economic welfare for all members of society. Influenced by the natural law tradition in philosophy, Smith also assumed that the economic world had reached its ideal form with the flourishing of competition in late eighteenth century England. Analysis of change was deemed irrelevant, because the "classical" economists believed they were describing the archetypal economic system that would henceforth prevail always and everywhere. In such a world, analysis of economic change could be restricted to the temporary movements away from competitive market equilibrium. The main question to be answered, then, was: When demand rises for one product or falls for another product, how will the market reach a new equilibrium price and quantity?

Veblen argued that an evolutionary model was more useful for understanding the economy. Writing one hundred years after Smith, and observing the economic changes that had so concerned Marx, Veblen, like Marx, declared that the social universe was not fixed and immutable. Smith had described a transitory epoch, according to Veblen. Writing in an age in which a Darwinian model of evolution was being adopted in the biological sciences and imitated in the social sciences, Veblen adopted an evolutionary model to explain the cumulative causation and constant change that he observed.[2] Indeed, during the period that Veblen wrote most of his major works, 1898 to about 1923, evidence abounded that economic and social change was a permanent feature of the economy. New technologies allowed for mass production of goods and services, transforming industries that may have once conformed to Smith's model of atomistic competition, into industries now dominated by a few large multinational firms. Moreover, a huge wave of mergers and acquisitions at the turn of the century created huge national and multinational business firms that dominated their industries and transformed the nature of competition. The economists who clung to Smith's theories and applied them to the greatly changed economy of the late nineteenth century assumed that the natural order of the world (in the form of placid price competition) would quickly restore Adam Smith's ideal economy.

Veblen's use of the Darwinian approach did not mean that Veblen believed in survival of the fittest, despite the fact that Veblen actually studied under William Graham Sumner, one of the architects of social Darwinism. Veblen took from Darwin and Sumner a different scientific method, "which studies humanity in its process of continuous adaptation to both its social and natural environment and which sees the conditions of human existence as subject to ceaseless change." (Tilman 1993, xxvi) It is not survival of the fittest that is relevant to understanding economic and social change, but rather the simple fact of evolution itself. As a simple example, the modern practice of men wearing ties—a non-utilitarian adornment that fits tightly around the neck of most men who move in professional circles—for important social or professional occasions, dates to an era where men used their ties or cravats to wipe their faces while eating. Over time, ties evolved into the quintessential symbol of the gentleman of business, even though the modern businessman would no sooner wipe his face on an expensive silk tie than he would appear in public with a cheerful checked napkin wrapped around his neck. Less obviously, perhaps, but more importantly, Veblen observed that the nature of the work performed by entrepreneurs, or to use his word, "undertakers," also evolved considerably as large multinational firms came to dominate the U.S. economy. Businesspeople in the mid-nineteenth century conducted the financial and managerial affairs of their businesses, but also spent time on the shop floor working alongside their own workers. Thus they had constant exposure to the working conditions of the average production worker. By the end of the nineteenth century, the undertakers had become "captains" of industry and finance who managed their operations for their own pecuniary gain rather than to meet the needs of the community.

THE LEISURE CLASS

To understand why Veblen, and other heterodox economists after him, saw analysis of economic change from an evolutionary approach as crucial to understanding the dynamics of any economic system, we will look at his most important economic ideas in their appropriate context. Veblen wrote at a time when many social scientists (but few economists) were beginning to use evolutionary narratives to examine social phenomena. Veblen began his analysis of the economy with the concept of the "leisure class." which he singled out as "an economic factor in modern life." He presented this in his most famous book, *The Theory of the Leisure Class*, which set forth many of the basic concepts of his analytical system, and made explicit use of his evolutionary understanding of the modern economy. The book was written as the excesses of the Gilded Age of the late nineteenth century began to reveal themselves in the form of the lavish entertainments and opulent mansions enjoyed by the wealthy capitalists of the era. However, Veblen began his analysis not with these wealthy robber barons, but with the feudal cultures of Japan and medieval Europe, because he believed that modern economic behavior had evolved slowly from those beginnings. In Veblen's view, any careful analysis had to unearth the long historical roots of our modern institutions. (Lerner 1976, 22)

A common theme ran through economic history, according to Veblen: "Wherever the institution of private property is found, even in slightly developed form, the economic process bears the character of a struggle between men for the possession of goods." (Veblen 1973, 34) The word "struggle" conveys Veblen's view of competition—not merely placid price competition of the sort described by Smith, but the "slash and burn" competition more common in our modern business landscape. Veblen also recognized that property had held a dual role throughout history: one economic, one symbolic.

In that struggle for subsistence, according to Veblen, there has always been a "warrior" or "leisure class" and a "menial" or "productive class." This taxonomy is similar to the class distinctions made by Marx. The leisure class first emerged in early hunter-gatherer societies. Veblen defined this group as the class of persons exempt from menial labor and for whom the "honorable employments" of hunting were reserved. (Veblen 1973, 21) In these early cultures, the gender division of labor between men and women was strictly observed: the men hunting for food, the women gathering and farming and preparing the food. Both sets of activities were, of course, equally indispensable to economic survival, but not equally honored.[3] The hunters constituted the first leisure class: "in [the hunter's] own eyes, he is not a laborer, and he is not to be classed with the women in this respect; nor is his work to be classed with the women's drudgery, as labor or industry." (Veblen 1973, 23)

Over time, the leisure class came to include the entire class of persons who were exempt from the more routine and menial tasks necessary for economic survival; the leisure class was not exempt from all work of any kind, but was instead exempt from menial labor. These invidious distinctions between different lines of work have persisted over time, Veblen insisted, meaning that our modern ranking of methods of making a living is rooted in our deep anthropological past. While a modern industrial economy no longer depends on a class of hunters to provide a large portion of society's means of subsistence, the higher honor accorded those engaged in "predatory" pursuits has endured, and the low repute accorded those engaged in actual productive work has also persisted. The modern day robber barons were, in Veblen's analysis, the economic descendants of the warring nobles of medieval Europe and the warrior class of Japan, struggling not against nature or against other clans for control over land and property, but against other robber barons for control of their industries. We can see similar struggles today. The U.S. government's antitrust trial against Microsoft exposed Bill Gates' ruthless tactics to increase use of Microsoft's Internet Explorer (IE) and prevent new competition from threatening its monopoly, such as forcing computer manufacturers to install IE on their computers or withholding Windows from manufacturers, such as IBM, who were building operating systems that might compete with Windows. Similarly, when faced with foreign competition in the 1970s, the U.S. auto industry used its political clout to lobby for protectionist measures, and ignored the emerging demand for quality small cars because they were not sufficiently profitable in the eyes of the Big Three. It is evident to all industry observers that the bankruptcies of GM and Chrysler in 2009 originated not in the spike in oil prices that preceded these actions three years earlier, but in the several decades worth of decisions to manufacture large gas guzzlers and to lag behind in the best technology that finally caught up with these famous brands.

In the Veblenian system, then, the modern leisure class consists of those whose ownership of wealth and whose control of the means of production permits them to engage in the same kind of relentless competition and predatory activity carried out by their barbarian forefathers, and more importantly, to be exempt from the menial jobs performed by ordinary workers. Modern leisure-class activities include high finance, corporate law, management, and other activities undertaken by those concerned mainly with "conversion of goods and persons to [their] own ends, and a callous disregard of the feelings and wishes of others, and of the remoter effects of his actions." (Dorfman 1961, 184) The modern menial class thus consists of those who are not owners of property and thus must work for someone else to obtain wages or salaries.

For Veblen, the leisure class was also the wealthy class, and that too has historical precedents. In ancient cultures, Veblen believed that wealth came to be equated with social status: as he argued, "possession of wealth confers honor." (Veblen 1973, 35) Initially, wealth consisted of the booty dragged back from wars with neighboring clans or nations; the items seized, be they treasures or slaves, were the spoils of battle and therefore served as a very public sign of physical prowess. Possession of wealth came to represent "a trophy of successes scored in the game of ownership carried on between the members of the group." (Veblen 1973, 36-7) Over time, mere possession of wealth came to confer reputability on the possessor, as if the wealth itself signified the superior strength of the leader of the household. By the late nineteenth century, robber barons such as Rockefeller, Vanderbilt, and Morgan were considered both successful and honorable largely because they were wealthy, despite their destructive and often dishonorable business practices. Moreover, ownership of property came over time to be seen as an indication of the prowess of the owner. With wealth thus equated to esteem, humans strove to emulate and surpass the wealth of their neighbors: as Veblen concluded, "[I]t becomes indispensable to accumulate, to acquire property, in order to retain one's good name....A certain standard of wealth in one case, and of prowess in the other, is a necessary condition of reputability, and anything in excess of this normal amount is meritorious." (Veblen 1973, 37-8)

CONSPICUOUS CONSUMPTION

Of course, mere possession of wealth does not confer upon the possessor an honorific position in society unless the rest of society perceives that wealth. Therefore, the wealthy must engage in "conspicuous consumption." Conspicuous consumption was an important element of Veblen's understanding of human behavior. To quote Veblen at length on this point:

> The quasi-peaceable gentleman of leisure [by which Veblen means the modern robber baron 'descended' from the early warrior], then, not only consumes of the stuff of life beyond the minimum required for subsistence and physical efficiency, but his consumption also undergoes a specialization as regards the quality of the goods consumed. He consumes freely and of the best, in food, drink, narcotics, shelter, services, ornaments, apparel, weapons and accoutrements, amusements, amulets, and idols or divinities....Since the consumption of these more excellent goods is an evidence to wealth, it becomes honorific; and conversely, the failure to consume in due quantity and quality becomes a mark of inferiority and demerit. (Veblen 1973, 64)

Conspicuous consumption is the way the wealthy demonstrate their wealth, and thus their success in war—or in business. By purchasing the finest houses, autos, suits and shoes—all visible and public signs of financial success—they gain the respect and admiration of their peers and subordinates. Today, the BMW parked outside the office, the Armani suit for everyday wear, and the designer handbag slung casually across a shoulder, tell the casual onlooker that the owner is a successful (i.e., wealthy) person.

Veblen referred to this as "conspicuous waste" because, "in order to effectually mend the consumer's good fame, [a conspicuous expenditure] must be an expenditure of superfluities." (Veblen 1973, 77) Those expenditures are "traceable to the habit of making an invidious pecuniary comparison"—to demonstrate the level of income and wealth held by the conspicuous consumer. (Veblen 1973, 79) In other words, the Lexus owner would be as ably transported around town by a Ford, or the Range Rover owner would have his or her needs just as efficiently and dependably met by a Chevy truck. The point of making an expensive purchase is precisely to demonstrate to those who cannot afford the Lexus or the Range Rover the superior social status of the conspicuous consumer. Robert Frank recounts how some "nouveau" millionaires in both Silicon Valley and suburban Chicago have demolished large modern homes, valued in the hundreds of thousands of dollars, so they could build even larger homes on the same sites to suit their elevated social status. As one new executive for America Online declared, the "scraper" that he razed "was definitely livable. I just wanted something bigger." (Frank 1999, 28-39)

While luxury SUVs or demolition of perfectly good homes carried on by the wealthy may be obvious examples of waste, Veblen even disparaged those forms of conspicuous waste that were practiced on a daily basis. Conspicuous waste in his view was anything that did not contribute to a "fuller unfolding of human life." (Veblen 1973, 94) For instance, Veblen argued that our tendency to prefer hand-wrought items to machine-made goods was based on the honorific status imparted by the costlier, hand-made item. In other words, our preference for a hand-crafted spoon over an ordinary spoon found in a diner was not based on the beauty of the hand-crafted item, but rather "a gratification of our sense of costliness masquerading under the name of beauty." (Veblen 1973, 79) Veblen himself once received as a gift an expensive brooch from a woman student who had become alarmed at his habitual use of a safety pin to hold together his jacket. When presented with the gift, Veblen simply chided, "You haven't listened to a word I have said all semester." (Dorfman 1973)

PECUNIARY EMULATION

Mainstream economic theory has long taught that consumers make purchases based on rational assessment of the intrinsic utility of the item in question. Veblen rejected that analysis as overly simplistic in one of his most famous paragraphs:

> The hedonistic conception of man is that of a lightning calculator of pleasures and pains, who oscillates like a homogeneous globule of desire of happiness under the impulse of stimuli that shift him about the area, but leave him intact. He has neither antecedent or consequent....Self-imposed in elemental space, he spins symmetrically about his own spiritual axis, until the parallelogram of forces bears down upon him, whereupon he follows the line of the resultant. When the force of the impact is spent, he comes to rest, a self-contained globule of desire as before. (Veblen 1919, 75)

The mainstream theory of consumer choice reduces all of the complex processes and influences involved in human consumption to a simple and overtly rational choice. The mainstream preconception is that products generate utility, e.g., that the smoker derives utility from consumption of his or her cigarette. Consumer tastes and preferences are then taken as given, with the relative price being the main factor that causes consumers to buy more or less of some commodity, such as shoes or cigarettes. Veblen recognized that this approach ignored the social influences on consumption: advertising, peer pressure, the symbolic nature of commodities in a capitalist culture, and many other external influences.

In particular, Veblen argued that mainstream economics ignored a powerful motive for consumption, the motive of pecuniary emulation: the imitation of the spending habits of our peers and those above us on the social ladder. As Veblen argued, "Goods are produced and consumed as a means to the fuller unfolding of human life....But the human proclivity to emulation has seized upon consumption of goods as a means to our invidious comparison." (Veblen 1973, 94) Consumption decisions are driven by the need to fit in with our peers or, in popular parlance, to keep up with the Joneses. Again, to quote Veblen:

> [T]he standard of expenditure which commonly guides our efforts is not the average, ordinary expenditure already achieved; it is an ideal of consumption that lies just beyond our reach....The motive is emulation—the stimulus of an invidious comparison which prompts us to outdo those with whom we are in the habit of classing ourselves...each class envies and emulates the class next above it in the social scale, while it rarely compares itself with those below or with those who are considerably in advance. (Veblen 1973, 81)

Veblen thought that this "propensity for emulation" was among the strongest economic motives. Juliet Schor confirms that this motive still dominates in our modern era in her 1998 book, *The Overspent American.* The ubiquitous "visible logo"—be it the Nike swoosh, the Hilfiger label, or even the Starbucks name on a disposable paper cup—tells observers that the purchaser has bought the real deal. (Schor 1998, 46) One nationwide poll of women revealed that half of the respondents participated in status buying, with 80% of the respondents—a percentage that would not have surprised Veblen at all—admitting that purchases were more often based on the designer label than on the intrinsic quality of the goods.

Veblen's argument that conspicuous consumption and pecuniary emulation are the driving forces behind much of the consumption we observe in capitalism is persuasive. But Veblen should not be interpreted as condemning *individuals* who engage in these behaviors. This is true for two reasons. First, human beings are social beings and we cannot help but to emulate much of the behavior of those around us, and in fact, to try to outdo others. (Lerner 1976, 24) Second, and perhaps more importantly, pecuniary emulation, or our emulation of the spending habits of our peers and those above us on the social ladder, takes place in a context of capitalism. In capitalism, social status is heavily tied to income and wealth, and is demonstrated visibly by the accoutrements of wealth—fancy clothes, luxury cars, and stately houses. To maintain our status in our desired communities, we endlessly strive to "keep up with the Joneses." Imagine for a minute the businessperson who arrived at an important meeting in a polyester suit, wearing coke-bottle glasses and carrying papers in a plastic shopping bag rather than in an expensive leather briefcase. Would he or she be given the same attention at that meeting, or receive promotions in due course? Similarly, the student who wanted to join the most popular sorority or fraternity on campus, but showed up for rush events in sweats and sneakers would most likely be hastened out the door. While both individuals might have much of substance to contribute, their outward appearance would signal their desired peers that they just wouldn't fit in.

MARGINAL PRODUCTIVITY AND INDUSTRIAL EMPLOYMENTS

Another tenet of neoclassical economics that Veblen disputed was the theory of marginal productivity. This theory, that the wage earned by any given worker would naturally tend to be equivalent to the marginal productivity of that worker, was articulated by Veblen's own former professor, John Bates Clark.[4] At the time Veblen began to write his *Theory of Business Enterprise,* many economists considered the high incomes received by the robber barons to be simply their fair returns, the hard-earned fruits of their intense and stressful labors. As entrepreneurs, they organized the production process, and their earnings were the equivalent of their contributions to the firm, just as the factory worker or the shop clerk earned his or her wage in proportion to the productivity that they contributed to the firm.

Marginal productivity theory is still a central element of mainstream labor economics; it is used, for example, to explain the high salaries of professional athletes: as the argument goes, they receive high salaries because they sell tickets and advertisements. Marginal productivity is also used to argue that it would be inefficient to raise the minimum wage. In recent years, marginal productivity theory has been used to justify the enormous and growing pay gap between CEOs and workers—a gap that reached 500 to 1 in 2000—and to justify the growing inequality of income. According to this argument, top management has increasingly had to make tough decisions to protect the competitive position of their firms, thus earning the millions of dollars that they are paid.

Veblen argued for a different taxonomy to compare the work of the robber barons to that of ordinary workers. Within the modern firm emerging at the turn of the century, Veblen saw two basic groups of workers: those who made goods (those engaged in industrial activities, as he called them) and those who made money (those engaged in pecuniary activities). This is not quite the same as the breakdown between the owners of property and the propertyless described by Marx, for Veblen includes among those engaged in pecuniary employments many who hold no property at all—for example, people working in advertising, middle managers, even corporate lawyers. In other words, Veblen thought that the modern-day businessman or businesswoman, even if they were not the actual owners of the enterprise, had the same class identity as a capitalist. Veblen argued that the work of the typical businessperson was directed at making the product of their firm vendible—i.e., marketing and selling the product. Thus they were engaged in buying and selling, negotiating and contriving, merging and financing, but not actually involved in producing anything.

For Veblen, this distinction between different kinds of work and workers—some involved in production, others acting as "undertakers" in managerial, administrative, and financial positions—reflected facts about people's social functions and interests. He argued that businesspeople—the captains of industry, financiers, lawyers, CEOs, and others at the top ranks of Wall Street or corporations today—were chiefly concerned with the distribution of wealth and the fattening of their own wallets. They were not concerned with providing needed goods and services to consumers. To quote Veblen, their concern was with the "exchange values of goods and...the vendibility of the items with which they are concerned, and on the necessities, solvency, cupidity, or gullibility of the persons whose actions may affect the transaction contemplated." (Quoted in Dorfman 1961, 193)

By contrast, actual production was carried out by those engaged in "industrial pursuits"—engineers, craftsmen, assembly line workers. These workers were, in Veblen's view, actively furthering the "material interests of the community," or more precisely, "adapting the material means of life, and the processes of valuation constantly involved in the work run on the availability of goods and on the material serviceability of the contrivances, materials, persons, or mechanical expedients employed." (Dorfman 1961, 192-3) Taken to its logical conclusion, this dichotomy suggests that profit-seeking businesspeople can be at least as interested in marketing products in clever and creative ways as they are in improving the actual product. As an example, consider the following: in the 1990s, Nike spent more to hire Michael Jordan to hawk its shoes than it paid to its entire Indonesian work force to produce the Air Jordans. Nike contracts out most of the production work for its shoe lines, relying on labor-intensive production technologies and low-cost labor, leaving Nike as little more than a large marketing company. The important work, for Nike, in other words, is not the work of engineering and producing the perfect athletic shoe but instead is the work of marketing very expensive shoes to impressionable young athletes based on brand-recognition and their identification with sports stars.

Veblen analyzed the changes in business firms since the halcyon days of Adam Smith in the same evolutionary terms he used to explore the evolution of consumption. In the early stages of manufacturing, dating back to the British Industrial Revolution and even before, the typical owner-entrepreneur was also a producer, who often manufactured or at least handled the goods that he sold. The master who crafted horseshoes, for example, might spend a portion of his day checking bank statements and logging orders, but would also work side by side with his journeymen and apprentices making the actual product. To quote Veblen here, this early "captain of industry" "was business manager of the venture as well as foreman of the works, and not infrequently he was the designer and master-builder of the equipment, of which he was also the responsible owner." (Veblen 1997, 103) As firms became larger and the management of those firms required more and more of the owner-manager's time, "industry and business gradually split apart." (Veblen 1997, 106) The captain of industry—originally "a cross between a business man and an industrial expert"—became removed from the shop floor and did not deal with matters of production, spending more and more of his time engaged in financial management of the firm. (Veblen 1990, 59) He became a "captain of finance," rather than a captain of industry, far removed from the production lines. As his daily activities changed, so did his interest, as he became less interested in production and more interested in profit. To quote Joseph Dorfman, Veblen's biographer:

> The modern captain is not interested in the permanent efficiency of the in-
> dustrial system or of any plant, but in the control of a segment of the system
> for the strategic purpose of influencing the security market for the flotation
> of securities, the maneuvering of a coalition or any other well known method
> of manipulation ....The modern captain does not create opportunities
> for increasing industrial efficiency, but only watches for opportunities to put
> his competitors in an uncomfortable position; cut-throat competition, rate
> wars, duplication, misdirection, wasted efforts and delay of improvements
> long after they are advisable are the price the community pays. (Dorfman
> 1961, 125-6)

In a later, famous passage, Veblen described this watchful waiting carried out by modern businessmen as being similar to the activities of toads sitting on a country road:

> Doubtless this form of words, 'watchful waiting,' will have been employed in
> the first instance to describe the frame of mind of a toad who has reached
> years of discretion and has found his appointed place along some frequented
> run where many flies and spiders pass and repass on their way to complete
> that destiny to which it has pleased an all-seeing and merciful Providence to
> call them; but by an easy turn of speech it has also been found suitable to
> describe the safe and sane strategy of that mature order of captains of industry
> who are governed by sound business principles. There is a certain bland suf-
> ficiency spread across the face of such a toad so circumstanced, while his
> comely personal bulk gives assurance of a pyramidal stability of principles.
> (Veblen 1997, 109-10)

With captains of industry making no direct contribution to production, Veblen argued that their salaries could not be attributed to marginal productivity.

INDUSTRIAL SABOTAGE

According to Veblen, it is not placid Smithian price competition that characterizes the modern industrial economy. Instead, it is savage and predatory competition. The efforts of John D. Rockefeller to smash his competition in the late-nineteenth-century United States exemplify Veblen's ideas of competition and business sabotage of the industrial processes.

By 1869, at the age of 30, Rockefeller was already a major oil refiner in Cleveland, the early center of the oil refining industry in the United States. He came up with the idea of negotiating lower shipping rates from several key railroads to gain a competitive advantage over rival oil refiners. At the time, most of the markets for refined oil were on the eastern seaboard of the United States; thus transportation represented a major cost for oil refiners. Using his clout as Cleveland's largest refiner and therefore an important bulk shipper of oil, Rockefeller secured preferential rates for shipping his oil. (Recall that the railroads during this same period were raising the rates charged to farmers.) This gave him an enormous cost advantage over smaller competitors who could not guarantee bulk shipments to the railroads. Rockefeller believed that he was simply exploiting his "economies of scale," but critics at the time argued that he was instead using his "special power to compel railroad-freight concessions." (Chernow 1999, 114)

In 1872, Rockefeller devised an even more ambitious scheme, innocuously named the "South Improvement Company," or SIC. Under SIC, all refiners who joined their operations with his would receive up to a 50% rebate from the railroads on their shipping costs, not only for their own oil but for all oil shipped by rail, including oil shipped by their competitors.[5] The SIC included most of the major refiners and all the major eastern railroads, in effect forming a double cartel. The SIC in turn guaranteed the major railroads a steady flow of oil shipments. To quote Ron Chernow, "the railroads acquired a vested interest in the creation of a giant oil monopoly that would lower their costs, boost their profits, and generally simplify their lives." (Chernow 1999, 113) The provision that the SIC refiners would receive rebates for oil shipped by their competitors has been described by one Rockefeller biographer as "an instrument of competitive cruelty unparalleled in industry." (Chernow 1999, 136) In fact, the SIC oil refiners would now have a huge advantage over their smaller independent rivals: "the harder their competitors worked, the more money Rockefeller and associates would make." (Dillard 1967, 410) Moreover, this same provision in the SIC agreement would give SIC members precise pricing and shipping information about their competitors, permitting the SIC oil cartel to undercut their rivals at every turn.

While it is true that this SIC contract violated no actual law (this was two decades before the first federal antitrust laws were passed), rumors leaked out about the "scheme of gigantic combination among certain railroads and refiners to control the purchase and shipment of crude and refined oil from [western Pennsylvania]." (Chernow 1999, 138) A firestorm swept the local newspapers in the affected regions; the railroads abandoned the agreement; and the Pennsylvania legislature canceled the SIC's charter in 1872. So the SIC never actually went into effect. However, during the six weeks in early 1872 that the SIC rumors were spreading, the remaining competition realized that if they didn't sell out, they would be driven out of the industry. Twenty-two of the twenty-six remaining Cleveland refiners sold their operations to Rockefeller during that six week period, most of them later acknowledging the implicit SIC club held over their heads by Rockefeller. (Chernow 1999, 154ff; Dillard 1967, Ch. 23; Porter 1973, Ch. 3)[6] This was not the friendly competition between small local blacksmiths that drove prices down, as Adam Smith had described. Instead, Veblen saw that the nature of competition had changed, and he used words like "sabotage" to describe the brutal tactics of Rockefeller and the other robber barons.

More generally, during the period Veblen wrote, most of the firms that were to become important American corporations, like John D. Rockefeller's Standard Oil, began to employ modern mass production technologies. These relied increasingly on the use of knowledgeable engineers and trained personnel to keep the production lines running. (Porter 1973) One feature of mass production—what Veblen referred to as the "machine process"— was the need for standardized production processes and interchangeable parts. For Henry Ford's assembly line to run smoothly and efficiently, every part had to be made precisely to the same specifications, so that an individual worker could simply insert the widget into the gizmo as it rolled across the work station. Interchangeable parts eliminated the need for hand crafting of each automobile from top to bottom and greatly improved both the quantity and quality of output. Parts suppliers—firms supplying the steel chassis, the nuts and bolts, the frames and engines—were required to meet exacting specifications. Production became less and less a matter of individual discretion and craftsmanship and more a matter of technological expertise and mechanization.

The mass production that accompanied the Second Industrial Revolution in late-nineteenth-century America created both huge productivity gains and great economic growth. (Ratner, Soltow, and Sylla 1993, Ch. 12) Specifically, American dominance in the machine tools industry, which promoted mechanization of hand-crafted tasks, and its early use of industrial research to develop new products and manufacturing processes, led to large production and distribution facilities, new technologies, and the big business that we know today.

However, in Veblen's analysis, these vastly superior machine technologies and improved capacity remained under the control of the captains of finance, who managed them with an eye toward greater profits rather than greater productivity. Productive capacities were great indeed, but Veblen believed that the captains of industry prevented industrial capacity from becoming even greater. Observing the great merger movement that occurred at the turn of the century, when nearly 3,000 firms disappeared into mergers with larger rivals, Veblen argued that businesspersons were taking control of large segments of the nation's industrial apparatus in order to carry out "industrial sabotage" on a large scale. For Veblen, industrial sabotage was a "conscientious withdrawal of efficiency." More fully, industrial sabotage could consist of "any degree of obstruction, diversion, or withholding of any of the available industrial forces, with a view to the special gain of any nation or any investor." Such sabotage "unavoidably brings on a dislocation of the system; which involves a disproportionate lowering of its working efficiency and therefore a disproportionate loss to the whole; and therefore a net loss to all its parts." (Veblen 1990, 73)

This was sabotage in Veblen's view because the increasingly interconnected industrial system needed rapid and reliable flow of goods and services from one sector to another—steel to the auto and rail industries, raw materials to the chemicals producers, railways transporting disposable food stuffs—and needed to be free of all obstructions to those necessary inter-sectoral flows. However, businesspeople could often profit from disrupting those flows or holding up supplies, raising prices and increasing profits.

Industrial sabotage for the purposes of pecuniary gain continues into our modern era. For instance, Microsoft Corporation was found in its antitrust trial in the late 1990s to have engaged in a wide variety of predatory and exclusionary activities to promote its own operating and desktop software at the expense of competitors and its own customers. In one example brought out at the trial, Microsoft waited until the last possible moment to make a deal with IBM for its Windows O/S, and then raised the price by nearly 900%. This, of course, placed IBM machines at a huge disadvantage compared with its PC competitors. Enron, in similar fashion, was accused of manipulating electricity supply in California—in particular, creating 'phantom congestion' on power grids in 1999. This manipulation exacerbated, or even created, the famous California energy crisis that summer, and produced enormous profits for Enron until its accounting crisis brought the firm to bankruptcy court. The subprime crisis of the first decade of the 21st century assumed its catastrophic proportions not simply because so many risky loans were made to marginal borrowers, but because large and well-respected financial institutions embarked on a plan to securitize and repackage these loans in their own relentless search for more profits and commissions, all the while ignoring the growth of a substantial housing bubble in the U.S. during this time. As a final example, the transgenic revolution in agriculture has transformed the very nature of the seeds used by farmers—the essential ingredient for sustaining the food system—turning them from what once were public goods to patent-protected private goods, thus allowing large agribusiness companies to genetically modify the food supply into a monoculture rather than to serve the nutritional needs of global consumers.

Veblen also believed that businesspeople engaged in sabotage when they chose to rely on obsolete but profitable methods of production rather than to move to more modern and innovative production techniques or to produce products that would better serve the consumer. In a famous example, J.P. Morgan, a captain of finance par excellence in Veblen's time, gathered hundreds of previously competing steel producers into a new behemoth, U.S. Steel, that dominated all segments of the steel industry. Having removed most of the relevant competition by merging with them, U.S. Steel was able to curb its costs by slowing its pace of innovation to a crawl. This set the stage for a pattern of sluggish innovation and noncompetitive behavior that persisted for the rest of the century. By the early 1980s, the American steel industry spent less as a percentage of sales on research and development than any other American industry except textiles. (Adams and Mueller 1986) Similarly, as noted earlier, one has only to ponder the story of the American automobile industry during the second half of the twentieth century or the dismal performance of corporate giants such as GM and IBM in the 1980s to see what Veblen meant. It was not the diligent efforts of GM engineers that prompted GM to develop more fuel efficient cars, but the gradual erosion of GM's market share and the superior cars made by foreign competitors that finally prompted some changes. (Adams and Brock 1995, 65-92)

By using the term sabotage, Veblen did not mean that the captains crept by dark of night into the factories that they controlled and meddled with the machines. He took a broader view of sabotage, one grounded in the notion that modern production technologies were so productive that they could allow humankind to produce sufficient goods and services to alleviate all poverty and human want. However, Veblen believed that modern business practices subverted these possibilities by prizing profit over production and thus keeping industrial plants operating inefficiently (i.e., below full capacity).

Veblen argued that industrial sabotage was pervasive and that it had serious macroeconomic effects. In his view, businesspeople valued pecuniary or profit-making activities over industrial or productive activities. Given those priorities, he argued that industrial depressions occurred when "the business men engaged do not see their way clear to derive a satisfactory gain from letting the industrial process go forward on the lines and in the volume for which the material equipment of industry is designed." (Veblen 1978, 213) In other words, Veblen saw business cycles as primarily caused by business sabotage of industry. For that reason, Veblen disparaged the term "overproduction," believing the term instead referred to the business "difficulty...that not enough of a product can be disposed of at fair prices to warrant the running of the mills at their full capacity, or running them at a rate near enough to their capacity to yield a fair profit." (Veblen 1978, 217) In other words, businesspeople would rather reduce production or close plants until supplies dropped and prices were restored to profitable levels.

For Veblen, sabotage was also waste, albeit a different form than conspicuous consumption: it was the consequence of deliberate idling of production and labor, and a direct consequence of the businessperson's profit-seeking. Idle capacity and waste were systemic and substantial, argued Veblen, and harmed the community welfare. Hence the irony observed by Veblen in many of his writings on the captains of industry and finance. As Veblen observed, the tremendous productive capacity of modern industry should have eliminated the problem of unemployment and privation by the turn of the 20th century, but the predatory and pecuniary practices of modern business seemed if anything to have exacerbated them. In short, for Veblen, modern business organization and the quest for profits created an inevitable tendency toward idle industrial capacity and unemployed labor.

Veblen's writing on sabotage recalls Marx, who also acknowledged the enormous productive capacity of modern technology. Veblen and Marx also agreed that modern capitalism placed pecuniary values above all others, so that greed, corruption, and invidious consumption eroded the productive potential of modern industry. Thus, capitalism generated enormous inequality and universal dissatisfaction with the goods already possessed. Both believed that if pecuniary values could somehow be displaced and the common welfare honored, enormous productivity could be harnessed for all peoples. It is a utopian view of an economy, surely, but one that has merit as we contemplate the growing inequality in our modern world and the great need still faced by so many. In fact, a 1997 UN report argued that we would need to redistribute no more than one percent of global income to eradicate poverty in the world. (UNHDR, Human Development Report, 1997) In other words, as Veblen argued one hundred years ago, we have the material means to provide a decent living for every person on the planet. The question is, how to permit sufficient output of the needed goods and services, ranging from basic foodstuffs to good schools, and how to distribute these goods and services to meet the basic needs of all people on the planet.

Veblen's analysis of sabotage also resonates with Marx's analysis of the reserve army of the unemployed, and the relentless drive of the bourgeoisie to keep wages low and profits high. Veblen adds to Marx's arsenal of capitalist strategies the use of mergers, buy-outs, and all other business tactics that are used to garner profits rather than benefit consumers or workers. To quote Veblen, "in no such community that is organized on the price system...can the industrial system be allowed to work at full capacity for any appreciable interval of time, on pain of business stagnation and consequent privation for all classes and conditions of men. The requirements of profitable business will not tolerate it." (Veblen 1990, 43) In other words, it is imperative for business interests who serve pecuniary and not industrial ends, to use Veblen's terms, that industrial capacity be kept below its potential. Otherwise, supply would increase too rapidly, prices would fall, and profits would suffer. Was he referring simply to business downturns? Veblen argued that even in periods of high profits, business interests would act to make those high profits even higher: "it is considered doubtful whether an increased production, such as to employ more workmen and supply the goods needed by the community, would result in an increased net aggregate income for the vested interests which control these industries. A reasonable profit always means, in effect, the largest possible profit." (Veblen 1990, 45)

CONCLUSION

Veblen saw that the economy was constantly evolving, and he strove to understand the nature of economic and social change. At the same time, he understood that our deep cultural roots influenced our modern economy in important if unrecognized ways. Most importantly, he argued that the predatory nature of competition, the prevalence of pecuniary standards of success, and the failure to use modern technologies to alleviate human want and misery were all symptoms of a capitalist economy that placed pecuniary values above all others. As a consequence the economy no longer functioned primarily to provision all its inhabitants. Veblen is remembered today mostly for his colorful analysis of the leisure class, but his criticism of business interests, his understanding of the importance of economic change in economic analysis, and his belief that the economy could be used to meet all the genuine needs of all human beings, remain his important if ignored contributions to the discipline of economics.[7]

Veblen's writings not only contain trenchant critiques of the received economics of his day, but also offer alternative forms of analysis that could lead economists to new conclusions. Veblen was critical of the view that human beings were merely self-interested. In his many other writings not reviewed above, he expanded on his affirmative view of human nature, and argued that what really promoted human welfare was not self-interest, but rather the instinct of workmanship and the parental bent. To state these ideas briefly here (the reader can read Veblen's *Instinct of Workmanship* to learn more), the parental bent extended beyond concern for one's own children, and, according to Veblen, was a culturally instilled proclivity to provide for the next generation and to contribute to the common good. The instinct of workmanship was the human proclivity to improve things, to make things work, to be both creative and efficient. We can only imagine how different mainstream economics might be if it had started from these alternative premises.

5
John Maynard Keynes
and the Turbulent Birth of Macroeconomics

INTRODUCTION

No human frailty is more complex than our ability to believe strongly in things that are clearly not true. As examples, those prior to Columbus who believed the earth was flat had the same kind of blindness that afflicts mainstream economists who ignore the complex web of social classes that leaves unfinished, if not absurd, all of their work. It can be quite costly to trudge forward into the cold and piercing winds of life on the basis of wrong ideas, and especially so if we are experts with an audience.

Another such costly idea was held for almost two centuries by the classical school of economics and, like so much of modern thinking about the economy, this one has origins in the early 18th century. Its most famous advocate was Jean Baptiste Say, a French businessman who coined what became a famous claim, that "supply creates its own demand." He meant by this phrase that when businesses pay for the goods produced they produce a flow of income to business, government, and wage earners adequate to buy all of the output. The natural, internal forces that automatically end over-production before it becomes a recession or depression (and we will have a more detailed explanation of Say's model below).

This theory was greatly at odds with the observable fact that capitalism is an unstable system in which every expansion of the total output is followed with the inevitable decline, or what we call, downturns, recessions, or depressions. Though historians differ about the exact number, there have been over 40 such recessions/depressions since 1800. There have been eleven of them in the past fifty years, including a deep recession (what some would call a depression) in 1982, and what has been called the "great recession" that started in 2007. These kinds of downturns spread a decline in employment, income, crucial public spending, and increasing public unrest across the globe. Further, the most serious ones have never ended without massive public intervention that give lie to the theory that economies will return to equilibrium on their own.

Despite this unchallenged history of the ups and downs of capitalist states, the classical theory held sway in economic thinking roughly from the late eighteenth century until the middle of the Great Depression in the 1930s. It was John Maynard Keynes who dealt it a crushing blow in a 1936 book, *The General Theory of Employment, Interest, and Money*, sometimes abbreviated as simply *The General Theory*. This book swept away much of the debris of classical thinking about business cycles, and what to do about them.

To economists in the classical school, the self-regulating character of capitalism meant that the government's role in the economy should be limited. Adam Smith wrote his famous treatise *The Wealth of Nations* in 1776 primarily as a tract against the "mercantilist" thinking of his time. The mercantilists believed in government economic policies that would foster favorable trading conditions with other nations. This required a mosaic of government rules and regulations, including favoring monopolies in crucial trading industries. Under mercantilism, the state was an instrument for the benefit of a few industries and individuals, often to the detriment of everyone else. Smith's biggest fans, members of the emerging capitalist class in Britain and France, believed that unregulated capitalism would, in contrast, benefit all groups in society. By allowing members of all economic classes to seek their self-interest in a competitive system, capitalism would produce the most productive outcome possible. Though, as we have seen, Smith allowed for a few government functions, such as education, police protection, and national defense, he thought an economy that was largely unregulated by government would be both superior and self-regulating.

In the central tradition of economics[1] between 1776 and 1936, business cycles were ignored as a legitimate subject of study, and public policy to lessen their damaging effects was consequently out of the question. In the United States during these years, the classical school's domination of economic thinking among both academics and capitalists claimed countless victims. President Herbert Hoover, responding to the ravages of the Great Depression in the early 1930s, could only proclaim to a disbelieving public the classical article of faith: "Prosperity is just around the corner." Irving

Fisher, among the most respected U.S. economists of the time, no doubt helped to confuse Hoover by declaring, just prior to the 1929 stock market crash that began the Great Depression, that the economy was on a "permanently high plateau." It was into this theoretical morass that Keynes stepped in 1936 with *The General Theory* to change forever the way we all think about the capitalist business cycle.

So, who was this Keynes fellow?

JOHN MAYNARD KEYNES, THE PERSON

Keynes was an Englishman who lived from 1883 to 1946, and after 1913 produced a torrent of books and articles about the economic world. In the course of his 63 years he was: a brilliant student at England's most famous prep school; an equally brilliant student and then professor at Kings College in Cambridge; a financier who made a fortune for himself, and later for Kings College by overseeing its endowment fund; president of a life-insurance company; patron of the arts; husband of a famous Russian ballerina; member of the influential "Bloomsbury set" of intellectuals; esteemed official of the British Treasury; and a board member of the Bank of England. He was also the British, and quite prominent, participant in a conference in Bretton Woods, New Hampshire, in 1944, where the allies in the war against Germany and Japan designed what would become the post-war system of system of international finance. Most important to his lasting fame, Keynes's writing held the rapt attention of the political and intellectual world during his adult life, and continues to have lasting influence over half a century after his death.

The General Theory is only the most famous of his many economic writings. One of Keynes's earliest works was an acclaimed book on probability theory. Another early book, *The Economic Consequences of the Peace* (1919), catapulted him into an international spotlight that never dimmed while he was alive. In this book, Keynes argued with impressive foresight that the victorious allies in World War I had exacted such heavy reparation payments from the Germans that the German economy would sink into ruin, producing dangerous political chaos. From the 1920s on, Keynes focused mostly on economics and, as we shall point out later, he often paused to write sharp critiques of the methods and analyses of other mainstream practitioners.

While Keynes was a powerful critic of some aspects of mainstream economics, his work was clearly different from the political economy practiced by Marx and Veblen. Keynes never gave up the idea that capitalism was the best of all possible modes of production. Indeed, given what he saw as human nature, he believed that competitive markets in capitalism were uniquely designed to minimize the often-deadly effects of human competition. Keynes championed government intervention in capitalism because he believed that without it, the system he preferred would collapse into economic and political chaos. In other words, Keynes wanted to save capitalism from itself.

Marx called for revolutionary overthrow of the capitalist class and the development of a socialist system rather than the reforms of the sort Keynes sought in government policy. And Veblen imagined an industrial democracy, guided by engineers and scientists who, compared to the capitalists, would organize the economy for production rather than profit. Therefore, if we look only at the political policies Keynes called for, in comparison to those advocated by Marx and Veblen, we can see that he was a very different kind of political economist than they were. Despite their fundamental differences, all three shared two principal conclusions that set them aside from most of those in the central tradition. The first is their view that unregulated capitalism, for various reasons, is a disaster waiting to happen; and second is their belief that economists in the central tradition had so narrowly defined their discipline that they had come to misunderstand, or completely ignore, crucial dimensions of capitalism. We will discuss these two points later in this chapter, but first we turn to Keynes' critique of the classical explanation of business cycles.

DEFINING OUR TERMS

Business cycles have such enormous effects on life in capitalist societies that economists have developed an array of names for them. In the early nineteenth century, some economists referred to economic declines as "gluts" or "overproduction." Later in the nineteenth century, these gave way to the more ominous "economic crises," a term popularized by Marx.

During the 1930s, the collapse of U.S. capitalism was so deep and prolonged that it came to be known permanently as the "Great Depression." However, when the economy took another dip in 1937-38, after four years of slow growth, economists came up with "recession" as a way to distinguish that dip from the Depression. A few mainstream economists, their thoughts clearly under the mesmerizing spell of the classical school, tried in the 1950s to popularize a peculiarly hopeful term, "rolling readjustments." Fortunately, this term didn't stick but it is useful to note that profoundly different political ideologies are embedded in the concepts "economic crisis" and "rolling readjustment."

We will use the term "business cycle" in a general sense, and we will use other terms—gluts, recessions, depressions, or crises—as they fit the scenario that we are discussing. As with all descriptive language, one's choices among these terms often reveal personal biases. One oft-quoted analysis of these choices roots them completely in subjective circumstances: "If you lose *your* job, we're in a recession; if I lose *mine*, we're in a depression."

No matter what they were called, capitalist business cycles produced a long-standing debate throughout the nineteenth century, and the two sides can be succinctly expressed:

The Classical School: Economic recessions and depressions are natural and localized consequences of capitalism that are automatically self-correcting.

The Alternative Schools: Economic crises are complex, inevitable, and unpredictable consequences of the capitalist order that come with tremendous costs.

THE CLASSICAL SCHOOL AND BUSINESS CYCLES

Until Keynes exploded their theory, economists in the classical school believed that "overproduction"—the production of goods that cannot find buyers—was impossible except in the very short run. Economists in this school believed that when some firm, or even an entire industry, produced too many goods, automatic adjustments would occur that would put the economy back on track. We briefly describe the analysis, but the ideological importance of this claim is easily explained. Classical economists, like most of their successors in the central tradition, did not question that capitalism was the best of all possible economic systems. This firm stance gave them the inclination to ignore unsightly aspects of capitalism, such as social classes and the dominance of the state by the capitalist class. It also encouraged them to try to explain away obvious imperfections in the system. An imperfection such as the business cycle, both obvious and potentially politically destabilizing, needed explanation. How did the classical economists explain away the business cycle?

To answer this question, we will construct a hypothetical model of an early nineteenth century capitalist economy with three classes of economic actors: wage earners, capitalists, and landlords. Let's suppose that during a given year, the owners of capitalist firms produced $10 billion of goods and services and were successful in selling it all during the same time. To produce that level of output, the capitalists would have had to buy materials and labor time, and rent space from landlords. Thus they would have paid out most of the receipts from their sales in material costs, wages, and rents. Whatever was left after making all the payments to these "factors" of production could be kept as profits.

The process we are describing here is a key one to understand for this reason: at the aggregate level of the economy, the process by which the capitalists produce goods is the same as the one by which participants in the economy receive income to buy back the output from the capitalists. If we break into this flow of income and spending at the beginning of production and look at just one part of the stream during a particular month, we can see that, in exchange for their members' labor time, households received wage payments. And during the same month that they receive this income, they will send most of it back to the capitalists in exchange for consumption goods and services. This interdependence between producers, consumers, and workers is now called the "circular flow of income and output," and you were part of it the last time you cashed your paycheck and headed off to buy something. The circular flow is so crucial to an understanding of aggregate economics that there is always a circular flow diagram early on in principles of economics textbooks, and we have reproduced one below (see Figure 5.1). Because it is the conceptual center of macroeconomics, it will help the beginner to study such a diagram long enough to understand its basic meaning (perhaps before you go on here).

Now, let's go back to our earlier example and assume that as the $10 billion in sales revenue flowed into the capitalist (business) coffers during the year, they paid it out to individual households as follows:

$7 billion went to laborers as wages

$1 billion went to the landlords as rents

$2 billion was kept by capitalists as profits

We are going to suppose that the laborers spent *all* their $7 billion of wages on goods and services (products), and the landlords spent *all* their $1 billion on consumer goods, too. This $8 billion, as you now know, will have gone back to the capitalist producers during the same year, and it will be the biggest part of what they have in order to start up the next year's cycle of production.

Now consider the $2 billion going to the capitalists this year. Let's suppose they spent $1 billion on consumer goods for themselves, and "saved" $1 billion. We'll also make the reasonable assumption that the $1 billion they saved was soon put back into the spending stream when they purchased—"invested in"—new capital goods, such as machinery and factories. Machines wear out and new technologies emerge that could lower costs for the capitalist, so that each year capitalists use up part, or all, of that year's

Figure 5.1 The Circular Flow Model of the Macroeconomy

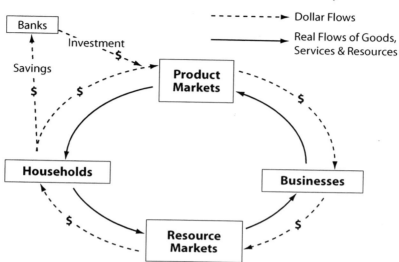

Businesses produce goods and services for sale to individual buyers in product markets in exchange for money. Households provide resources (labor, land and capital) for sale to businesses in resource markets in exchange for money. Some household money gets saved, and this money is returned to the circular flow of the economy via investment.

savings to buy these new capital goods. This process is sometimes called "capital accumulation." In our model, the upshot is that the capitalists will have put all their profits back into the spending stream by purchasing $1 billion of consumer goods and $1 billion of capital goods. Capitalists might also save some of their profits in banks, but we will assume that the banks automatically lend out these funds to consumers, governments, or to other capitalists to use for their own investments.

We can sum up the results of our hypothetical model in this way: during the year, capitalists produced $10 billion because they thought they could sell it. They actually did sell it all because every dollar they paid out in the form of wages and rents, as well as the profits they paid themselves, came right back to them in the form of someone's consumer spending, plus their own spending for capital goods.

This model embodies the theory that all output will find a buyer—a theory that formed the core of classical thinking about the business cycle until Keynes's *General Theory*. As we pointed out, this theory became known as

"Say's Law," named for the French economist Jean-Baptiste Say. What's the basic problem with this theory? *Not all savings are automatically converted into spending during the same year, month, or six months, or whatever time period we might be analyzing.* Going back to our example, let's take a closer look at the $1 billion saved by our capitalists. What might the capitalists in our economy have done with that $1 billion if, during the year, threatening events—such as epidemics, war, catastrophic weather, or a financial crisis—had produced a sweeping wave of pessimism among them? Such events might also have frightened the other potential savers in the economy, the landlords, and what would be the effect of their fears on their own spending? Both of these classes might reasonably have responded to fears about the future by saving for the coming bad times, rather than using all of their income to buy consumer or capital goods. If they had done this, that is, not put back all the $3 billion we gave them in our model, there could only have been one result: the capitalists would have produced goods that were not then sold, causing them to accumulate unwanted, unsold goods—inventories—and very likely to produce less output during the next time period. An economic downturn—initiated by overproduction or a glut of goods—would have begun because all of the supply would not have created its own demand.

Despite the reign of a modified version of Say's Law in the central tradition up to the 1930s,[2] some economists saw through the classical error. Thomas Malthus in the early part of the nineteenth century, Karl Marx in the middle, and John Hobson at the turn of the twentieth century, are only the most well-known who argued that savings not returned to the income stream quickly enough could cause a downturn. Marx undoubtedly spoke for many of these ignored economists by referring to Say's analyses of the aggregate economy as "trivial," "tedious," and "insipid nonsense." Whatever they might have thought about Say and his law, however, these critics could not break its transfixing hold on classical economists. That break would have to wait for Keynes in 1936.

We now turn to a second foundation of classical thinking: the idea that sustained involuntary unemployment in capitalism is not possible.

THE CLASSICAL THEORY OF UNEMPLOYMENT

The classical economists believed, with good reason, that work for capitalist wages was essentially irksome. This meant that, below a certain level of wages, nobody would work and that as wages rose more people would offer their labor power to the highest capitalist bidder. Given the two sides of this labor market, if the supply of labor were to remain constant, for instance, but capitalists decided to increase their output, they would need more workers and this would drive up wages. Alternatively, if the supply of labor remained constant, but the demand for labor time fell, wages would fall.

To connect this theory of a single labor market to the classical theory of unemployment, consider the following example: take a hypothetical large city with an active labor market for skilled carpenters. Let's assume that the going wage is $15 an hour, and as we begin our analysis there are 10,000 carpenters on the job. Suppose that, for whatever reasons, there is a substantial decline in the demand for construction throughout the whole region. This event will likely reduce the selling prices of construction projects and thus the value of the output of the carpenters who work on them. As the value of what carpenters produce declines, their services will also be less in demand, and in turn, we would expect their wages to fall. However, suppose that these wage rates don't fall because the carpenters make it clear they will fight wage cuts individually, or collectively through labor unions, or in other ways. This kind of resistance produces the well-known, real-world phenomenon called "wage rigidity," and in response to it, if the decline in construction demand is steep enough, some employers will lay off some of the carpenters.

Suppose the capitalists lay off 2,000 carpenters, and the remaining 8,000 of them continue working for the old wage. Now, in terms of the classical theory, here is a crucial question: are these 2,000 laid-off carpenters "unemployed?" According to the classical economists they are unemployed, but *voluntarily* so. That is, they are *choosing* to be unemployed, and if they would lower their wage demands enough, construction firms would once again find it profitable to hire more carpenters. Perhaps, if all the carpenters were willing to take a cut in pay from $15 to $10 an hour, and if that wage fit the new market conditions, it would again be profitable for the capitalists to hire all 10,000 of them. In other words, as long as carpenters are unwilling to accept lower wages in the face of falling demand for their services, there will be voluntary unemployment but not involuntary unemployment. That is to say, their unemployment is their fault! The implicit and connecting idea here is that hiring the carpenters at a lower wage will allow the builders to sell their output at a lower price. This lower price will produce a greater demand for the projects, and that will lead to an increase in the demand for carpenters. In other words, our unemployed carpenters are out of work because of their resistance to wage cuts.

The classical school generalized this theory—that without wage rigidity all individual markets were always at, or tending towards, full employment—to the entire economy. So strong was the hold of this model on the minds of economists in the central tradition that it was, as Guy Routh reports, "maintained right into the depths of the depression of the 1930s," when unemployment in both Britain and the U.S. was about 25%. As a prominent example, consider the comments made in 1932 by the president of the Royal Economic Society, the principal organization of the British classical school: "General unemployment appears when asking too much is a general phenomenon.... [The world] should learn to submit to declines of money-income without squealing." (Routh 1986, 57)

To sum up this quick review of the classical school's explanation for economic downturns and the consequent unemployment, we have the following: (1) aggregate supply will always equal aggregate demand, except temporarily, because capitalists will automatically use any savings out of the income stream to purchase capital goods; and (2) deviations from full employment in *all* individual labor markets result from worker resistance to falling wages in contracting industries. How, then, did Keynes go about putting these models more or less into the dustbin of history?

THE BROAD OUTLINES OF THE "KEYNESIAN REVOLUTION"

We want to be clear about our purposes in this section. The central structure of the Keynesian macroeconomic framework is formed by interrelated theories of consumption, investment, government spending, net exports, and the way in which behavior in these various sectors causes a capitalist economy to expand and contract. Such a framework is central to any introduction to modern macroeconomics, and all economics students will thus be made to learn its structural outlines and most important details. We will leave to economics courses the proper development of macroeconomics and take up only what helps us to explain the broad impact of Keynes' ideas on economics and on public policy, and of course, the relationship of these to political economy.

In 1936 when Keynes published *The General Theory*, many economists eagerly seized its details and implications, especially their relation to the causes of the Great Depression all were living through. Most of these economists were young and from the United States, many from Harvard's economics department. At the same time, the book produced a great debate among economists throughout the capitalist world, and many were not then, nor are they now, convinced of its usefulness. However, enough economists in the United States and Britain were converted to his way of thinking to begin to sink the classical ship. One such young economist, Harvard's Paul Samuelson, legitimized Keynesian economics by putting it on a par with classical microeconomics in a 1948 introductory textbook that remains the model for most economics textbooks.

Another reason that Keynes' critique took hold was that others outside the central tradition, who understood and accepted his principal conclusions, had already developed much of his critique. As early as the 1700s, thinkers outside the mainstream had already advanced arguments about savings, involuntary unemployment, and the policy measures that might solve the problem of depressions. In the 1860s, Marx had developed a number of ideas about business cycles, including that they resulted in part from an imbalance of spending in the investment and consumption sectors of the economy. Similarly, in 1899, the Englishman John A. Hobson had argued that unemployment was caused by "over-savings." Hobson, however, was soon to realize that he had made a heretical argument and would be punished for it. As he later wrote, there were several negative responses to the book:

> The first shock came in a refusal of the London Extension Board to allow me to offer courses of Political Economy. This was due, I learned, to the intervention of an Economics Professor who had read my book and considered it in rationality as equivalent to an attempt to prove the flatness of the earth...[The second came] when suddenly, without explanation, the invitation [to offer a course to a charitable organization] was withdrawn. Even then I hardly realized that in appearing to question the virtue of unlimited thrift [savings] I had committed the unpardonable sin. (Quoted in Keynes 1936, 365-6)

By the late nineteenth century it had become, at least according to Hobson and Keynes, an unpardonable sin not to agree with the classical explanation of the business cycle! And as we have seen, right up to the point when Keynes was writing *The General Theory*, Britain's most widely respected economists were still telling the world that the only way out of the Great Depression was to lower wages all around.

More substantive than these largely ignored critiques of the classical theory were the actual practices of one European country, Sweden, which had implemented its own "Keynesian" policies before *The General Theory* was published. John Kenneth Galbraith has described how, since the early part of the century, Swedish economists and government planners had instituted policies that made sure that "over-saving" in the Swedish economy was offset by government expenditures. (Galbraith 1987) Swedish fiscal policy, in practice before Keynes argued for it, was part of the Swedish "middle way" we discuss in Chapter 9.

All this theory and practice was well known by Keynes, a fine student of history and of his own discipline, and he drew upon both to build his own system. He also chose as a specific strategy in *The General Theory* to explain his analysis in the terms of the conceptual foundations of the classical school. If you were to try to read the book, you would almost certainly be cornered by confusion. Yet, if you plowed on you would find that the book opens up at the end because, quite intentionally, Keynes wrote the closing chapters for the general public. There he took up the implications of his theory for public policy in a discussion that justifies his renown for eloquence as a writer.

THE KEYNESIAN CRITIQUE OF SAY'S LAW

A major contribution of Keynes's *General Theory* was its critique of Say's Law. Keynes argued conclusively, in terse theoretical parts of his book, that this "law" was the wishful thinking of those who dreamed of a self-regulating capitalist system. The assumption that savings would always be spent on capital goods during the same production period was not quite so far-fetched when made by Adam Smith. In his time the merchant and land-lord classes did virtually all the saving, and it appears that usually—but certainly not all the time—they quickly converted their savings into capital goods in order to profit from rapidly expanding capitalist markets. However, Keynes noted that by the nineteenth century, and certainly by the early twentieth century, industrial capitalist systems had become vastly more complex.

Even in a world in which the economic role of government was supposed to be minimal, governments had become ever more involved in economic affairs. Thus, the saving "leakage" from the economy was joined by the "tax leakage," because whatever governments took in taxes reduced the circular flow of income. Like savings, these taxes could lead to underconsumption if the tax leakages were not put back into the income stream by government. Still a third leakage occurs when, for example, people in the United States buy imports which, dollar for dollar, reduce the amount they would have bought from U.S. firms. In fact, from the point of view of Say's Law, we can think of taxes and imports as identical to savings: they are a drain from the system that must be returned or overproduction will occur. Figure 5.2 illustrates the circular flow model of the economy with all of the leakages included. We can express Keynes' idea more clearly if we consider the magnitudes of these leakages from the spending flow in our own economy. Take 2003 for example (and it doesn't matter what recent year you use). In 2003, U.S. business firms employed over 137 million people and these people produced output that was sold for nearly $11 trillion. As this $11 trillion flowed through the

U.S. economy, most of it, about $7.8 trillion, was put back in by household consumption spending. However, much of it was drained out of the expenditure stream as leakages:

> More than 10 million businesses firms saved—"accumulated"—about $1.5 trillion to help finance their expenditures for capital goods.3
> More than 110 million household units saved about $176 billion and put most of that in banks or other financial institutions to be lent out to others.
> All the levels of government took a total of about $2.0 trillion out of the expenditure stream through taxation.
> Households and firms spent about $.5 trillion on imports, another leakage from the domestic expenditure stream.

Figure 5.2 The Complete Circular Flow Model of the Macroeconomy

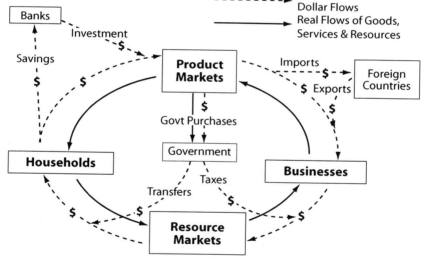

This means that during 2003, the tax, savings, and import leakages out of the flow of income were almost $4.2 trillion, or about 38% of all the expenditures! Of course, at the same time that these leakages were occurring, "injections" were taking place as well. Governments were putting money back into the expenditure stream by spending on such things as military hardware and education; business firms were adding to the stream by buying machinery and equipment; banks were lending the savings out to all kinds of spenders; and there were exports sold to foreigners.

These figures lead us to the relevant theoretical point: while U.S. capitalists were deciding to produce the $11 trillion of output during 2003, they had no idea, of course, how much of the income they generated would be lost to leakages, and how much would be gained back by injections. *The reason is that these leakages and injections result from an impossibly large number of decisions by people who, at the time they save, tax, or spend, do not typically know anything about how others are putting money into, or taking it out of, the income stream.* The capitalists in this process are not operating in total darkness, because they have past sales experiences to draw upon. However, the volume of output that the capitalists produce for sale, say, for next month, depends upon hunches, or other best guesses, about something they *cannot know*: the level of leakages and injections that will occur as the income their production generates flows through the economy. If their estimates of sales are not realized—which, in theoretical language, will occur if there are too many leakages that are not offset by injections—they will likely accumulate inventories, and during the subsequent time period they will likely produce less total output. Thus, when the *typical* business firm is not selling all the output it is producing, there will be general overproduction, and this general overproduction will ultimately lead to a decline in output, employment, and income.

The Multiplier and the Liquidity Trap

Two other parts of Keynes' critique of Say's Law merit a brief description here. Keynes developed the first of these, called the "multiplier," with other Cambridge economists, and it was a powerful addition to his model of the macroeconomy. We will explain the multiplier with a simple example. Imagine a rosy scenario in which the local billionaire decides to pay back the community by giving the first person he or she sees a $100 bill. Suppose you are the lucky recipient, and you spend it on that tattoo of your favorite professor you've been aching to put on your arm. Your purchase alone increases spending in the economy by $100, and it also increases the income of the tattoo parlor by $100. Suppose the owner of the parlor spends $80 of it for a new hairdo. This will add $80 of new spending and income to the $100 spent for the tattoo, both of them additions to spending brought about by that initial $100 the billionaire gave to you. The beautician now has some more money to spend, and on down the line each new level of spending creates multiples of its own.

These successive transactions thus "multiply" the first round of spending—the $100 spent on the tattoo—and make the total change in spending some multiple of that first round. The multiplier adds a certain speed and energy to upward and downward movements of the economy, and it added to the new macro theory that Keynes used to undermine the classical theory. It also carries with it depressingly bad news for those committed to laissez-faire because it implies that government spending can have a large, positive effect on the economy: our $100 bill would have produced a similar multiplier effect had it been new government spending for goods and services, or simply handouts to needy citizens. We'll say more about that later.

The theory of the "liquidity trap," another of Keynes' principal ideas in *The General Theory*, has resurfaced in public discussion in relation to the long-term depression of the Japanese economy during the 1990s and the financial crisis of 2007. In trying to explain the depth of the Great Depression, Keynes argued that societies could wallow in a slump for long periods of time even if interest rates—which at low levels are supposed to induce capitalists and consumers to borrow more, and in turn to spend more and end the downturn—fall to zero. He called this problem a "liquidity trap," and argued that it would occur if there were a collapse in confidence among consumers and capitalists that encouraged them to seek "liquidity," meaning they would choose to hold on to their money, rather than buy things, until they perceived that the economy was improving.

KEYNES AND THE CLASSICAL THEORY OF UNEMPLOYMENT

Keynes developed several critiques of the classical claim that there could be no long-lasting *involuntary* unemployment, and we will concern ourselves with the two most prominent ones. Remember that for classical economists, lasting unemployment resulted when workers were not willing to take lower wages in declining product markets. Thus, their suggestion for unemployment policy—even in the middle of the Great Depression, when the unemployment rate was 25% in both the United States and Britain—was for the working classes to take lower wages. Keynes saw two fatal errors in this thinking. The first had partly to do with the relative power between workers and their bosses, for it was apparent to Keynes, and almost everyone else, that unless there was a sustained and deepening downturn, workers mightily resisted wage cuts. However, because the classical economists ruled out government intervention as a way to lower wages, nothing was left to do except to wait for workers to see the light and accept the necessary wage cuts. When they didn't—which was almost always—this meant that wages never fell quickly in recessions, preventing the economy from self-adjusting as the classical theorists believed it would. To the classical school, this resistance from workers to falling wages also meant that the recessions should be blamed on them, rather than on the system itself.

The second error of the classical school can be explained like this: suppose that an economic contraction becomes deep enough, and sustained enough, to lower the demand for labor in all the principal labor markets. There would be a point in such a contraction at which wages would begin to fall, when and by how much depending on countless conditions. We have already pointed out that, according to the classical economists, falling wages would lower costs and prices, thus inviting a greater demand for goods and services. In turn, they believed that this greater demand would *automatically* turn around the economic decline. Keynes pointed out, however, that a *general* fall in wages—the largest single part of national income—would likely cause an eventual *decline* in the demand for goods and services that workers buy, rather than an increase encouraged by lower prices.

Keynes offered several other possible consequences of a fall in wages, some of which might be expected to raise expenditures by business firms, but he did not see them as having the capacity to offset the decline in total spending that would come from falling wages. Falling wages, if they did have the effect of reducing total consumer demand, could also greatly reduce the optimism of the capitalists and lead them to reduce their spending on new equipment. This latter possibility was important to Keynes because he knew that the sustained and deep depression of the 1930s had, by 1936, done exactly that in the leading capitalist countries. In general, such a progression would mean that the decline in consumption spending, along with the decline in capitalist spending on capital goods, would send the economy spiraling downward even further.

To Keynes, then, the levels of employment and unemployment depended on a series of factors: the collective decisions of people to spend as consumers and capitalists and to fund government spending programs, the decisions of foreigners to buy U.S. products, the multiplier, and all the remaining parts of his theoretical framework. That is, in his model the unemployed are victimized by crises in capitalism, *and the classical solution of lower wages would only make the crises worse.* In his argument, Keynes came closer than he probably would have liked to Marx's idea of an "industrial reserve army" of unemployed that we discussed in Chapter 3. What these two theories share is the conclusion that unemployment is an inevitable feature of capitalism over which workers have no control and not a matter of voluntary choice on the part of the unemployed. Unemployment goes up when aggregate spending declines, and thus if we are looking for culprits to blame, it would have to be the millions and millions of individuals in households and business firms deciding to cut back on their spending. Unemployment in capitalism, therefore, is *systemic and inevitable*, rather than the result of individual decisions to work or not to work at market wages. It is hard to imagine a more resounding rejection of classical economics than this Keynesian conclusion about unemployment.

THE CURRENT STATUS OF KEYNESIAN ECONOMICS

Aside from pushing from the limelight central parts of classical economics, the principal long-term influence of *The General Theory* has been to broaden the focus of macroeconomics. Today, aggregate sectors of spending, and their dynamic interrelationships, are understood as central to the study of the capitalist business cycle. Keynes had no particular qualms about the microeconomic models that his own mentor, Alfred Marshall, had been so important in bringing to the mainstream; and his principal work in 1936 built on many of the theoretical foundations of the classical school. For this reason, as we have said, Keynes never really left the central tradition of economics. In fact, the macro theory he produced gradually became part of the mainstream, a process that led Paul Samuelson to write in the 1964 version of his textbook that:

> [Today] the broad fundamentals [of Keynes' theory] are increasingly accepted by economists of all schools of thought, including, it is important to notice, many who do not share Keynes' particular policy views and who differ on technical details of analysis. (Samuelson 1964)

Samuelson's point here does not mean, by any stretch of the imagination, that there have not been challenges, before and after 1964, to Keynesian ideas. These have come particularly from economists unhappy with his conclusions about the need for government intervention in the economy. Two of these challenges, called "monetarism" and "rational expectations," have come from the economics department at the University of Chicago, which has been one of the strongest bastions of anti-Keynesian sentiment in the United States academy since the 1930s. There are also "post"-Keynesian economists who believe Keynes' ideas constitute the best understanding to date of capitalism, and they compete for the attention of other academic macroeconomists and the policy makers in government.

It is far beyond the scope of this essay to go into the current academic debate about macroeconomic theory.[4] But there is fresh evidence of the fact that, even after more than 70 years of challenges from some mainstream economists, Keynesian ideas continue to play a role in current academic debates about the macroeconomy, as we shall see later when we discuss the economic policies of Barack Obama.

KEYNES, THE POLITICAL ECONOMIST, I: ECONOMIC METHODOLOGY

We now want to expand our argument for having included Keynes in a book on political economy. The Keynes you will encounter in your regular textbook will seem to conform to the "scientific method" used by mainstream economists. But there was another important political economy side to Keynes' thinking—a side that demonstrates the broad sweep of his ideas. We will let Keynes demonstrate this by speaking for himself at some length here and below. Writing in 1931, (and using the characteristically sexist language of the time) he said:

> The study of economics does not seem to require any specialized gifts of an unusually high order. Is it not, intellectually regarded, a very easy subject compared with the higher branches of philosophy or pure science? An easy subject, at which very few excel! The paradox finds its explanation, perhaps, in that the master economist must possess a rare *combination* of gifts. He must be mathematician, historian, statesman, philosopher—in some degree. He must understand symbols and speak in words. He must contemplate the particular in terms of the general, and touch abstract and concrete in the same flight of thought. He must study the present in the light of the past for the purposes of the future. No part of man's nature or his intuitions must lie entirely outside his regard. He must be purposeful and disinterested in a simultaneous mood; as aloof and incorruptible as an artist, yet sometimes as near the earth as a politician. (Keynes 1963, 140-1)

Referring more precisely to the quantitative techniques of the mainstream economists, Keynes wrote in *The General Theory*:

> Too large a proportion of recent "mathematical" economics are mere concoctions, as imprecise as the initial assumptions they rest on, which allow the author to lose sight of the complexities and interdependencies of the real world in a maze of pretentious and unhelpful symbols. (Keynes 1936, 98)

As an example of the kind of ideas that Keynes was willing to entertain, consider his explanation of what motivates economic actors in capitalism.

In the following passage from *The General Theory*, where his specific focus is what motivates capitalists to invest in capital goods, note that Keynes implicitly dismisses the constricted creature called economic man as a misleading description of human behavior.

[A] large proportion of our positive activities depend on spontaneous optimism rather than on a mathematical expectation, whether moral or hedonistic or economic. Most, probably, of our decisions to do something positive, the full consequences of which will be drawn out over many days to come, can only be taken as a result of *animal spirits*—of a spontaneous urge to action rather than inaction, and not as the outcome of a weighted average of quantitative benefits multiplied by quantitative probabilities.... Thus if the animal spirits are dimmed and the spontaneous optimism falters, leaving us to depend on nothing but a mathematical expectation, enterprise will fade and die—though fears of loss may have a basis no more reasonable than hopes of profit had before....In estimating the prospects for investments [in capital goods], we must have regard, therefore, to the nerves and hysteria and even the digestions and reactions to the weather of those upon whose spontaneous activity it largely depends. (Keynes 1936, 162-3, emphasis added)

If we take these three passages together, we can see in Keynes' methodology a far-flung net—or a particularly big vacuum cleaner, if we use the metaphor of U.S. economist Robert Solow—in which to catch things that might help his analysis. For Keynes, apparently, the entire universe of ideas and knowledge had potential for helping theorists understand the world outside the swirl of prejudices and confusions inside their heads. His methodology for studying economic activity broke all the self-imposed bonds of the central tradition. Though he insisted often that economic *theory* was a matter of simple logic, it seems hardly to have mattered to him whether economics was a science. In other words, though Keynes's ideas about the economic world were in some ways deeply embedded in classical thinking, they were outside it in critical ways. Perhaps now, after reading about Veblen and Marx, one can see how much closer his research impulses were to theirs than to those of the economic mainstream. His method of work was that of a political economist with a broad scope and an understanding of the instability and uncertainty that characterize the actual economy.

KEYNES, THE POLITICAL ECONOMIST, II: THE POLITICAL KEYNES

By the early 1920s, Keynes had come to believe in the need for government intervention in certain areas of economic life, and thus the policy prescriptions he offered in *The General Theory* merely extended ideas he had held for some time. The specifics of his antirecession policies will not come as a surprise to readers at this point. When an economy is mired in an economic contraction, Keynes argued, it is a consequence of inadequate spending in all the key sectors. Economic downturns were most likely to originate from a decline in capitalists' purchases of capital goods, because volatile and unpredictable "animal spirits" ruled these expenditures. When the spirits led the capitalists to reduce their spending on buildings and equipment, all those who had been supplying such products before would now be out of jobs and income, and the effects of their declining spending would spill over into the consumption sector, causing a decline there as well. Further dragging the economy down would be a negative multiplier effect, and soon enough an economic crisis would be underway.

Given this theory of how the aggregate economy could quickly slide into a recession, the solution seemed obvious to Keynes: as investment and consumption spending fell, the government should take up the slack in demand by borrowing money to increase its own expenditures, or reducing interest rates to encourage spending in other sectors of the economy. And it didn't matter for what those expenditures were made. As this spending worked its way through the economy, it would ultimately produce a better outlook for businesses, which meant more investment on capital goods. With the help of the multiplier, this would start the whole process moving back upward to recovery and economic growth.

Aside from the Swedes, who succeeded with this kind of fiscal policy before Keynes argued for it, other capitalist governments did not readily jump on the Keynesian bandwagon. The New Deal in the United States generated a spate of new government programs such as unemployment compensation, federal welfare, and public works projects that gave jobs to the unemployed, but the government was not ready to risk the huge deficits that Keynesians were urging as the way to end the Depression. However, starting in about 1940, Keynesian policies were "tested in the field" by most capitalist governments during World War II. In the United States, government leaders tossed aside the classical school's admonition against government intervention in the economy, including its rule against deficit spending, to fight the war against Japan and Germany. Running massive deficits to finance the construction of bombs, planes, and ships, federal government spending led to a massive recovery. By

1943-44, the unemployment rate fell to its lowest recorded level, about one percent of the work force.

With the war as a gigantic lab experiment that seemed to prove the Keynesian theory, most in the scholarly and political world gradually came to adopt it. After World War II, almost all capitalist nations passed laws, such as the Employment Act of 1946 in the United States, making the maintenance of stable prices and full employment a responsibility for the federal government. These were laws in part written by, and certainly reflecting the views of, Keynesian economists. A symbolic high point of the influence of Keynes occurred in 1963, when in a speech at Yale University John Kennedy used the idea of the Keynesian multiplier to justify the cut in personal income taxes that he was urging upon the Congress as a way to cause a sluggish economy to grow faster. The essentially Keynesian basis of domestic U.S. economic policy remained in place for about 25 years, and in 1971 an economic conservative, Richard Nixon, argued that "we are all Keynesians now."

Even as Nixon spoke, the U.S. economy had already begun to develop a number of structural problems, particularly pockets of hard-core unemployment and rising inflation, that could not be readily resolved by Keynesian policies. These problems in the United States and in Britain in the 1970s deepened through the decade and they propelled into power Margaret Thatcher in Britain in 1979 and Ronald Reagan in the United States in 1980. The public elected these two because it succumbed to their espousal of the old laissez-faire slogans of free enterprise, individual initiative, and especially the sentiment that government in principle was a bad thing for the economy. By the middle of the 1980s, the U.S. Republicans and British Conservatives held sway with an increasingly antigovernment rhetoric that became the stated economic philosophy of the major political parties in both countries. After the early 1980s, it became virtually impossible in the United States to be elected to public office at any level if one championed higher taxes. According to some political analysts, George H. W. Bush was pushed from the presidency by Bill Clinton in 1992 because he went back on his famous "read my lips" pledge not to support tax increases.

For his part, Bill Clinton jumped on the bandwagon when he came into power as a "new Democrat," claiming that "the era of big government is over." His economic policies—including "ending welfare as we know it"—were largely indistinguishable from those of the Republicans. Together with Robert Rubin, his treasury secretary and economic advisor, Clinton squelched efforts in the late 1990s to regulate the financial industry. These two latter day robber barons also led the international drive to open the world to globalization by giant capitalist firms. This sort of catering to business and financial interests was now considered sound "economic policy," justified by the specious argument that their good fortunes will trickle down to the rest of us by creating a climate "hospitable" to business interests. Partly, Clinton moved toward the Republicans in order to get elected and re-elected; partly he did so because, more than any Democratic president before him, he aggressively and successfully financed his campaigns with money from rich individuals and powerful corporations.

Not surprisingly, given his family background and his conservative economic policies as Governor of Texas, George W. Bush continued to pour out the laissez-faire rhetoric, although he contradicted it with his actions such as installing hefty duties on steel imports and signing legislation providing multi-billions of dollars to agribusiness. For all these politicians, sloganeering about the evils of government works as a political strategy. Their actions, however, reveal that they are no more antagonistic to government action than was Keynes, if not being so fits into their re-election strategies, or can add to their personal gain in other ways.

This widespread involvement of government in capitalism is the political reality in all modern capitalist countries, no matter what their politicians say in speeches or at press conferences about "keeping government off of peoples' backs." These same people expect their governments to manage the macroeconomy, and presidents who have failed to do so in the public perception—Jimmy Carter and George H. W. Bush are two recent examples—don't get a second term. In other words, the so-called Reagan revolution in domestic economic policy is considered a success to all those conservatives, including many mainstream economists, who saw it as reversing the Keynesian ideas that for the previous four decades had a been a principle foundation of those policies.

The Democrat, Barack Obama, became U.S. president in 2009 knowing well enough that unregulated capitalism was dangerously unstable and aware, too, that his Republican predecessor had worked with his Congressional allies for eight years to eliminate as many of the rules and regulations as they could. Obama also knew that, in the previous three decades, the U.S. economic order had become increasingly unequal. His schooling at Harvard, including his law degree, and his community organizing in low income areas of Chicago, had kept him from becoming yet another fan of laissez-faire. However, his experience in the classrooms and in Chicago neighborhoods did not prepare him for what he was to face as president.

When Obama took office in January 2009, the financial crisis which had exploded in 2007 was already pushing the U.S. economy towards a major downturn. Declining GDP, rising unemployment, and mortgage failures were principle harbingers of a major collapse, one that was spreading around the globe. The public infrastructure—schools, hospitals, roads—was ever more unattended as state governments lost tax revenue and no longer could afford to finance such projects.

In the face of this crisis, the Obama administration pursued a strategy with two central elements, the first of them to make risky loans of hundreds of billions of dollars to a few of the major banks, insurance companies and investment firms to keep them from total collapse. There was wide-spread resistance, mostly outside the government, to this policy because the public saw it as taking care of the banks before taking care of working people. The public reached this conclusion in part because the policy was pressed on Obama by principal economic advisers who were political conservatives, most of them from the banking industry. They included his chief economic advisor, Larry Summers, who had strongly urged Clinton not to regulate derivatives, and had declared that Milton Friedman's "greatest contribution may have been in convincing people of the importance of allowing free markets to operate." Also, at the White House as a special advisor was Henry Paulson, Bush's Treasury Secretary who had come to government from being the CEO of Goldman-Sachs. Further, Obama picked as head of the Federal Reserve System Ben Bernanke, an ex-academic, who had claimed at Friedman's 92nd birthday party that, "Among scholars, Milton Friedman has no peers."

With such advisers, it was not surprising that Obama began his fight against the economic downturn by convincing Congress to approve a loan of $182 billion to the country's largest insurance company, A.I.G. In this process, among other favored recipients, Chase Manhattan Bank got $29 billion when it purchased the failing Bear Stearns. Obama also proposed to increase regulations in the financial industry, something the entire public, save that industry, wanted to have in place.

The second major element of Obama's anti-recession policy was passed in 2009 and he called it the American Recovery and Reinvestment Act (ARRA). It included federal tax cuts, allocated over $700 billion to expand unemployment and other social welfare benefits, and aimed to expand income and employment with spending on the public sector, including energy. With this proposal, Obama essentially brought Keynes back to the conference table at the White House where the government forges its economic policies, and many commentators in the media made note of this fact. Obama also proposed a complicated revision to the health care system, with central elements that further regulated insurance companies and funds allocated to try to guarantee insurance coverage to 31 million people without it.

By the middle of 2010, the overall effects of these policies were still to be determined. The giant financial firms were mostly safe and had resumed paying out huge bonuses, despite a public outcry against them. In March 2010, Obama signed into law the health care plan, but, as a measure of the kind of resistance he faced to all of his proposals, it was not supported by a single Republican member of the House of Representatives. It also ushered forth a screaming, sometimes violent opposition from a loose amalgam of conservatives opposed to what they considered the dangerous spread of federal government power. The new health care program is complicated, not well understood by most of the population, and many of its elements will come into effect slowly over the years. It will be a long time, indeed, before its efficacy can be determined.

Regarding the ARRA, in 2010 the unemployment rate, as measured by the federal government, fell below 10% for the first time in over a year. (Yet, remember that this measure is fatally flawed because it does not include workers who quit seeking jobs and those who work part-time but want full-time work.) Rising GDP and other measures beside unemployment rates indicate that the economy has stopped its free fall. But, most economists, from all persuasions, predicted that unemployment rates at recession levels would be around for at least two years. Many prominent liberal economists believed the AARA was well-intentioned but was doomed at the beginning because its allocations were far too small given the severity of the crisis.

Whatever are the ultimate consequences of the Obama anti-recession policies, his administration has reinstated Keynes as part of the dialogue by his willingness to expand the role of government in responding to a major economic crisis. ARRA and his health care plan, in particular, represent a clear break with the neo-liberal policies that most recently originated with Ronald Reagan and which no president since 1980 had vigorously, nor successfully, challenged. Yet, Obama faced a sea of problems: a major economic crisis, the relative and steady decline of the United States in its power to have its way in the world, a rebellion by the Republican Party committed deeply to his failure for a host of reasons, and the abiding disappointment of many of his one-time supporters who saw him worrying more about bankers than about working people. Keynes was back at the White House table, but was this enough of a change? Many political economists, however much they might enjoy Obama's resistance to certain elements of neo-liberalism, see his administration as badly misled by the comforting illusion that U.S. capitalism can be civilized by modest, liberal reforms.

KEYNES AND INTERNATIONAL CAPITALISM

As we have written above, Keynes also was one of the principal designers of the post-World War II system of international finance, with its two major institutions, the International Monetary Fund, (IMF), and the World Bank. It is true that Keynes's proposals on key elements of the system were rejected by delegates from the United States, in particular his idea that the international system should be overseen by an international bank especially geared to encourage economic growth. The United States, however, dominated the conference, and it preferred the IMF with the more restricted goal of working only to encourage price stability. Such a policy, of course, favored the United States, with its booming war-time economy, and penalized most of the other 43 allied countries, whose societies had been torn asunder by the war. And, as we shall see, both the IMF and the World Bank would eventually become a monumental barrier to growth in many poor nations.

Nevertheless, there was a crucial ideological foundation to the IMF and the World Bank in its inception, one that remained in place at least until the 1970s. This foundation is the idea that capitalism is inherently unstable, it therefore necessitates both domestic and international regulation, and governments are what John K. Galbraith called a requisite "countervailing" power to that of private corporations. This matrix of regulations at both the domestic and international level was an assault on the classical system because "free trade" was, in that system, the analog to an unregulated domestic economy. One observer, looking back on the effects of the system the delegates produced, has written:

> Between 1945 and 1973, when the regime of [international] financial controls remained in effect, the war-ravaged economies of Europe and Asia were rebuilt, and the developed world as a whole enjoyed annual economic growth rates exceeding four per cent, which translated into the virtual tripling of total output. (Cassidy 1998b)

After the 1970s, much in this regard changed. The ideology of "free trade" was a part of the Reagan/Thatcher *laissez-faire* agenda, and picking up where they left off, Democrat Bill Clinton campaigned more vigorously for unregulated international capitalism than any president since before the Great Depression. In their championing of "free trade," presidents Reagan, George Bush, and Clinton used the considerable authority and power of the U.S. government to dismantle the system of international controls established at Bretton Woods. Some regulations, such as those controlling the values of currencies, were dropped in the 1970s. Others, such as the regulation of capital flows across borders, were eliminated in the 1990s as developing countries come under pressure from the U.S. and other powerful capitalist nations to adopt their own "free trade" policies.

Though we cannot know now the ultimate effects of on the U.S. economy of the growing encroachment of *laissez-faire* policies, we can safely extract one conclusion from this comparison: the sustained period of economic growth in U.S. history, cited above by John Cassidy—1945-1970—occurred during the period in which both U.S. and international economic policies were most thoroughly Keynesian. It was also the only period in modern U.S. history that has produced a downward redistribution of income (albeit a small one). Since the mid-1970s, this distribution of income has become ever more unequal, and it is now the most unequal of all the industrialized capitalist nations.

As final words on Keynes, we have seen that the Bretton Woods agreement was most importantly embodied in the International Monetary Fund and the World Bank. As we described in our first chapter, for three decades—under the tutelage of Milton Friedman and his "Chicago Boys—these two institutions developed a policy of bullying poor nations seeking aid into trying to shape themselves into largely unregulated capitalist states. Deregulating the economies of poor countries has meant eliminating labor and environmental protections, "restructuring" government spending to starve social programs, and instituting an array of other reforms that serve the interests of corporations and Western governments. In 1995, the IMF and World Bank were joined by the World Trade Organization, made of up representatives of over 150 nations, with a principal goal of working out interstate agreements that facilitate unregulated international trade—that is, facilitating globalization.

Resistance to the WTO, an organization that is dominated by representatives from the United States and other large capitalist states, erupted in 1999 at its annual meeting in Seattle, Washington. A loose coalition of trade unionists, students, and organizers from a host of other groups, including anarchists and socialists, engaged in activities ranging from speeches and rallies to direct confrontation with the police and some of the organizers of the event. The conference was delayed, and over 600 protesters were eventually arrested for resisting the police, many of whom beat up peaceful protestors. This kind of resistance to the WTO and globalization has continued at most of its meetings, and has been joined by groups from all over the world. The message of the protesters is always the same: the spread of unregulated market capitalism is a boon to giant capitalist firms and can be utterly disastrous to hundreds of millions of people in poor countries, and to the environment.

It is hard to imagine unfettered globalization as an outcome Keynes intended—he was more interested in stabilizing currency values, promoting economic growth, and facilitating orderly trade. Like most mainstream economists, Keynes assumed that good policy based on good analysis would win the day. In fact, in unregulated capitalism, the capitalists almost always win the day, and in large part because—as political economists have known all along—they have already won the state before the day begins. Despite all his contributions, Keynes would have made richer ones yet had he spent more time studying economists from the other end of the political economy spectrum, most notably Marx. Doing so might have helped him see more clearly how the capitalists, and the politicians they buy, turn "good' economic analysis into yet another advantage they have on the playing field.

CONCLUSION

Keynes and his ideas are included in this book because he shared two important ways of thinking with political economists. For his study of economic life, no information was outside his purview. He was a thoroughly erudite man, a voracious reader and consummate conversationalist, and he believed that dependence on all the senses—what one had read, heard about, seen, could intuit, and even what one felt—was central to the work of any good economist. This is a far, far cry from the restrictive methodological stance that dominates mainstream economics. Unlike typical mainstream economists, who claim to be "making correct scientific judgments," Keynes never stopped giving his opinions to the day that he died. Keynes also shared with political economists the conclusion that unregulated capitalism is an unsustainable system, and for it to last over the long run its aggregate performance will have to be overseen by a strong government, ultimately more powerful than the most powerful corporations. In our view, Keynes' development of this argument has no worthy rival.

SUGGESTIONS FOR FURTHER READING

Alvin Hansen. *A Guide to Keynes.* New York: McGraw-Hill, 1953.

Robert Lekachman. *The Age of Keynes.* New York: Random House, 1966.

Guy Routh. *Unemployment: Economic Perspectives.* London: MacMillan, 1986.

Joseph Schumpeter. *Ten Great Economists, London:* Allen and Unwin, 1952.

Skidelski, Robert. *John Maynard Keynes: The Economist as Saviour,* 1920-1937. London: MacMillan, 1992. (This is part of an acclaimed and readable multi-volume biography of Keynes, his life and work.)

6
Social Class in American Capitalism

I. INTRODUCTION

The Class System at Our University

The catalog for Bucknell University, where we teach, is typical of such catalogs in that it contains a lofty "Mission Statement" telling the world that the university is dedicated to noble goals. Here is its final promise: "Bucknell seeks to educate its students to serve the common good and to promote justice in ways sensitive to the moral and ethical dimensions of life." Only the most churlish person could criticize such goals for a university. And how wonderful it would be for professors if students left our classrooms committed to justice and sensitive to the moral and ethical dimensions of theirs, and others' lives. Wonderful, too, if professors were that way themselves!

These goals, alas, are pronounced against a jarring social reality ignored at most universities: *social class*. The undeniable existence of an array of social classes at universities, among the students and among those who work as faculty, staff, and administrators, is a constant reminder that some of us are accorded more income, status, and respect than others. It is hard to know how a student might see her university "promoting justice" when it bestows benefits and status in glaringly unequal ways.

Students will learn from dorm life during the first week of classes that some are from very privileged backgrounds, some from merely privileged backgrounds, and some from considerably lower ones. Expensive cars and clothes, or the lack of them, and all the talk about one's family reveal the degree of social privilege each student enjoys. In turn, each student receives some added privilege simply by attending college: soon forgotten will be the roughly half of all 18- to 24-year-olds who have never attended college.

Most of these non-students will be engaged in low- to medium-skilled work or will be in the military.

Within all U.S. universities, striking income inequality illuminates the class structure. In 2010, Bucknell's president made a salary and benefits of about $500,000, or roughly three to four times as much as the other administrative bosses below him. The range of average faculty salaries was $114,000 for full professors and fell steadily downward through the hierarchy of professors to the lowly temporary ones, some of whom were paid less than $50,000.

Below these university luminaries are those people who are called, in a perfect word for a class system, "support staff." These employees do all the work that actually keeps the university factory open for business, and they include such employees as custodians, administrative assistants (secretaries), food-service workers, engineers, maintenance workers, and administrators of all kinds, a few of them the bosses of the others. It is hard to know with precision what they make because Bucknell does not readily make such data available. But the range of their annual income is from about $120,000 for the heads of various departments all the way down to below $20,000 for food service workers and janitors, which is less than a living income in the region. There is, then, a gradient of pay for Bucknell employees that is typical of a private corporation. To top it all off, the president lives in a mansion just off campus that is about three hundred yards away from the cafeterias where food-service workers toil for wages that don't allow them to pay all their bills.

In a word, despite the self-aggrandizing language about its mission statement, Bucknell University contains an income distribution that demonstrates less of a commitment to justice and moral sensitivity than to a rigid system of social classes. Some people would argue—those at the top of such pay scales can be counted on for doing so—that the wage and salary scale at Bucknell reflects the guiding meritocracy that determines such scales in a free-market economy like our own. We won't pause here to point out the many glaring deficiencies of that argument, some of which we consider in other parts of the book. We will note that, since Bucknell's grossly unequal income distribution reflects those of almost all U.S. colleges and universities, it provides key evidence to critics who see such institutions as little more than a self-deluding extension of corporate America.

These income numbers, whatever you make of you them, are only the gaudiest element of Bucknell's class system. Consider the effect of Bucknell's income inequality on the children of this university community. The higher salaries of leading administrators and faculty members unquestionably allow them to pass on to their children a number of advantages, such as better odds at attending the higher status schools; access to superior food, clothing, doctors, and dentists; and a better environment in which to learn the linguistic styles and the cultural prejudices of other elites who will eventually hire them for better jobs. As the children might put it, and they tend to begin to understand these things at an early age, "That's not fair!" Why, then, this lofty language about justice in the University's catalog? Is it simply a guise to attract unwary students, to pry lucre from their parents' pockets?

Not altogether. Bucknell's university catalog is not lying to the world—at least not beyond generating the half-truths that, like all vendors, it publicizes to attract its customers. Americans have worked mightily to explain away the system of social classes that shapes our lives and whose ugly consequences are routinely acknowledged in every other industrial society in the world. The myths of the "melting pot" and the "American Dream" figure prominently in Americans' denial of social class. The first of these suggests that, once on U.S. shores, all people meld into a similar kind of being: American! And the second promises that anyone can make it to the top with a little guts and gumption—a notion that contests the very idea that class barriers exist.

Meanwhile, as history has unfolded, the structure of social classes brought here by Europeans has remained more or less intact. The highest social classes remain inhabited mostly by rich white men and their families, who are at the top because they dominate the economic order, and the political order along with it. At the bottom of the social order are disproportionate numbers of women, people of color, and white men who are considered unskilled and uneducated—precisely the people who were there in 1800.

Social Class in More General Terms

The system of social classes is interesting because of its complications, its layerings, and its changes over time. It is also consequential for what happens to any of us, whether we recognize it or not. In the United States, the subject of social class is yet more compelling because the directive to deny its existence gives a hint of the illicit to discussions about it.

The first part of this chapter briefly reviews central ideas in the broad literature about social class. In the second part we will discuss the consequences of social classes, particularly the differential effects of social class on the physical and emotional health of people in modern capitalist societies. We will find in this section good evidence that the lower your social class, the more likely you will suffer from serious psychological and physiological disease, and the shorter your life is likely to be. What could be more conse-quential? In the last part of the chapter we look briefly at the issue of "up-ward mobility" in capitalist societies, and challenge the popular myth that the road upward is available to most, if not all, and always fulfilling to those who make it.

Finally, before we turn to the theorists, we want to emphasize what this essay is *not* about. In isolating social class as a determinant of our behavior, we do not mean to ignore the other factors that mold and make us. We all know that race and gender are two other powerful shaping forces in our lives, and both of these act interdependently with social class. Black and Latino families in the United States, for example, make a little more than 60% of the income of whites because ingrained and unrelenting racism has for all our modern history denied most in both groups access to the best schools, neighborhoods, and jobs. Further, while the interdependence of race and gender are obvious and powerful determinants of who we are and what happens to us, they do not stand alone. Here, we seek only to bring into a sharper focus one element among a number which shape us into the people we are becoming.[2]

II. THEORIES OF SOCIAL CLASS

The two predominant ways that people today think about social class come from Karl Marx, writing in the middle of the nineteenth century, and Max Weber, who wrote at the turn of that century. We will introduce their ideas on social class, along with those of Pierre Bourdieu, a recent interpreter of Weber. Our focus on these three writers means, of course, that we are not providing the broad survey that one might find in textbooks on social class. However, we will introduce all the important categories and dimensions of the current scholarly discussion of the issue. Along the way, and at the end, we will mention a few other authors our readers might want to look at for greater depth and details.

Marx and Social Class

Marx developed his idea of social class at the same time that many others were theorizing on the topic. The use of the word "class" to describe people's roles in a social hierarchy emerged in the early eighteenth century in the work of Daniel Defoe, an English political pamphleteer best known for writing *Robinson Crusoe*. Soon, theories of class found their way into French analyses of society, fueling the French Revolution and the overthrow of the French aristocracy in the late eighteenth century. The most influential writers in the British classical school of economics, Adam Smith and David Ricardo, both recognized that the different streams of income in capitalism—wages, profits, and rents—flowed into the households of separate groups, or classes, of people: laborers, capitalists, and landowners. Ricardo was especially important in shaping modern conceptions of social class because he argued that conflict between the social classes was inevitable. He saw capitalists and workers ever engaged in a struggle over the distribution of what was left to them after rents were paid to the landlords.

Marx was aware of these earlier French and English theories of social class and, typical of all his work, he built on such theories to develop his own. At least two things distinguished his ideas about social class from earlier ones. First, they formed the center of a larger, more complex analysis of capitalism that continues to attract significant attention. And second, Marx and his frequent co-author, Frederick Engels, argued that class conflict would ultimately generate a revolution that would bring an end to capitalism.

In a brief section on social class in our earlier chapter on Marx, we quoted economist Teresa Amott's comment that "Marx's original conceptions continue to define and shape the argument" about social class in capitalism. To refresh memories, in Marx's analysis the capitalist class (or bourgeoisie) rules in capitalism: it owns the firms that dominate the economic order, and this preeminence provides the money and power to rule the political order as well. We also described Marx's argument that the income and wealth of the capitalist class derive from "surplus value," that part of the workers' output that goes to the capitalists in profits rather than to the workers in wages or salaries. These wage-workers, by far the majority, comprise the other major class in capitalism, and the continual struggle between capitalists and laborers over their wages and working conditions is the dynamic center of the system.

Marxists say that class position is defined by one's "relationship to the means of production"—the factories, equipment, and other productive assets used to produce goods and services. If you own these, or manage them in the very top positions in corporations, you are in the capitalist class. If you don't, you are in the proletariat. Marx was aware, and those who have extended his work were aware, that his two-part class system was a broad abstract construct used as a way to see the most essential structural features of capitalism, as well as its likely direction. However, when Marx wrote about events of his own time he would always introduce a host of highly specialized class groupings, including the dominant capitalists and their allies in struggle against an unruly amalgamation of working-class groups. What has happened to his theory of social class in the hands of later theorists?

Max Weber and Social Status

Max Weber was a German social theorist who lived from 1864 to 1920 and whose writings were central to the development of modern sociology. He constructed a carefully reasoned and complex theory of social classes, in which he introduced several key terms such as "social class," "status hierarchies," and "lifestyle." Importantly, Weber replaced the idea of two classes endlessly struggling against each other with the image of social "stratification." This metaphor implied that classes are more like layers of rocks at a geologic site than the two warring classes of owners and workers in Marx's model. Weber's social geology is responsible for the current popular image, where the "upper class" rides atop a hierarchy of classes that descends to the "middle classes" and on down to the "underclass." Weber's theorizing about social class is currently more influential among U.S. academics than Marx's, importantly because radical views of U.S. society, whether they are right or wrong, have been marginalized for most of the past century.

Weber did not abandon Marx's position that employment, one's relationship to the economic order, mattered greatly in determining class position. He argued that a person's kind of participation in the economic order determined *social class*, and that played the dominant role in determining *life chances*. However, Weber wrote that a person's overall class standing also depended on what he called *social status*, how one's economic position, activities, and possessions are perceived by others in the community.

Dennis Gilbert has summarized Weber's ideas about how one's status is interdependent with one's economic class. Gilbert writes that:

> Because of class position, a person earns a certain income. That income permits a certain lifestyle, and people soon make friends with others who live the same way. As they interact with one another, they begin to conceive of themselves as a special type of people. They restrict interaction with outsiders who seem too different (that may be too poor, too uneducated, and too clumsy to live graciously enough for acceptance as worthy companions). Marriage partners are chosen from similar groups because once people follow a certain style of life, they find it difficult to be comfortable with people who live differently. Thus, the status group becomes an ingrown circle. It earns a position in the local community that entitles its members to social honor or prestige from inferiors.…To preserve their advantages, high status groups attempt to monopolize those goods that symbolize their style of life—they [might] band together to keep Jews or blacks out of prestigious country clubs or universities. (Gilbert 1998, 9)

As an example of the social exclusion Gilbert describes, the men who run the Masters Tournament at a fancy golf club in Georgia apparently see women as a threat to all that is hallowed at their club and, to this day, do not allow them as members. It does not take much analysis to see clearly that the class system is rigidified by the exclusion of women from plush golf courses dominated by elite men, almost all of them white.

It is useful to see that in the Weberian system, one's economic class is *objectively* determined, meaning that what matters is what you do in the economy, along with the power and benefits you get from it, rather than how others might value it. On the other hand, social status is *subjectively* determined, meaning that our views about where in the status hierarchy we abide, and the place where others might be, rest on a complex, shifting mosaic of attitudes. Weber realized the interdependence between economic class and social status, and that the former always shaped the latter. Elite groups, such as the socially prominent families in a city, typically get their income and wealth from an economic and political order they dominate by owning factories, banks, and service companies. They translate this advantage into a lifestyle not affordable for most others, and they consider themselves better than others because the evidence that this is the case seems so obvious to them. Finally, they use schooling and networking to protect their privilege into the future, making sure that their children will be more likely to dominate the economic and political order, and thus the world of status. A critical feature of status groups, Weber argued, is that they bond together to construct boundaries between themselves and others, and the higher the status of a group, the thicker are the walls that separate it from all the others.

Over the years, Weber's followers have gradually replaced his distinction between the economic basis of social class and the lifestyle basis of social status; they widely accept that the term "social class" includes both elements. This means, for example, that you can improve your "social standing"—another phrase for class position—either by getting a more highly paid job, or keeping the same job and moving into a more prestigious neighborhood. In most such cases, of course, higher pay will be the reason for moving to a more prestigious neighborhood. In other words, Weber modified and made more complex Marx's theory of social classes, but he retained the preeminent role that Marx assigned to one's place in the economic order.

Pierre Bourdieu: Class Position and Cultural Capital

In the 1960s, the French sociologist Pierre Bourdieu interviewed 1,200 French men and women about their living and spending habits, and collected the information in his work *Distinction: A Social Critique of the Judgment of Taste* (1979). Bourdieu analyzed his data in terms of ideas about social class derived from those before him, especially Max Weber. However, Bourdieu added an extended discussion of what he called "personal capital," which proved useful to subsequent theorists and commentators in illuminating barriers between social classes. Personal capital can take several forms, including economic capital (income and/or wealth), educational capital (years of education and institutions attended), and social capital (the network of family and associations). All these "capitals" are implicit in the work of Weber and his followers, but Bourdieu enriched the old mix by focusing on what he called *cultural capital*. Douglas Holt, an interpreter of Bourdieu, has described cultural capital as being "fostered in…the social milieu of cultural elites." In simple terms, it is elite cultural know-how acquired by spending time in elite circles. Holt writes that cultural capital includes the following crucial elements:

[U]pbringing in families with well-educated parents whose occupations require cultural skills, interaction with peers from similar families, high levels of formal education at institutions that attract other cultural elites studying areas that emphasize critical abstract thinking and communication over the accumulation of particularized trade skills and knowledges, and refinement and reinforcement in occupations that emphasize symbolic production. (Holt 1999, 3)

Bourdieu focused on styles of consumption as manifestations of cultural capital, arguing that consumption was one way that cultural elites draw distinctions between themselves and others. For instance, in his book, *Distinction: A Social Critique of the Judgment of Taste*, Bourdieu discussed the different ways that social classes "consume" such cultural items as newspapers, literature, food, and clothing, and at one point he pays special attention to commercial films. (Bourdieu 1984, 27ff) Even the language used to discuss such a cultural product as a film can be inaccessible to non-elites, as an example will demonstrate.

Try to imagine yourself the daughter of parents with high-school educations, your father a brick layer, your mom a clerk in a small business, and yourself a college freshman. The mother of your assigned roommate is a professor and her father a high roller in the financial industry, perhaps under indictment but not yet incarcerated. Now, imagine spending a weekend with your friend at her parents' country home. At dinner, the subject of the film "Juno" comes up, and someone at the table asks you what you think about it. You say you really liked it because it had different ideas about pregnancy, love affairs, and lots of interesting characters. And, you loved the end of it. Then, mom and dad weigh in with a few ideas about films, commenting on the director's choices, the many unrealities the film portrays, and its odd casting. Dad sighs with a dismissive gesture that the film was "overwhelmed by typical Hollywood sentimentality," and mom closes things off by dismissing all Hollywood films as being that way, and, additionally, always inferior to French films. Perhaps before dinner, you might have felt out of place because of the differences between your families' house and contents, cars, and lawns. After dinner, you might also realize you're in a world of ideas you didn't know existed.

As a guest at this country home, you might also have concluded, and kept to yourself, that your own father possessed more useful knowledge than your friend's father, and that your mother had a much more coherent and comfortable sense of design than your friend's mother. You might well have been right on both counts. However, and this is the point, the people who control the world into which you are moving—the schools and job markets, for example—will likely share the cultural values of your friend's parents. In other words, different forms of cultural capital are neither better nor worse, inherently. They are, however, valued differently by social elites, and therefore they differ crucially in how they aid or retard one's ability to navigate the class system.

We can already guess which of our two first-year women will most likely be a cultural elite in the next generation. Clearly, the daughter of the professor and finance-industry high roller has already accumulated enough educational and social capital to have a great advantage over her roommate. By not living in a house with elite consumption items, and not learning the way in which such items are used and talked about, our working-class student has already fallen far behind in accumulating cultural capital.

It is apparent that all these kinds of capital—economic, educational, social, and cultural—are more readily accessible to the children of the privileged than those of the middle and working classes. None of this is to say, of course, that we can know which of the two young women in our example will work her way highest up the social ladder and how life will be there. Our privileged student might fall into the grip of a destructive eating disorder, while our bright and persevering working-class student works her way to the top of a corporate ladder. Our argument is only that the richer your family, the greater your odds of accumulating crucial kinds of personal capital. We shall see some stunning consequences of these odds in a later discussion of social class and health.

Regenerating Social-Class Privilege

The United States Department of Agriculture (USDA) publishes data each year that explain more directly how the children of the privileged acquire more personal capital than other children. In 2008, the USDA report entitled *Expenditures on Children by Families,* included the information summarized in Table 1 on expenditures on children by "husband-wife" families of varying incomes.

Table 1

Annual Family Income	Average Expenditures on each child to Age 18
Under $56,870	$159,870
$56,870–98,470	$221,190
Over $98,470	$366,660

The numbers in Table 1—showing that the parents in the top third of the income distribution spend more than twice as much money on each child to age eighteen as parents in the lowest third—mean simply that richer kids get more and better food, clothing, health care, schooling, travel, and all the rest. And, directly or indirectly, these material advantages allow them to develop more economic and social capital. Taking the full extent of economic inequality in the United States into account, and adding race and ethnicity to the mix, we can get an even richer version of how class works in the United States. In 2007, the average white family had an income of $64,000, while the average income of Black and Hispanic families was about $40,000. This means the average white kid lived in a family with 60% more family income than the average Black and Hispanic children.

None of our argument is meant to say that a larger family income necessarily leads to a more productive life or a better sense of well-being. In fact, economist Juliet Schor, in her engaging book *The Overspent American: Why We Want What We Don't Need* (1998), reported that 39% of people in U.S. families with incomes between $75,000 and $100,000, and 27% of those with incomes over $100,000, told interviewers they did not have enough money to buy all they needed. We all know unhappy rich people as well as people who gain contentment with modest means. Indeed, aside from extreme wealth compared to extreme deprivation, there is probably no way to know whether more money typically makes for a more satisfying life. Nevertheless, most people in our society would prefer more income to less, and few parents would turn away the opportunity to give their children better health care and education, or more cultural experiences.

Without question, cultural capital is one way—along with the other advantages of being richer—that social classes tend to "reproduce" themselves from one generation to the next. The best way to get into the most prestigious and privileged positions in the economy remains having wealthy and high-status parents.

III. CLASS POWER AND ECONOMIC POWER

Economic power does not just make the upper classes rich: it gives them unrivalled political power. Because the upper classes dominate the political order, the government shapes its economic policies to help them maintain and increase their social and economic advantage. As a prime example, consider the massive redistribution of income that has occurred in the past three decades. During this period, while the real income of most families in the United States has grown only modestly, the richest 5% of the families has increased its share of total income by hundreds of billions of dollars per year. Alice H. Amsden, describing the enormous redistribution of income that occurred in the 1990s, sums up key ways that public policy ensured this result:

> With so much money sloshing around [in the 1990s], contributions by business to politicians increased. With more campaign funding, deregulation resumed where Reagan left off. [The] effective federal tax rate for the top 1% of families fell from 69% in 1970 to about 40% in 1993, with plenty of loopholes remaining. Over the same period, the tax rate for the median family increased from 16% to 25%. Between 1950 and 2000, corporate taxes as a percentage of total tax receipts fell from 27% to 10% while [social security] taxes, mostly paid for by the middle class, jumped from 7% to 31% ...(Amsden 2002)

Amsden argues that the Reagan deregulation "revolution" unleashed a tidal wave of greed, exemplified by the fact that the ratio of CEO pay to average wages went from less than 100 to 1 to over 500 to 1. For his part, Bill Clinton's administration allowed the accounting industry to relax auditing standards, freeing corporations to defraud workers and investors. And, as we pointed out in our first chapter, he quashed the efforts among some of his own advisors to regulate the derivatives markets which, when they collapsed, ushered forward an economic collapse. The George W. Bush tax cuts of 2001-03 granted the largest reductions in taxes to households in the top 1% of all taxpayers. (Mishel et al, 85-86) He also appointed as heads of key regulatory agencies, such as the E.P.A., people from business who shared his antipathy to government regulation of the economy. This tidal wave of money pouring into to the rich and the corporations allows them to continue their inexorable re-shaping of the U.S. power structure into a genuine plutocracy. That process was undoubtedly quickened in 2010, and in the middle of an economic crisis, when the Supreme Court decided, by a 5-4 margin in *Citizens United vs. Federal Election Commission,* that corporate spending on political campaigns was "free speech." This meant that private firms could spend as freely as they liked to back their favorite candidates for public office. The five members of the majority in the Citizens United case were either appointed by Ronald Reagan or served as high officials in his administration.

To indicate the likely effect of this decision on the distribution of political power, the IRS estimated in 2005 that American corporations had assets of roughly $23 trillion, to which they can now turn to get by ever more politicians at every level of government. This decision, not surprisingly, expands the reach of the Reagan revolution to deregulate the U.S. economic order and thus allow corporations to have their way.

IV. THE LIVING CONSEQUENCES OF SOCIAL CLASS
Mainstream economists ignore social class in part because you can't quantify key aspects of the analysis, and its existence conflicts directly with their benign view of capitalism. Both of these prejudices lead them to perceive themselves as "dispassionate experts" with the professional obligation to offer policy solutions for problems that arise in capitalism, rather than to consider the relative merits of the system itself. As a modern "scientific" economist might put it, "Our job is to study *what is,* rather than *what ought to be,*" without ever considering whether there *ought to be capitalism* as opposed to some other system. In this way of thinking, and especially in the United States, nasty aspects of capitalism—such as its inevitable ruin of the envi-

ronment, gross inequality, its directive that we be as greedy as we know how to be, and its rigid and damaging hierarchy of classes—are necessarily kept out of sight. In ignoring social class, they are also refusing to consider inequality and a system of power that shapes everything. We now turn to examples of that shaping process.

Life Itself

Consider the relationship between health and social class. In 2005, the *New York Times*, abandoning for a while the avoidance by the U.S. media of meaningful discussion of social class, ran a five-part series on the matter. One of the five articles, "Life at the Top in America is Not Just Longer, it's Better" (May 16, 2005), by Janny Scott, contains the following succinct review of what we consider the principal ways that one's social standing affects one's health and longevity:

> Class is a potent force in health and longevity in the United States. The more education and income people have, the less likely they are to have and die of heart disease, strokes, diabetes and many types of cancer. Upper-middle-class Americans live longer and in better health than middle-class Americans, who live longer and better than those at the bottom. And the gaps are widening, say people who have researched social factors in health.
>
> As advances in medicine and disease prevention have increased life expectancy in the United States, the benefits have disproportionately gone to people with education, money, good jobs, and connections. They are almost invariably in the best position to learn new information early, modify their behavior, take advantage of the latest treatments and have the cost covered by insurance. . . .
>
> [S]ome researchers now believe that the stress involved in so-called high-demand, low-control jobs further down the occupational scale is more harmful than the stress of professional jobs that come with greater autonomy and control. Others are studying the health impact of job insecurity, lack of support on the job, and employment that makes it difficult to balance work and family obligations.

How did Janny Scott come to these conclusions? First, there was a foundation for them in the work of Marx. He and Engels, other social theorists, and novelists such as Charles Dickens, wrote extensively about the dire circumstances that limited the lives of the working classes in 19th-century Britain. In *Capital*, Marx presented considerable data from British

Parliamentary studies showing that the health and the life span of British workers depended importantly on what they did for a living and where they did it. In the United States, a few scholars extended Marx's early arguments, and none of them more notably than Vincente Navarro at Johns Hopkins.[3] As an example of his wide research on the issue, in 1991 Professor Navarro explained why U.S. health experts were just then discovering a relationship between health and social class that should have been apparent all along:

> The way in which the U.S. government collects health and vital statistics reflects [the fact that class is rarely discussed in the scientific and mainstream media]. The government collects statistics about mortality rates and causes of death by race, gender, and region, but not by class. The overwhelming majority of other developed capitalist countries do collect mortality statistics by class. (Navarro 1991)

As an example of Navarro's point, for some time it has been widely known that in the United States black men, on average, live shorter lives than do white men. This result, as is also widely known, can be traced to a mixture of socioeconomic class background and racism. However, if we control for income—that is, for example, compare black and white men who made annual incomes of $100,000—we find that their longevity is about the same. As Navarro points out, because the U.S. government doesn't look at these matters in terms of social class, those who use government statistics must explain them all in terms of race.

Navarro describes a 1986 report on the relationship between social class and health care as "one of the few occasions" that the U.S. government reported on this relationship. The report broke people down into several categories, and listed their mortality rates for heart disease, per 10,000, as shown in Table 2.

Table 2

Occupation	Heart Disease Mortality Rates, per 10,000
Management/Professional	37
White Collar Workers	43
Service Workers	59
Craft Workers	69
Blue Collar Workers	86

As we travel down the hierarchy in Table 2, we descend into a world in which people have less and less control over their work. While it is difficult precisely to rank the amount of control held by what the government calls service, craft, and blue collar workers—and in many cases, these categories seem to overlap—the much higher rates of heart disease among these workers tell a chilling story, to which we will return shortly.

Personal Capital and Access to Health Care

One explanation for these data on health and social class can be explained in terms of Pierre Bourdieu's idea of personal capital. Having more educational and cultural capital, such as the typical professional, makes it easier to negotiate in public life. Knowing how to get health care when you need it includes reading skills, access to information and understanding what to do with it, and regular contact with others who have the same skills and have sought the same health care you seek. Then, of course, having more economic capital allows you more readily to pay for the care. Further, most professionals have health insurance, while more and more wage earners don't; professionals take longer vacations; and professionals seek health care from other professionals, thus people like themselves who have the same linguistic habits and may be "on the same wavelength" in other respects. Finally, because they have more education, income, and access, professionals are much more likely to participate in stress-reducing leisure activities at sports clubs, golf courses, and similar places where one can simultaneously work off the fat and have fun.

Social Class and Emotional Health

The evidence gathered by scholars over many years concerning mental health and social class is persuasive. Before we present the evidence, however, we want to make certain readers do not confuse our point. All of us know people from different social classes, and we can all cite instances where someone from the working class seems more satisfied with his or her life, and more emotionally sound, than someone who is rich and privileged. Here, our argument is comprised of generalizations with no power of prediction whatsoever about a single individual, or even a small group of individuals. We will be discussing qualitative aspects of the behavior of large groups of people, and these are always relatively imprecise and given to many conflicting interpretations. Nevertheless, we believe the data at this general level comprise a persuasive and powerful argument.

Scholars John Mirowski and Catherine Ross produced an especially important study of the relationship between social class and mental health in their analysis of a broad survey done in Illinois in 1985. (Mirowski and Ross 1989) Though Mirowski and Ross's original study is more than 20 years old by now, its conclusions have, in the meantime, been confirmed by a great body of additional research in the United States and Europe. Mirowski and Ross did indepth interviews with 809 people in Illinois about their lives, their feelings, and the extent to which these could be identified as symptoms of depression. The researchers broke the data down into "deciles," ascending from the bottom 10% to the top 10%, where those in the bottom 10% had the least income and the least education, respectively. Their conclusion in this regard is straightforward enough: the less income you have, the more likely you are to be depressed; and the less education you have, the more likely you are to be depressed.

On the matter of "severe psychological distress," Mirowski and Ross wrote the following:

> Social factors account for a great deal of distress, but do they account for severe psychological distress? To address this second question, we defined extreme distress as a level of symptoms greater than that evidenced by 95% of the population. Approximately 61% of these people would qualify for a psychiatric diagnosis. If we split society into two halves, socioeconomically, better and worse, the worse half of society has 83.2% of all the severe distress. The advantaged half has only 16.2%. Stated another way, the odds of being severely distressed are 5.9 times greater in the worse half than in the better half. (Mirowski and Ross 1989, 17)

Mirowski and Ross give as major reasons for these outcomes the fact that rich people are more likely to detect mental illness in its earlier stages, more likely to know how to seek treatment, and better able to afford better treatment than their less advantaged counterparts in the class system. All these factors would produce statistical evidence that mental illness is less a burden for the rich than for all others, particularly the poor. For example, many researchers have found that schizophrenia is much more common among the low income than among the rich.

In this kind of research, we must be wary of the enormous practical difficulties that exist, such as defining mental illness, the limitations of interview data, and imperfect record keeping by hospitals and mental health workers. Nevertheless, since Mirowski and Ross reported their findings in 1989, its major implication—that the best way to avoid mental illness is to be born into the upper classes—has been seldom challenged by subsequent research both in the U.S. and abroad.

The Central Role of "Control" in Health and Longevity

Here we will focus attention the amount of control one has over one's work and its relationship to one's health and well-being. Central to this issue is the fact that workplaces in the United States have been designed such that in most of them (as Marx once put it), "the hand is separated from the brain." In other words, managers design and control the work, while workers actually perform it. This separation began long ago. Adam Smith remarked about it in depth in *The Wealth of Nations*, and Marx saw it as a principal cause for what he called "alienated labor."

However, this "division of labor," or what we call "specialization," began to spread across the industrial landscape in the United States more rapidly in the early twentieth century. This happened because of the increasing complexity of machinery, but also because of the writings of Frederick Taylor, the originator of what is called "scientific management." Taylor convinced the owners of many of the largest firms to use techniques like time and motion studies to divide production processes into their simplest components. The goal was to establish workplaces where jobs were simple, mindless, and repetitive, and where workers were told what to do, when to do it, and how to do it. Thus, U.S. firms increasingly developed ways to produce goods and services where specific tasks were imagined and designed by a relatively small number of professionals, such as engineers and management specialists, and overseen by top officers, including financial specialists. The work of producing the goods or services, though, was mostly done by wage earners whose jobs were "deskilled" by the process. This production process gradually spread its way through the economy. Indeed, it became known as the "American Way" of production, or what we now call a "bottom line mentality."

What are the consequences of this lack of control over work, which is the basic fact of life for most employed adults in our society? Consider first this very general statement from the World Health Organization in a report published in 2003, entitled *The Social Determinants of Health: The Solid Facts, Part II*:

> Several European workplace studies show that health suffers when people have little opportunity to use their skills and low decision-making authority. Having little control over one's work is particularly strongly related to an increased risk of lower-back pain, sickness absence and cardiovascular disease. These risks have been found to be independent of the psychological characteristics of the people studied. In short, they seem to be related to the work environment.

This study about stress in European workplaces confirms such research about the American workplace by two of the subject's most influential writers: Robert Karasek, a professor Sociology and Labor Relations at University of Massachusetts at Lowell, and Tores Theorell, a physician and professor at Sweden's National Institute for Psychosocial Factors and Health. In their book *Healthy Work: Stress, Productivity, and the Reconstruction of Working Life* (1992), Karasek and Theorell paid particular attention to what they call "decision latitude," a measure of the degree to which workers control their work. College professors always rank high on the scale of those with substantial control over their work, and waitresses and sales clerks always rank low. Concerning, for example, the effect of control at the job site on blood pressure, Karasek and Theorell wrote:

> If an employer increases the demands on employees while concomitantly decreasing their decision latitude, the employees will experience rising blood-pressure levels. Only some of them will react, and they will probably be the best workers—highly motivated and cooperative. Certainly the toll of badly designed jobs is high: our evidence builds a strong case that the work environment can become a biological prison that the average human being cannot endure without adverse physiological effects in the long run. (Karasek and Theorell 1990, 157)

Karasek and Theorell divided jobs on a grid in terms of two dimensions, "low/high psychological demand" and "low/high decision control." They found the breakdown summarized in Tables 3 and 4 consistent with their data on heart disease.

Table 3

Examples of jobs under the most stress (high psychological demand/low control):	
Sales clerk (female)	Freight handler
Waiter and waitress	Garment stitcher
Fireman	Mall worker
Telephone operator	Cashier
Cook	

Table 4

Examples of jobs under the least stress (low psychological demand/high control):	
Sales clerk (male)	Peddler
Architect	Auto repair man
Natural scientist	Forester
Dentist	Skilled machinist

A study done by Dr. Peter Schall, director of the Center of Social Epidemiology at the University of California at Irvine, confirms the data from Karasek and Theorell on job strain and hypertension (high blood pressure). According to Delores Kong, a *Boston Globe* reporter:

> [Dr. Schall] cites an automobile plant in California, where the assembly line is sped up so much that employees were timed spending 58 seconds out of every 60 seconds working. "Every second of every minute of every working hour is accounted for in plants like this," Schall said....[Schall and his colleagues] monitored the blood pressure of nearly 200 men for 24-hour periods. Those who had the highest job strain had on average a systolic blood pressure (the upper number) nearly 12 points higher and diastolic blood pressure nearly 10 points higher than those with the least strain....Dr. Schall said, after looking at all possible causes of high blood pressure, job strain was found to be more important than smoking or salt in the diet. (Kong 1999)

This kind of research is, of course, subject to challenge, especially because it is based on such variables as "high psychological demand" and "high/low control." Yet the work of Karasek, Toress, Schall, and the studies at the World Health Organization combine compelling logic and considerable empirical evidence to support their conclusions. Further, these findings do not bode well for the health of workers in the United States in the next century because the federal government predicts that some of the fastest growing job sectors will require cashiers, sales clerks, waitresses and waiters, and mall workers. Karasek and Theorell argued in their book that the United States was woefully behind other countries in studying the relationship between stress on the job and health. In 1999, Professor Karasek, just back from a year advising the government of Norway on the issue, told Delores Kong in 1999, "The government used to fund large-scale occupational health studies but stopped about 20 years ago," which, our readers may note, coincides with the election of Ronald Reagan.

Precisely because the jobs at the top always pay much better and are the healthiest places to be, most everyone in the lower classes tries to get there. When those from the bottom half get to the upper half, it is considered an example of significant "upward mobility," and this event in someone's life is often known as realizing "The American Dream." This dream, which depends on the idea that anyone can pull himself or herself up "by the bootstraps," is presented as a powerful antidote to the damages wrought by the class system. If anyone can "make it" by trying hard enough, no matter how deprived life had been down below, the awful effects of work in the different social classes are presented as, somehow, justified. We need to look at this claim carefully.

SOCIAL CLASS AND THE AMERICAN DREAM

The claim that upward mobility allays the damages of the class system is actually composed of two related arguments. The first of these is that anyone can make it to the top with enough effort, and the second is that those who do make it are, in fact, delivered into the Promised Land. We will look at these separately.

How Much Mobility Is There?

Though data on this important question are surprisingly sparse, Dennis Gilbert, in *The American Class Structure*, has produced what we consider the most comprehensive look at the trends over the last 50 years.[4] But, before we get to Gilbert's data, we need to discuss the limitations of all the figures on mobility. Two limitations have to do with gender and race. As Gilbert points out, most U.S. studies on mobility have focused on men, although the available data on women demonstrate a similar mobility pattern to that of men. The picture is also more complicated when it includes blacks. As we might expect, blacks have greater numbers in the lower class categories and less upward mobility than whites, but the rate of their upward mobility has increased since 1960.

A third limitation of social mobility data is more fundamental. Some writers believe that factors other than social class are so influential as to outweigh it; most notably, they point to the influence of the media and of U.S. subcultures, arguing that these determine behavior and social position at least as much as social class does. For instance, recently some writers have pointed to the rapidly changing way in which status symbols emerge, confer their magic on this or that group of people, then are lost from sight. Because an all-encompassing media is the principal agent by which status is hyped and publicized, these writers see a weakening in the lasting power of status symbols and thus, to some degree, less rigidity in the class system. As examples, reality shows on television make celebrities, even lasting ones, of people not known until the first episode. And, the media's broadening focus on personal scandals of people from all classes is a vehicle through which more people can get celebrity status. The aimless boyfriend of a seriously unbalanced pop singer (or actress or whatever) ends up abandoned with the kids, but writes a book about it all and is off and running, perhaps even toward being an unbalanced pop star. It thus appears that, with a bit of luck, anyone can make it, and more and more people do so without the usual mix of background, school, and connections.

However, other scholars see our society as continuing to have genuine class boundaries. When we began our own research on these matters two decades ago we concluded that significant upward social mobility (which we define more precisely below) occurred for no more than 10% of the working population, a figure that, among studies on social mobility, is quite low.[5] Many readers of this early research, including some scholars and journalists, criticized how low our figure was; others, however, saw it is as quite reasonable.

In other words, scholarly studies on the ratio of upward mobility produce figures that range all over the place.[6] The researcher can literally select whatever ratio fits his or her agenda. Given this situation, we have chosen to use the work of Dennis Gilbert because, in our view, he gives the widest and the fairest reading of the literature on social mobility. He is aware of the limitations of these data and would be the first to advise accepting his own conclusions as tentative.

In his survey, Gilbert compared data from several studies over the years, and their different classifications made it necessary for him to compress them all into one set of categories. After doing that, he ended up with the following five-class system:[7]

Upper white collar: professionals, managers, officials, non-retail sales
Lower white collar: proprietors, clerical workers, retail sales workers
Upper manual: craftsmen, foremen
Lower manual: unskilled workers (services & other), operatives (semiskilled machine operators, truck drivers, etc.), non-farm laborers
Farm: farm workers, farmers

The figures below are about males only, and they indicate the percentage of all U.S. workers that ended up either above, the same or below the economic position held by their fathers. (These data relate to the period from 1995 to 2004, and the percentages are roughly similar to those in other studies done since the 1960s.)

Up: 41%
Stable: 33%
Down: 26%

As simple figures, these confirm the idea that there is a great deal of mobility in the U.S. economy, with more than 40% of the sons achieving a higher standing in the economy than their fathers. Most of this mobility, however, was the movement across one class barrier, such as the movement from lower- to higher-manual labor, or lower- to higher-white-collar labor. Crossing a single class boundary is hardly the stuff of the American Dream, which promises a transformation from "rags to riches." Such success stories imply movement across several class barriers. What can we say about these bigger leaps?

We will define *significant upward mobility* as moving from the bottom of Gilbert's classification to the top. An example would be the son of an unskilled laborer who becomes a doctor, or the daughter of a cashier who becomes a corporate executive. The following numbers express in percentage terms what kind of jobs were attained by the sons of men who were lower-manual workers:

Upper white collar: 20%
Lower white collar: 22%
Upper manual: 20%
Lower manual: 36%

How many people from the bottom actually make it all the way to the top? We can see from the data above that 20% of lower-manual workers actually made it into upper-white-collar work, ending up with jobs as professionals, managers, officials, or non-retail sales workers. However, these data don't tell us how many of these sons became, say, high-status doctors and how many became lower-status managers in small firms. Some additional information on how hard it is to make it to the top can be found in a 2006 report entitled *Understanding Mobility in America* by Tom Hertz of American University. Hertz reports that children born into the poorest 20% of U.S.

households have a 1% chance of getting rich, which he defined as making it into the top 5% of income earners (with annual incomes over $166,000). Also interesting is Hertz's data that the middle 20% of income earners have less than a 2% chance of becoming rich, indicating that even members of the middle class have very little chance of making it to the top.

For most people, the most frequent outcome is simply staying at the same level as their parents. For example, 56% of the lower manual workers *remained* manual workers. This means that there is for the sons of most manual laborers a consignment to wage-earning manual labor. It is also true, according to Gilbert, that 61% of all those who are in upper white-collar jobs had fathers who worked in white-collar jobs.[8] It is hard to conclude from these data anything other than this: *real structural barriers to upward mobility exist in the United States, and the best pathway to success is not merit or hard work but being born to parents with socioeconomic privilege.*

Nevertheless, if we grant Gilbert his conclusion that about one fifth of U.S. workers experience significant upward social mobility, one might reasonably decide that, comparable to most societies over time, our system is remarkably open. However, Hertz reports that it is much more difficult for poor people to make it to the top in the United States than in all other high-income countries for which data are available, except for the United Kingdom. For example, while a poor person in the United States has only a 1% chance of becoming rich, a poor person in Denmark has a 22% chance. The primary reasons for this huge difference in opportunities seem to be the superior education, training, health, and welfare services provided for poor people in Denmark. A poor person in Sweden, Denmark, and other social democracies, where quality education, training, and health care are available to all citizens rather than just the well-off, has a better chance of realizing his or her full potential. Also disturbing has been the decline in class mobility in the United States in recent years. Gilbert's data indicate that the number of lower-manual workers making it into upper white-collar work declined from 27% in the 1980s to 20% in the 1990s. A study by Katharine Bradbury and Jane Katz at the Federal Reserve Bank of Boston showed that the percentage of U.S. families staying at the same income level across generations was 35% in the 1970s, 37% in the 1980s, and 40% in the 1990s, while the percentage of families moving up declined during the same periods. Thus, it seems to be getting more and more difficult for those at the bottom to make it to the top in the United States.

Interestingly, even those from the lower classes who do have the great fortune to make it to the top don't always enjoy the full measure of their success. Thus, we must also consider a key question: once they get to the top, what actually happens to the sons and daughters of factory and service workers who became doctors, lawyers, and bosses?

Strangers in This Fine Place So Far from Home

What does happen, say, to a person from a working-class family who ends up at an elite university, then accumulates enough educational capital to land a job with a Wall Street firm dominated by fancy Ivy League types? That's an important question for two principal reasons. The first of these is that upward social mobility actually lessens the genuinely unfair constraints of social classes. Since the distribution of opportunities closely mirrors the distribution of income, and is thus greatly unequal, mobility allows at least some people to make their up way out of lower class standing. Second, upward mobility allows for more political stability than would be possible without it: if everyone in the bottom half was consigned there for life, particularly in a society claiming itself as free, rebellions would always be just beneath the surface of social life. Much depends, then, on whether upward mobility "works" as it is supposed to for those who achieve it.

Does, in fact, upward mobility work for those who try to achieve it? Though the results of studying trying to answer the question are mixed, there are some important conclusions that scholars have reached who have done the most influential studies. Consider, as a general statement, a dramatic claim from one of the most influential books written in the field, *Social Class and Mental Illness: A Community Study* by August Hollingshead and Fredrick Redlich. They conclude this about "social climbers," those upwardly mobile people who appear to have made their move "successfully":

> The climber may impress an observer as pleasant, successful, and very able if he is successful and appears well integrated. Only on longer acquaintance and after a deeper search does one become aware of the climber's conflicts and defenses. His deeper anxieties become manifested when his mobility drive becomes blocked; then his defenses do not function properly....When these social climbers were rejected by those who "are there" socially, their reactions were characterized by severe anxiety, depression, sometimes by antisocial acting out, and in... extreme cases by suicidal attempts... (Hollingshead and Redlich 1957, 368)

The tone and the overall conclusion of this quote are more important to us than its specific claims, because they signal that the literature on upward mobility is always in part about the stressfulness, called "status dissonance," that comes with it for so many who make the trip. One body of research that encompasses all the relevant issues about upward mobility focuses on essays by college professors who have working-class backgrounds. By going from the lower- or upper-manual classes to becoming a college professor, such people have clearly made a substantial upward movement from their family backgrounds. In the books from which we will draw examples, there are dozens of different voices, and they all tell different stories. Some of these professors, for instance, expressed relief at having been lifted up from the drudgery of wage work; others found pleasure at having a foot in two worlds; while still others found having their feet in two worlds wrenching and painful. Four studies that make up part of this research, each with a different focus from the others, are: Ryan and Sackrey 1984, 1996; Tokarczyk and Fay 1993; and Dews and Law 1995.

While all these voices were unique, there were unmistakable dominant themes, of which one can find examples in virtually all the essays. One theme was a genuine feeling of alienation from professional (often in these essays called "middle-class") life. The first voice here expresses this alienation as anger about colleagues, most of whom came from middle- or upper-class backgrounds:

> My friends have been a handful of fellow outsiders who share my contempt for the rest of "them." I feel quite unapologetic about these prejudices. I feel "they" are all deeply worthy of contempt. They parade a sense of inflated self-importance; take pleasure in feeling smarter than students; pretend they contribute meaningfully to GNP; dance for favors; create parochial empires; cower before symbols of authority; wallow in bogus professionalism; and submerge themselves in their narrow expertise, which, for many, is their ticket to a legitimate place in the academy. The tone and the anger in what I've written above give some indication of the depth of my alienation. (Ryan and Sackrey 1996, 261-2)

Another voice from these collections carried a second theme, mixing recognition of the durability of one's class origin with hopefulness that the conflicts that come from class mobility can be mitigated:

> How can working-class academics begin to integrate the divided or split sense of self that arises from belonging (yet in some fundamental ways, not belonging) to two distinct class cultures? As members of a transition class, it is likely that working-class academics will always feel marginal to some degree. However, if this outsider status is to become a source of empowerment rather than a source of internal conflict, it is imperative that such faculty begin to validate

the working—and middle—class parts of themselves. To do so requires that they recognize and confront the ways in which they have internalized the classism of the larger society and, thus, their own oppression. This process is essential if working-class academics are to reclaim their power and develop an authentic or integrated sense of self. (Tokarczyk and Fay 1993, 54)

Another of these professors sounded a third theme that resonated in all the essays, about how long the path from home had become. She reflects on these matters by recalling the time when her parents were about to drive her back to her studies at Dartmouth, but her father was called back to duty at a paper mill.

My father left [for the mill] a bit earlier…and as my mother began the drive out of town with me in the passenger seat, I remember being struck with the feeling that my father was out there somewhere, driving too, but on a very different road. With the greatest clarity I have ever experienced about the question of mobility, I saw myself on the road to my life of bright and interesting friends, a glut of culture and ideas, comfort and privilege. My father was on the road he took every day to the paper mill. Huge and noisy and noxious, the mill was where my father spent lonely, dirty days among men who shared none of his interest in reading about ideas. (Dews and Law 1995, 157-58)

Alienation, anger, the unending reminder that your parents went down a different road, the unmistakable power of social class to stick with you all the way down your own path, mixed in with hopefulness and willingness to struggle for legitimacy—these are the themes common to the literature on upward mobility. You might get to another place, but once there, you need to figure out how to deal with the fact that, unlike most people, you have a dual-class experience. Therefore, whatever else might happen, whether you are happy for most of your days or miserably angry at the pretensions of life at the "higher reaches," you must construct a way to negotiate a new terrain. To go from the working classes to the more prestigious professions is both literally and figuratively to move from one neighborhood to another one. At first, people in that new world might not even notice you; or, worse, they might despise you and all your trappings. Upward mobility puts you in a world in which those already there have likely accumulated more of Bourdieu's personal capital than you have. They will have a greater ease with the neighborhood, and a built-in savvy about how to negotiate the terrain.

The upward traveler must, therefore, develop a strategy to survive. The literature on upward mobility is in agreement on this point, without exception. These strategies range from assimilation (trying to be like them), to separation (trying to keep your job while staying to the side), to war (fighting them tooth and nail until they fire you). The absolute necessity of such strategies makes our essential point that social class is, however ambiguous and hard to tie down, a powerful shaping mechanism in our lives. Social classes exist because of real differences in our work, income, education, habits, and all the rest. To cross class barriers, one must learn to navigate in enemy territory and, perhaps as a precaution, wear a helmet.[9] The alleged "freedom" of U.S. capitalism presumes some semblance of equality of opportunity: every Jack and Jill must have an equal chance to hit the big time. However, that kind of equality can only exist in a society in which most people have the opportunity to move upward significantly, and in which most of those who do find the trip worth the effort. Neither of these two conditions seems to exist in the United States. Most people stay where they started, bossed around by the same kind of people who bossed around their parents. And, if they do move up, they go to a new neighborhood in which they are at the bottom, often despised, isolated, or misunderstood. The fact of social classes makes the American Dream a particularly deceitful myth.

CONCLUSION

We hope that readers will come away from this chapter considering the likelihood that social classes exist and play a crucial role in determining who we are; that most people inherit the class position of their parents and stay there; and that numerical representations of social class, such as by income levels, badly understate the overall effects of the class system. On this last point, if we say, for instance, that the top 10% of the income classes has about four to five times as much income as the bottom 10%, the numbers understate our point. Access to four or five times as much income as the next person gives you multiple advantages beyond the income, including especially the kinds of personal capital we have described. Being at the top of the income system means more of life itself: healthier lungs, a stronger heart, straighter and whiter teeth, and more things about which to smile.

Given that critical dimensions of social class cannot be measured precisely, if at all, it is no surprise that mainstream economists simply ignore it, leaving the subject for sociologists or other "soft" scientists to study. Yet in the work of political economists such as Marx and Veblen, and in less radical social policies aimed at "civilizing" capitalism, such as those developed in Sweden, the idea of social class is central. We agree that the issue belongs at the forefront of any discussion of capitalism.

SUGGESTIONS FOR FURTHER READING

Bourdieu, Pierre. Distinction: *A Social Critique of the Judgment of Taste.* Cambridge, Mass.: Harvard University Press, 1984.

Christoper, Renny. A Carpenter's Daughter: *A Working Class Woman in Higher Education.* Sense Publishers, 2009.

Dahrendorf, Ralf. *Life Chances. Chicago:* University of Chicago Press, 1979.

Domhoff, William. *Who Rules America?* 4th Edition. New York: McGraw-Hill, 2002.

Fussell, Paul. *Class.* New York: Ballantine, 1983.

Gerth, H. H., and C. Wright Mills, eds. *From Max Weber: Essays in Sociology.* New York: Oxford University, 1946.

Gilbert, Dennis. *The American Class Structure in an Age of Growing Inequality.* 5th Edition. Belmont, Calif.: Wadsworth, 1998.

Kadi, Joanna. *Thinking Class: Sketches from a Cultural Worker.* Boston: South End Press, 1996.

Karasek, Robert, and Tores Theorell. *Healthy Work: Stress, Productivity, and the Reconstitution of Working Life.* New York: Basic Books, 1990.

Vanneman, Reeve, and Lynn Weber Cannon. *The American Perception of Class.* Philadelphia: Temple University Press, 1983.

Zweig, Michael. *The Working Class Majority: America's Best Kept Secret.* Ithaca, N.Y.: ILR Press, 2000.

7
John Kenneth Galbraith
and the Theory of Social Balance

The ideas of John Kenneth Galbraith are known around the world from his many books and articles, and his more than half a century in public life in the United States. But surprisingly, they are little known inside the mainstream of economics. Indeed, economist Ron Stanfield has called Galbraith "the most famous economist of the last half-century." Nonetheless, Stanfield notes, "he also represents a very obscure American institutionalist tradition. This paradox I cannot resolve for the reader... The Galbraithian Paradox puzzles me." (Stanfield 1996)[1]

As we go through this chapter, we think it will become evident that Galbraith's argument about social balance, made some fifty years ago, was prophetic and remains as current today as it was then. Why it has failed to have an impact on mainstream economics is a measure, we believe, of how deeply mired mainstream economists are in a limited view of what counts as "economics."

I. THE MYRIAD WORLDS OF JOHN KENNETH GALBRAITH

Galbraith, who was still writing books until his death at the age of 98 in 2006, said that Keynes, Marx, and Veblen were the economists who most influenced his own thinking. We shall see that, like these three, Galbraith worked mostly outside the confines of mainstream economics, and he was a prominent social critic and public servant for six decades. He taught economics for forty years, mostly at Harvard University, starting in the 1930s. During the first two years of the Second World War, Galbraith led the federal Office of Price Administration, a position that gave him the immense power to determine which U.S. companies could raise which prices. He was the U.S. ambassador to India during the John F. Kennedy administration in the early 1960s. He wrote speeches for, and advised, prominent Democrats including Adlai Stevenson, the party's presidential candidate in 1952 and 1956, Presidents Kennedy and Johnson, and Eugene McCarthy, a U.S. Senator who challenged Johnson for the Democratic presidential nomination in 1968.

Mostly, however, Galbraith was known for books and writings covering an immensely broad range of genres and issues. He wrote terse theoretical works, articles about economics for *Fortune Magazine*, twenty highly readable books analyzing the economics and politics of modern capitalist societies, three memoirs, and two novels. He co-authored a book on Indian painting, wrote and narrated a thirteen-part PBS series on the history of economic ideas, and produced countless shorter pieces for academic journals and the press. All his analytical books have typically focused attention on three matters: (1) the operations and effects on economic and political life of the giant corporations that dominate the world economy; (2) the failure of mainstream economics adequately to incorporate into its analyses of capitalism the effects of these large firms; and (3) the issue of whether the central value in mainstream economics—that "more is better than less"—is a reasonable guide to social policy. An especially prominent feature of Galbraith's writing and political activities is that he put them forward as an unapologetic liberal, always arguing from the perspective that public policy needs to countervail the immense powers of huge corporations and, more generally, that an unregulated capitalist economy is chaos in-the-making.

II. THE THEORY OF SOCIAL BALANCE

In his 1958 book *The Affluent Society*, Galbraith argued that the slavish commitment of people in advanced capitalist societies to private goods at the expense of public services, also called the "public infrastructure"—such as schools, roads, efficient government, clean air and water, beautiful cities—could bring them to ruin. He called this analysis of private and public spending the "theory of social balance," and he stated its essential meaning in the following well-known passage:

The family which takes its mauve and cerise, air-conditioned, power-steered, and power-braked automobile out for a tour passes through cities that are badly paved, made hideous by litter, blighted buildings, billboards and posts for wires that should long since have been put underground. They pass on into a countryside that has been rendered largely invisible by commercial art....They picnic on exquisitely packaged food from a portable icebox by a polluted stream and go on to spend the night at a park which is a menace to public health and morals. Just before dozing off on an air mattress, beneath a nylon tent, amid the stench of decaying refuse, they may reflect vaguely on the curious unevenness of their blessings. Is this, indeed, the American genius? (Galbraith 1958, 253)

What is the larger, structural, context of this statement? Here is how Galbraith describes that larger structure:

[The] disparity between our flow of private and public goods and services is no matter of subjective judgment. On the contrary, it is the source of the most extensive comment, which only stops short of the direct contrast being made here. In the years following World War II, the papers of any major city—those of New York were an excellent example—told daily of the shortages and shortcomings in the elementary municipal and metropolitan services. The schools were old and overcrowded. The police force was under strength and underpaid. The parks and playgrounds were insufficient. Streets and empty lots were filthy, and the sanitation staff was underequipped and in need of men. Access to the city by those who work there was uncertain and painful and becoming more so. Internal transportation was overcrowded, unhealthful, and dirty. So was the air. Parking on the streets had to be prohibited, and there was no space elsewhere. (Galbraith 1958, 252)

And, a bit later in his book, Galbraith argues that:

Every increase in the consumption of private goods will normally mean some facilitation or protective step by the [public sector]. [If] these [public] services are not forthcoming, the consequences will be in some degree ill. It will be convenient to have a term which suggests a satisfactory relationship between the supply of privately produced goods and services and those of the state, and we may call it *social balance*.

The problem of social balance is ubiquitous, and frequently it is obtrusive....An increase in the consumption of automobiles requires a facilitating supply of streets, highways, traffic control, and parking space. The protective services of the police and the highway patrols must also be available, as must those of the hospitals. Although the need for balance here is extraordinarily clear, our use of privately produced vehicles has, on occasion, gone far out of line with the supply of the related public services. The result has been hideous road congestion, an annual massacre of impressive proportions, and chronic colitis in the cities. (Galbraith 1958, 255, emphasis added)

Galbraith went on to cite other examples, including the prophetic one that there was delinquency everywhere because the growing absence of parents—more of them working to feed their consumption habits—meant that children, "in effect, become the charge of the community for an appreciable part of the time. [And] if the services of the community do not keep pace, this will be another source of disorder." These and other examples together embodied the theory that consumer-oriented societies will inevitably produce "private opulence and public squalor," as Galbraith put it in one of his more memorable phrases. Why does this happen?

The Dependence Effect
We begin with the "private opulence," whereby individuals shower themselves with more and more goods, at great cost to themselves and society. How does this come about? Galbraith's answer focuses importantly on what he called the "Dependence Effect," explained as follows:

As a society becomes more affluent, wants are increasingly created by the process by which they are satisfied. This may operate passively. Increases in consumption, the counterpart of increases in production, act by suggestion or emulation to create wants. Or producers may proceed actively to create wants through advertising and salesmanship. *Wants thus come to depend on output. In technical terms it can no longer be assumed that welfare is greater at an all-around higher level of production than at a lower one. It may be the same.* The higher level of production has, merely, a higher level of want creation necessitating a higher level of want satisfaction. There will be frequent occasion to refer to the way wants depend on the process by which they are satisfied. It will be convenient to call it the *Dependence Effect*. (Galbraith 1958, 158, emphasis added)

The point here is that in high consumption societies, wants come to depend on output, and for two major reasons that we now turn to.

The first reason wants come "to depend on output" is that increases in output will generate spreading consumer envy wherever new products or multiple units of other products come to rest in a private household or driveway, become the latest fashion styles, or otherwise gain the attention of consumers. As we discussed in an earlier chapter, social critic Thorstein Veblen called this process "pecuniary emulation" and considered it a consequence of our desire to mimic the habits of those with a higher social ranking. This is an easy idea to remember because now everyone calls it "keeping up with the Joneses," and of course because we all do it. For instance, five years ago, university students would not be bothered by lack of access to an iPhone or Blackberry, yet such devices are now regarded by increasing numbers as utterly essential. Similarly, most people in the United States regard enormous television sets, not long ago invented, as necessities.

The second cause of the Dependence Effect is the vast and corrosive influence of advertising, or, as Galbraith puts it more gently, "...producers may proceed actively to create wants through advertising and salesmanship." Modern U.S. society is abuzz, ever more loudly, with the noise of advertising. Indeed, as we point out in our first chapter, one educated estimate is that between the mid-1980s and the early 2000s, the number of ads to which American adults were subjected went from about 1,500 to 3,000 *per day*.[2] For an idea of the level of this intensity, consider these details from the *Washington Post*, in 2000:

> [C]ompanies are seeking ever more novel places to promote their goods and services. Parking meters, elevators, restaurant restrooms, portable toilets, golf course locker rooms—plus the handles of golf clubs and baseball bats—have all become eligible targets. ...A combination of factors is spurring advertising's aggressive movement into virtually every facet of daily life. The healthy economy continues to give companies both money and incentive to advertise. Yet, at the same time, many advertisers believe the traditional means of advertising have become less effective...particularly [in reaching] 20- to 30-year-olds. (Quoted in Mayer 2000)

This article provides a number of intriguing examples of places where advertising is penetrating the collective consciousness: television monitors that run short loops of programming in gasoline stations, convenience stores, elevators, and train platforms; and ads on cocktail napkins and glasses at bars, in restrooms above urinals and inside stall walls, on turnpike coupons and portable toilets, and on ATMs. Other bright ideas, so far rejected by producers, have been to place stickers advertising bras on melons and advertising condoms on bananas.

No less frenzied, and likely more deleterious, is the increasing number of ads aimed at children. *Business Week* discussed this trend in a 1997 article. Kid-centered ad campaigns, it argued:

> ... represent a quantitative and qualitative change in the marketing aimed at children....[V]irtually no space is free of logos. And traditional ads have more venues than ever, with a gaggle of new magazines, dozens of Web sites, and entire TV channels aimed at kids. From 1993 to 1996, alone, advertising in kid-specific media grew more than 50%, to $1.5 billion, according to Competitive Media Reporting.
>
> The cumulative effect of initiating our children into a consumerist ethos at an ever-earlier age may be profound. As kids drink in the world around them, many of their cultural encounters—from books to movies to TV— have become little more than sales pitches devoid of any moral beyond a plea for a purchase....Instead of transmitting a sense of who we are and what we hold important, today's marketing-driven culture is instilling in them the sense that little exists without a sales pitch attached and that self-worth is something you buy at a shopping mall. (Leonhart and Kerwin 1997)

A Brief Digression: The Dependence Effect and Mainstream Economics

A discussion of the corporate creation of demand inside the heads of toddlers is a good place to digress briefly and relate Galbraith's concept of the Dependence Effect to mainstream economics. In fact, the idea is a straightforward challenge to the central article of faith in mainstream economics that more output always makes people better off. Mainstream *micro*economists typically presume that, given the resource base, firms in competitive markets will produce the greatest possible output at the cheapest possible cost for "rational" consumers. These buyers will be best off by getting the most products at the cheapest prices and will choose these products according to their pre-determined "preferences." In *macro*economics, the central article of faith is that a growing GDP is good and grand, despite what it might be doing to the forests, lakes, streams, mountains, and seas that will be maimed a bit more with each increase in output.

This idea that more output automatically produces more welfare became the national religion—and is now becoming a world religion—by virtue of what Galbraith termed the "growth lobby." Conservative political leaders are members of the lobby because a growing economy provides greater revenue, profits, and economic power for the big firms that are their principal supporters, hefty defense budgets that most conservatives support, and (especially important) because growth affirms the conservative's central idea that capitalism is the best of all possible economic systems. Liberal politicians join the lobby because they, too, get generous support from corporations, and because more output also means more taxes for more public services. Further, until recently, they had ordinarily adopted Keynesian growth policies as the best way to create employment for, and increase the incomes of, the lower classes in capitalist societies. Politicians from both these camps also get crucial support from mainstream economists who use complex models to make their case, models put forward as "science" but that always carrying the crucial assumption that more is better than less. The fact that millions of their listeners are captive audiences of college students in their formative years helps to inculcate each generation with the religion.

Yet, despite the overwhelming adoption of the mainstream notion that more output means higher standards of living, in *The Affluent Society* Galbraith raised a question that continues to be fresh and challenging: How much extra welfare do we get from an additional 1% of GDP if it represents goods we did not know about last year (or even last week), *and* if their production and consumption spoil the environment in which we use them? We will not pursue this Galbraithian critique here except to suggest that, however astute, his critique turned out to have very little impact on mainstream thinking.

The Dependence Effect and the Big Firms

Why are the big firms compelled to continue turning up the volume of advertising? To begin with, in industries dominated by a few firms (what economists call "oligopolies"), price competition is generally replaced by product differentiation as the major way that firms distinguish their own output. This dimension makes it mandatory that, for example, consumers see Motrin as different from Advil despite the fact that they will describe identical contents on their labels. In the global economy, companies increasingly seek customers everywhere, and so must scream out their slogans loudly enough to be heard all over the planet. This feature of capitalism has not been lost on any economist who has studied it, whether in or out of the mainstream. What Galbraith and other political economists add to the mix is how this process is increasingly orchestrated by gigantic firms operating on a world scale.

In another of his major works, *The New Industrial State*, in which Galbraith gave careful attention to these big firms that dominate the modern economic and political life, he called them the "planning system." (Galbraith 1967) He argued that the big firms themselves are under the control of a host of professionals—technicians, engineers, accountants, lawyers, economists, and production, distribution, and sales executives, among others—whom Galbraith called the "technostructure" of the big firms. Circling around these mammoth suns are millions of smaller planets, the more or less competitive firms that make up the rest of the economy, and in some ways fit the description given them in mainstream microeconomics. Galbraith noted the broadly *anti-democratic* influence of the planning system on government at every level, with the big firms spending whatever it takes to get government officials to do their bidding. So it is, too, with their necessarily growing influence abroad: As the tentacles of the companies they control reach ever further into an ever more globalized world, the technostructure broadens its influence on the activities of people everywhere.[3]

The argument about big firms in *The New Industrial State* is, of course, thoroughly compatible with the theory of social balance. Most centrally, in order to shape consumer wants, these big firms can afford a well-paid cadre of skilled artists, designers, marketing specialists, psychologists, and others to design and to impose their message. As examples of the scale of this sales effort, in 2009, the two largest corporate advertisers in the United States, Verizon and Proctor & Gamble, each spent over $1 *billion* for ads, and together American firms spent about $158 *billion* to try to cajole you, me, and the rest of the population to buy their products. (Credit/Loan. com, *Infographics*)

In a later book, *The Anatomy of Power*, Galbraith developed a useful structural model to describe how corporations, or any organizations, wield power in the contemporary world. According to Galbraith, organizations accumulate and use two different kinds of power, "compensatory" and "conditioned," to get their will done. Regarding firms, the first of these is simply paying for things, particularly labor and materials, which gives corporations control over people and resources. The second, *conditioned* power, is the ability of the large corporations to use persuasion through public relations and advertising to affect the views of the citizenry, and lobbying to affect the views of politicians about the general beneficence of corporate activity. Of course, compensatory and conditioned power come together in the capitalist firm's "power of the sack," its ability to hire and fire workers at will. This immense power means that those who work for capitalist firms—most of us—are conditioned to think the corporate way, at least in public...or else. (Galbraith 1982) The omnipresent *laissez-faire* ideology, challenged by the world-wide economic crisis that began in 2007, attests to the power of the capitalist class to "condition" the rest of us to believe that "What's good for General Motors is good for America," as General Motors CEO Charles Wilson put it in the 1950s.[4]

Big firms must condition consumers with ad campaigns because the bigger the corporation, the greater are the stakes of not selling its output. Consider, for example, a company like GM. Assume, for instance, that it produces 10,000 cars a week that cost $20,000 each to produce, a total expenditure of $200 million to buy labor, materials, and other inputs, and to pay interest on the loans borrowed to finance capital expansions. Those costs of $200 million explain why consumer demand for these cars *must* be created. Smaller firms also need to advertise, and from their perspectives, the stakes are the same: Convince the public to buy the output or fold the tent. However, the smaller the firm, the fewer funds it has available for advertising, another reason why the larger firms end up dominating, absorbing, or driving out of business their smaller rivals.

To Galbraith, then, the effects of pecuniary emulation, along with the unceasing imperative that the dominating firms sell their products, constitute what he calls the "Dependence Effect." Consumers develop a dependence bordering on addiction for the products generated by these firms. Of course, we should remember that all this producing, advertising, and emulating mostly takes place in the *private* sphere of the economy, and a growing private sector inevitably creates a need for goods in the *public* sphere. But, according to the theory of social balance, the supply of goods forthcoming in the public sector will always lag behind, leaving pollution, congestion, poor schooling, and all the rest in its wake. Why is that true, according to Galbraith?

The Public Sector as "Inferior"

In *The Affluent Society*, Galbraith makes the following argument for why the public sector inevitably lags behind the production and consumption of private goods:

[The consumer] is subject to the forces of advertising and emulation by which production creates its own demand. Advertising operates exclusively, and emulation mainly, on behalf of privately produced goods and services. Since management and emulative effects operate on behalf of private production, public services will have an inherent tendency to lag behind. Automobile demand which is expensively synthesized will inevitably have a much larger claim on income than parks or public health or even roads where no such influence operates. The engines of mass communication, in their highest state of development, assail the eyes and ears of the community on behalf of more beer but not of more schools. ...

The competition is especially unequal for new products and services. Every corner of the public psyche is canvassed by some of the nation's most talented citizens to see if the desire for some merchantable product can be cultivated. No similar process operates on behalf of the nonmerchantable services of the state....The scientist or engineer or advertising man who devotes himself to developing a new carburetor, cleanser, or depilatory for which the public recognizes no need and will feel none until an advertising campaign arouses it, is one of the valued members of our society. A politician or a public servant who dreams up a new public service is a wastrel. Few public offenses are more reprehensible. (Galbraith 1958, 260-1)

And, later Galbraith adds this about the proper role of government:

In this discussion a certain mystique was attributed to the satisfaction of privately supplied wants. A community decision to have a new school means that the individual surrenders the necessary amount, willy-nilly, in his taxes. But if he is left with that income, he is a free man. He can decide between a better car or a television set. This was advanced with some solemnity as an argument for the TV set. The difficulty is that this argument leaves the community with no way of preferring the school. All private wants, where the individual can choose, are inherently superior to all public desires which must be paid for by taxation and with an inevitable component of compulsion. (Galbraith 1958, 268)

In sum, a social imbalance arises from an increase in the production and consumption of private goods that is not matched by the public services required by their use and where "all private wants...are inherently superior to all public desires." The tendency becomes an imperative in capitalist societies that are dominated by giant firms because of their great need to sell their products and because of the enormous sums of money they use to market them. Last of all, it leads down the road to "private opulence and public squalor."

Galbraith's Solution: The New Class

Close to the end of *The Affluent Society*, Galbraith expressed hopes for a better social balance coming from a growing "new class" of mostly educated people. He believed that this new class would see the problem clearly and fight politically for adequate public services and against the overpowering need of the giant firms to blind us with ads and bury us with products. This hope led him to call for broader and deeper education, as "our hope for survival, security, and contentment." (Galbraith 1958, 355)

Indeed, Galbraith saw citizen organization and mobilization as the primary hope for checking the massive power of corporate interests. As Galbraith observed, historically "the problem of corporate power was solved in practice...by creating another, opposing and thus annulling position of power." (Galbraith 1981, 282) He thought that the best source of "countervailing power" would emerge in part in citizens groups, such as trade unions and what he called, "spontaneous organizations." But "where the organization necessary for the requisite annulling of economic power was too difficult to achieve, the assistance of government was invoked." (Galbraith 1981, 282) Galbraith's analysis implies that when the government, laborers and consumers work together, they can develop sufficient countervailing power to rein in corporations and to force them to work in the public interest to achieve social balance.

Unfortunately, for myriad reasons, particularly the abiding mistrust of government that has characterized most of our nation's history, Galbraith's hopes for a "new class" to establish countervailing power and bring us to our senses have not been realized. So ingrained now is the sentiment against government in the United States that it is extremely difficult for a candidate who campaigns for higher taxes and more government spending to get elected in the United States at any level of government. The push to demonize government received great momentum with the election in 1980 of Ronald Reagan, who championed tax cuts for the wealthy and a rollback of federal regulations of the economy. He, and the events of the time, succeeded in legitimating to a large segment of the population the dream of a return to the "good old days" before the New Deal social-welfare programs of the 1930s.

With the attacks on New York on September 11, 2001, there was a clamoring for more federal government action regarding national security. Supporters of such spending can relatively easily find supporters in the White House and in Congress. This is also true of war spending, or maintaining our imperial military presence around the world (where we had over 700 military bases in 2010). It now seems also true for banks "too big to fail," which, in the 2007-2009 financial crisis, received billions of dollars of bailout money, and the public saw them as receiving priority in a crisis in which working and middle class people faced high levels of unemployment, mortgage failures, and declining income. Other government programs, such as the health care reforms proposed by both Clinton and Obama faced relentless resistance from conservatives in and out of the government. In Chapter Five, we described that gauntlet in the case of Obama's health care program, which became law in 2010 despite the fact that not a single Republican member of the House of Representatives supported it. In other words, except for national security, bailing out banks, and pet projects of powerful politicians, government spending at all levels continues to face that relentless resistance. Such resistance, along with the obvious facts of an ever expanding consumption sector would suggest that Galbraith's theory of social balance remains a body of ideas worth our time and attention. Is that the case?

III: THE THEORY OF SOCIAL BALANCE: A GUIDE FOR OUR OWN TIME?
Galbraith's View
In a special edition of *The Affluent Society* published in 1998 to commemorate the fortieth anniversary of its publication, Galbraith made very few changes, letting the book stand on its own. In an "Introduction" to this edition, he wrote the following:

> On two matters this book was right, and before its time.…[One of them is that] forty years ago I stressed the compelling difference between public and private living standards. We had expensive radio and television and poor schools, clean houses and filthy streets, weak public services combined with deep concern for what the government spent. Public outlays were a bad and burdensome thing; affluent private expenditure was an economically constructive force.
>
> My case is still strong. The government does spend money readily on weaponry of questionable need and on what has come to be called corporate welfare. Otherwise there is still persistent and powerful pressure for restraint on public outlay. In consequence, we are now more than ever affluent in our private consumption; the inadequacy of our schools, libraries, public recreation facilities, health care, even law enforcement, is a matter of daily comment. The private sector of our economy has gained enormously in role and reward and therewith in political voice and strength. No similar political support is ac-

corded the public sector, the weaponry and corporate welfare as ever apart. In civilized performance it has lagged even further behind the private sector.

So, Galbraith agrees with Galbraith, and this is hardly a surprise. What's the evidence for his continuing advocacy of his theory of social balance? We will present a body of representative evidence to show that, despite his being ignored by the great majority of economists, Galbraith was, for the most part, on target all along.

Robert Reich about the Decline of Public Goods, in 1999

Robert Reich, a professor of public policy, was Bill Clinton's Secretary of Labor from 1992 to 1996 and in 1998, forty years after *The Affluent Society* was published, Reich gave his view about the book's argument regarding the public sector. He wrote that:

> [By] some estimates, two-thirds of our elementary and secondary schools are in disrepair, and too few of them are providing our children with adequate education. Comfortable movement along public roadways and over bridges now requires the most sophisticated of automobile shock absorbers. Public recreational facilities are fast disappearing. More than one in five of the nation's children lives in poverty—lacking adequate housing, clothing, and nutrition. An ever-growing number of and percentage of Americans have no access to health care. Publicly supported basic research is on the wane. After rising through the 1960s and 1970s, federal investments in education, infrastructure, and research as shares of GDP have continued to fall over the last three administrations. They represented...sixteen per cent in 1998, lower than at any time since 1962. (Reich 1999, 89)

Like many other people who believe that a broader and more efficient public sector will allow us better to enjoy our private riches, Reich sees freedoms lost in bad schooling, poverty, and sick kids without recourse to good health care. It is not simply the inability to choose health care that is costly to freedom. Freedom also implies the ability to choose a society where one's own health is protected because *everyone else* has ready access to quality health care. Particularly troubling is that in the "affluent society" all this squalor is unnecessary. With gargantuan wealth in the U.S. relative to the rest of the world, Reich's estimate that two-thirds of all public schools are in disrepair and that our roadways and bridges suffer the same fate, suggests a genuine collapse of our collective rationality.

The American Society of Civil Engineers (ASCE) 2009 Report Card

Every five years, the ASCE presents a "Report Card" assessing the status of the nation's infrastructure of public goods. Its report card carries the usual values that students are used to, where A is exceptional, B is good, C is mediocre and D is poor. They make their ratings on the basis of a systematic review of related data on such issues as the number of highway miles available given the number of cars, the number of run-down schools, and how many toxic waste dumps are not being cleaned up. Here is the ASCE grade sheet for 2009:

Aviation	D
Bridges	C
Dams	D
Drinking Water	D
Energy	D+
Hazardous Waste	D
Inland Waterways	D
Levees	D
Public Parks and Recreation	C
Rail	C
Roads	D
Schools	D
Solid Waste	C+
Transit	D
Wastewater	D

How in the world did they come up with such a thoroughly grim list? Here are some details from two of the seven categories:

> Roads: Congestion on the nation's roads is increasing and the cost to improve is ever rising, causing the roads grade to decrease to a D- in 2009. Americans spend 4.2 billion hours a year stuck in traffic at a cost to the economy of $78.2 billion, or $710 per motorist. Poor conditions cost motorists $67 billion a year in repairs and operating costs. One-third of America's major roads are in poor or mediocre condition and 45% of major urban highways are congested. Current spending of $70.3 billion per year for highway capital improvements is well below the estimated $186 billion needed annually to substantially improve conditions.

Hazardous Waste: Hundreds of thousands of contaminated sites exist across the country, representing millions of dollars of untapped economic potential. Redevelopment of brownfield sites (places polluted from previous use) over the past five years generated an estimated 191,338 new jobs and $408 million annually in extra revenues for localities. In 2008, however, there were 188 U.S. cities with brownfield sites awaiting cleanup and redevelopment. Additionally, federal funding for "Superfund" cleanup of the nation's worst toxic waste sites has declined steadily, dropping to $1.08 billion, its lowest level since 1986. Since little has been done to clean up these sites since the last *Report Card*, hazardous waste again earned a grade of D.

The ASCE Report Card also points out that in the previous five years, grades for only one of the fifteen categories improved. The two examples above, along with the rest of the Report Card, describe a public sector starved for funds. Thus, ten years after Robert Reich made his assessment, he and ASEC tell us a similar story about continuing "public squalor. As a final comment on the ASCE Report Card, the civil engineers might not be the most impartial judges on these matters, given that much of the $2.2 trillion they claim are needed to repair our infrastructure would go to firms where some of them work. Yet their report is consistent with a mountain of information, much of it regularly printed in the media, confirming their claims. As an example, one from an impeccable academic source, Ernst Frankel, professor emeritus of mechanical engineering at the Massachusetts Institute of Technology (MIT), summarized his own assessment with the following comment:

> Most of our road, rail, water, sewer, electric power, wired telephone, and other distributed systems infrastructure are old and in need of repair. Our ports, airports, and rail terminals are archaic, ill designed, badly run, and poorly maintained. (MIT, *Faculty Newsletter*, October, 2007)

These assessments by Robert Reich, the ACSE, and Ernst Frankel seem to confirm the principal tenet of Galbraith's theory of social balance, that private wealth and public squalor had become, and would likely remain, a key characteristic of U.S. capitalism. However, it is not so easy to confirm Galbraith's explanation that the imbalance occurs only because of what he called the "dependence effect"—a torrential rain of advertising, stronger with each season, and the need to keep up with the Joneses next door—along with the increased pressure on state and local officials to follow the anti-tax ideology that had gripped the nation since the late 1970s. Apparently, the facts of the matter are more complicated.

In 1990, the Federal Reserve Bank of Boston, in response to the steady decline in infrastructure spending in the 1980s, held a conference attended by about one hundred economists, federal bankers, business representatives, and others, on the matter. The bank published the proceedings as *Is There a Shortfall in Public Capital Investment?*, which is an excellent compendium of data, theories, and history about the public investment, how it comes to be and how we might evaluate it. (FRBB, 1990) The participants mostly agreed about the decline in the quality of public services, but their explanations for why it was happening, that included certain aspects of those advanced by Galbraith, produced no comparable consensus. Two of those presenting papers at the conference even challenged the popular notion that the anti-tax movement had scared off state and local officials from spending. They argued that such behavior on the part of such officials has long been typical. Further, in many instances, such as national highway building, the federal government, rather than state and local governments, does most of the funding, and is thus subject to different and less direct political pressures. There was no focused analysis about whether the problem was greater than it had been earlier, or that there was even a problem at the time. Some participants argued that the infrastructure problem was not the supply of public goods available but the inefficient ways in which existing ones were used and whether user fees and other such mechanisms would improve efficiency.

Michael Tarr, a historian, argued that public goods spending had historically been cyclical in the United States, and that the cycles were too often unpredictable. As the principal causes of spurts of growth in public spending, he gave the following ones: urbanization and demands of cities for public goods; epidemics that ultimately led to an enormous expansion of sewage and water systems everywhere; and technological changes, such as the use of railroads, airplanes, and, especially, automobiles. Indeed, another of the participants presented evidence that U.S. infrastructure spending actually increased in the early 1980s on highways, sewers, and water, despite the election of the anti-tax president in 1980 and the emergence of the anti-tax movement in the last 1970s.

The evidence and explanations given at this conference do not negate those made by Galbraith in his own theory of social balance. Galbraith's engaging writing style and the force of his arguments in *The Affluent Society* brought broad attention to the decline in public goods and services long before it had become a public issue. He was genuinely a pioneer in this regard. Therefore, the participants at the conference, and others since 1990 concerned with these issues have built upon the foundation that Galbraith erected.

Consumerism and Degradation of the Environment

Environmental degradation was a second major social problem to which Galbraith brought wide attention in 1958, and even before Rachel Carson wrote her famous book, *The Silent Spring*, in 1962. In 2010, virtually all of us agree that we are fouling our nest in the biosphere. Because clean air and water are the most crucial goods of them all, most nations have left their protection to governments and also charged them with protecting some other aspects of the environment, in particular its aesthetic qualities and its common public spaces. Who, for instance, would trust these matters to a profit-seeking corporation? Yet, despite this matrix of laws, most of which corporate owners resist as "intrusions on free enterprise," there is an enormous and growing body of evidence that high levels of production and consumption in the developed world, and the lack of adequate environmental controls in much of the developing world, increasingly threaten the planet.

Though there had been concern about effects of industrialization on the U.S. environment starting in the 19th century, it began to form itself into a movement in the United States in the 1960s. Rachel Carson's book gathered much focused attention, and environmental concerns grew rapidly, enough so that Democratic Senator Gaylord Nelson of Wisconsin declared April 22, 1970 the first "Earth Day." From there, the movement became a loose amalgamation of groups around the world. In 1992, Sir Michael Atiyah, president of the Royal Society of London, and Dr. Frank Press, president of the U.S. National Academy of Sciences, provided a broad view of the problem in a joint statement, "Population Growth, Resource Consumption and a Sustainable World." They argued that:

> [I]f population growth and patterns of human activities remain unchanged ... science and technology may not be able to prevent either irreversible degradation of the environment or continued poverty for much of the world....The future of our planet is in the balance....Sustainable development can be achieved, but only if irreversible degradation of the environment can be halted in time. The next 30 years may be crucial.[5] (*Rachel's Environmental and Health Weekly* #699, Sept. 23, 1999)

Examples of the problems that were derived from this "environmental degradation" were already all around us. Native Americans, throughout U.S.

history, have often wondered why the European invaders so "hated Mother Earth." When Europeans arrived, Native Americans had been living in what is now the United States for over 30,000 years. Their numbers and their understanding that their welfare depended upon the welfare of the land meant that when the whites arrived, the air and water and land were mostly pristine. That began to change, of course, because Europeans mostly had in mind conquest of the people, their land, and whatever other riches might be available for seizing. They, and those that followed, spent little time, indeed, for the next 500 years worrying about protecting the environment of the new world that they had conquered.

According to *Green Student U* (a well-researched web site constructed for college students interested in environmental issues), here are a few facts about what we Americans dump onto that land:

- Every year, one American produces over 3,285 pounds of hazardous waste.
- Land pollution causes us to lose 24 billion tons of topsoil every year.
- Americans generate 30 billion foam cups, 220 million tires, and 1.8 billion disposable diapers every year.
- We throw away enough trash every day to fill 63,000 garbage trucks.
- Every day, Americans throw away 1 million bushels of litter out their car windows.
- Over 80% of items in landfills can be recycled, but they're not.

Some of the consequences of this assault on the land affect water also. Here are a few salient facts about water pollution:

- Over two-thirds of U.S. estuaries and bays are severely degraded because of nitrogen and phosphorous pollution.
- Every year, almost 25% of U.S. beaches are closed at least once because of water pollution.
- Over 73 different kinds of pesticides have been found in the groundwater that we eventually use to drink.
- 1.2 trillion gallons of sewage, storm water, and industrial waste are discharged into U.S. waters every year.
- 40% of U.S. rivers are too polluted for aquatic life to survive.
- Americans use over 2.2 billion pounds of pesticides every year, which eventually washes into our rivers and lakes.

Regarding air pollution, David Pimentel, Cornell University professor of ecology and agricultural sciences, found that:

> About 40 percent of deaths worldwide are caused by water, air and soil pollution....Such environmental degradation, coupled with the growth in world population, are major causes behind the rapid increase in human diseases, which the World Health Organization has recently reported....Air pollution from smoke and various chemicals kills 3 million people a year. In the United States alone about 3 million tons of toxic chemicals are released into the environment—contributing to cancer, birth defects, immune system defects and many other serious health problems. (*Science Daily*, August 14, 2007)

Climate Change

Last in this exemplary listing of the sources of environmental pollution is the problem of climate change, or global warming, the direst threat of all over the long haul. It is caused by the "greenhouse effect" of sunlight striking the planet, turning into heat, and then being trapped by "greenhouse" gases. These gases, primarily water vapor, carbon dioxide, and methane, allow the sunlight in but do not allow all the resulting heat to escape, thus causing "global warming." The principal causes of global warming are the combustion of fossil fuels in cars, plants that use coal to produce electricity, and factory production. Other important contributors are methane from landfills and the digestive systems of grazing animals, fertilizers, and deforestation (because forests absorb carbon dioxide).

This list of causes is actually a derivative one, because all are themselves the consequences of rapid economic growth in a world where concern for the environment has not produced a movement strong enough to offset its effects on global warming. Not surprisingly, the big industrial nations are the main culprits in this assault on the biosphere, as the following list will demonstrate:

Country	Total Emissions of Carbon (billions of metric tons)	% of World Total Emissions
China	6.1	21.2
United States	5.8	20.2
European Union	3.9	13.8
Russia	1.6	5.5
India	1.5	5.3
Japan	1.3	4.6

The table is clear enough that the giant industrial nations are the prime culprits in global warming. Moreover, the list includes those countries with the largest average incomes--the United States, some members of the European Union, and Japan—and it is the riches in these nations that urge forward similar behavior in developing countries. If they succeed in following our path, and without a different way of thinking about what constitutes the good life, we could become a world where most societies are amassing ever-expanding private wealth and ever-expanding tracts of public squalor, all of them perched on a planet whose biosphere is gradually getting warmer.

Regarding the part about the planet getting warmer, most people all over the globe know at least some of the details about the current and predicted effects of global warming. They might also know that for most of his time in office, President George W. Bush led the charge to deny that it was occurring. We Americans were then left to decide whether we believe the president, along with the energy companies and right-wing radio shows that beat drums for him, or the great majority of the world's scientists pouring forth a cascade of evidence that climate change *was* occurring and that it posed a direct threat to life on earth. For that evidence, thoroughly convincing in our view, we will turn first to *National Geographic*, ordinarily considered a more-or-less neutral source on environmental reporting. Here is one of its summaries:

> The rate of [global] warming is increasing. The 20th century's last two decades were the hottest in 400 years and possibly the warmest for several millennia, according to a number of climate studies. And the United Nations' Intergovernmental Panel on Climate Change (IPCC) reports that 11 of the past 12 years are among the dozen warmest since 1850.
>
> The Arctic is feeling the effects the most. Average temperatures in Alaska, western Canada, and eastern Russia have risen at twice the global average, according to the multinational Arctic Climate Impact Assessment report compiled between 2000 and 2004.
>
> Arctic ice is rapidly disappearing, and the region may have its first completely ice-free summer by 2040 or earlier. Polar bears and indigenous cultures are already suffering from the sea-ice loss.
>
> Glaciers and mountain snows are rapidly melting—for example, Montana's Glacier National Park now has only 27 glaciers, versus 150 in 1910. In the Northern Hemisphere, thaws also come a week earlier in spring and freezes begin a week later. (*National Geographic,* June 14, 2007)

Complementary evidence comes from Britain's Hadley Centre for Climate Change, which has a large corporate clientele, and uses billions of calculations from the world's largest supercomputer in Berkshire, England. The Center published this terse statement on its website in March, 2010:

> It is now clear that man-made greenhouse gases are causing climate change. The rate of change began as significant, has become alarming and is simply unsustainable in the long-term.

Our last, sad list is based on information from *PlanetSave*, a website that is another excellent source for this kind of information. Below is our summary of their predictions for what is likely to happen because of global warming:

- Rising sea levels. One island nation, Maldives, is already looking for a new home, and many other such islands and most coastlines around the world could face a similar fate.
- More violent storms. Winds from big storms have been increasing since the 1980s, and other elements of many storms are ever more intense.
- Massive crop failures. In much of the world, there already is too much sun and too little water. Both of these imbalances will get worse, particularly in developing countries.
- Mass extinction of species. Polar bears might already be on the way out, and they will be followed by many others.
- Rapid decline in coral reefs. This decline will alter the sea's entire ecosystem and endanger the entire food chain from the small creatures that the fish eat, to us humans who eat the fish.

These predictions, if true, promise havoc for animal life on the planet. Some estimates—such as that 3 billion people will have to move within 100 years in order to feed themselves—exemplify a limitless number of such threats. Most forbidding to rich nations is that all the poor people living in the deserts and along the flooded coastal areas will begin a chaotic mass immigration to find food, water, and shelter that might trigger an unimaginable human conflict between the minority of haves and the giant encroachment of the have-nots.

IV: OUR ASSESSMENT OF THE THEORY OF SOCIAL BALANCE

To be begin with, we want to note that in his 1958 book, *The Affluent Society*, Galbraith saw far ahead of most other economists, who by then were receding into the thickets of algebra (as British economist, Joan Robinson, described mainstream economics at that time). These economists then, as now, were held tightly in the grip of a powerful ideological stance, the notion that our form of capitalism was superior, was getting better all along, and should be exported to developing countries whenever possible. This led them to turn a deaf ear to political economists, such as Galbraith, who suggested the future of our economic order might be less than superior, perhaps even miserable. Part of their inclination to ignore Galbraith was in response to his having become a harsh critic of mainstream economics, a habit that he would maintain for the remaining 50 years of his writing career.

More directly concerning his theory of social balance, we have presented adequate evidence, we believe, to demonstrate that his theory was prophetic and remains useful in understanding and evaluating modern capitalist systems. We recognize that Galbraith's "dependence effect" only partially explains why these nations are likely to develop private wealth and public squalor, but he played a key role in gathering in the public's attention to the matter in a book that was widely read in the United States and elsewhere.

Also remarkable is that Galbraith's theory of social balance remains plausible more than 50 years after he offered it in his book, and despite the fact that the world has changed enormously. The capitalist society that he was describing has, in one form or another, been spreading steadily around the world since he wrote the book, and especially in the past three decades. The inevitable expansion of capitalism was first detected by Marx, and he described it in 1848 with characteristic flair in *The Communist Manifesto*. There, he made the following prophetic claims, ones that could have been written for our own time:

> The bourgeoisie, by the rapid improvement of all instruments of production, by the immensely facilitated means of communication, draws all, even the most barbarian, nations into civilization. The cheap prices of commodities are the heavy artillery with which it batters down all Chinese walls, with which it forces the barbarians' intensely obstinate hatred of foreigners to capitulate. It compels all nations, on pain of extinction, to adopt the bourgeois mode of production; it compels them to introduce what it calls civilization into their midst, i.e., to become bourgeois themselves. In one word, it creates a world after its own image.

Our own times demonstrate well how prophetic Marx's words had been. Capitalism is engulfing the globe now for the following main reasons:

Capitalist economies greatly outperformed their rivals during the Cold War; the IMF and the World Bank, controlled by the United States and other major capitalist nations, imposed market economies on many developing countries; the United States financed and trained militia in opposition to development plans, in such countries as Guatemala, Cuba, and Chile, that did not get U.S. approval; and the United States worked endlessly—abetted by over 700 U.S. military bases in foreign countries—to resist any barriers to its spreading imperialism.

As the bourgeois of our own era "create a world after their own image," we can make use of the theory of social balance as a basis to make some predictions with confidence. One prediction would be that as developing countries build capitalism, either by choice or by force, ultimately they will have to contend with the loud shrieks and the smoke and mirrors of the sales effort. Otherwise, they, too, will become like we Americans: unable to stop buying things, most of which we don't need, even though we have been fouling our own nest for decades, and, along with the other major industrial nations, are now threatening all of humanity with global warming.

CONCLUSION

We believe that Galbraith's theory of social imbalance is an indispensable guide to understanding contemporary capitalism. His theory allowed us to back away from the noise and glitter and promises of the modern consumer society and to take a close look at the underlying forces at work on us when we shop. He urged us to ask ourselves about the true blessings of going to shop for things we don't need, and to have to travel there in congested traffic and surrounded by toxic air. It is a fine theory, indeed, about which to think, and study, and wonder.

Along the way in this chapter, we have mentioned, but not developed, the other side of the story, the conservative critique of Galbraith's theory. In this critique, the bedrock presumptions are that more is always better than less; that government involvement in the economy is at best a necessary evil; that with every reduction of this involvement, our freedom is expanded; that the dominant presence of the United States in world economic and political affairs attests mightily to the powers unleashed in the absence of an intruding, inefficient government; and that the alleged squalor in public services seen by liberals like Galbraith is caused by a blindness about what constitutes true freedom and liberty.

Each of us, of course, ultimately will judge which of these two assessments best describes the world we experience. Are we always better off when taxes come down, consumer spending goes up, and public services fail to keep up? If your community has more cars in family garages, are you likely to enjoy more "consumer welfare" than if you and your neighbors had fewer cars but your city had ambient air that was healthy for you, and for your children? Is there a richer and deeper meaning to "freedom" and "liberty" than the ability to buy anything you want, no matter the consequences to your neighbors, the world community, and the planet itself? Or, are we in a lemming-like march to the abyss, done in by a love affair with consumer goods?

SUGGESTIONS FOR FURTHER READING

Bowles, Samuel, Richard Edwards and William G. Shepherd. *Unconventional Wisdom: Essays on Economics in Honor of John Kenneth Galbraith*. Boston: Houghton Mifflin, 1989.

Federal Reserve Bank of Boston. *Is There a Shortfall in Infrastructure Investment?* Conference Series #34, 1990.

Hessions, Charles H. *John Kenneth Galbraith & His Critics*. New York: New American Library, 1972.

Montague, Peter, ed. *Rachel's Environment and Health Weekly.* Annapolis, MD: Environmental Research Foundation. You can receive this newsletter free and online by sending an email to: listserve@rachel.org, with the words, SUBSCRIBE RACHEL-WEEKLY [YOUR NAME] in the message.

Okoi, Loren J. Galbraith, Harrington, Heilbroner. *Economics and Dissent in an Age of Optimism*. Princeton, N.J.: Princeton University Press, 1988.

Stanfield, Ron. *John Kenneth Galbraith*. St. Martins Press, 1996.

Williams, Andrea, ed. *The Essential Galbraith*. Boston: Houghton-Mifflin, 2001.

8
U.S. Monopoly Capitalism:
An Irrational System?

INTRODUCTION

Is U.S. capitalism an "irrational" system? Despite its global economic and political domination, could the system be described in such negative terms? Two Marxist economists, Paul Baran and Paul Sweezy, thought so. In 1966, they offered a famous explanation of their conclusion in a book entitled *Monopoly Capital: An Essay on the American Economic and Social Order*. In the final chapter to this book, called "The Irrational System," Baran and Sweezy argued that the giant firms that dominate our economy were in a permanent war with their employees, customers, and the entire society.

Baran and Sweezy updated Marx's work by documenting the behaviors and effects of the huge multinational firms whose dominating power Marx saw on the horizon. Both Adam Smith and Marx had developed their ideas during a time when capitalism was considerably more competitive than it is now. Smith warned his readers in *The Wealth of Nations* that the "joint stock" companies (corporations) emerging in Britain threatened the atomistic competition he championed. The big firms he warned against were still consolidating power when Marx wrote almost a century later. Thus, it was left to contemporary Marxists to study and theorize about giant firms in their developed states.

None of these Marxists produced a richer analysis than Baran and Sweezy in *Monopoly Capital*. As they stated their central theme:

We must recognize that competition, which was the predominant form of market relations in nineteenth-century Britain, has ceased to occupy that position, not only in Britain but everywhere else in the capitalist world. Today the typical economic unit in the capitalist world is not the small firm producing a negligible fraction of a homogeneous output for an anonymous market but a large-scale enterprise producing a significant share of the output of an industry, or even several industries, and able to control its prices, the volume of its production, and the types and amounts of its investments. The typical economic unit, in other words, has the attributes that were once thought to be possessed only by monopolies. (Baran and Sweezy 1966, 6)

Baran and Sweezy observed that although many industries go through a competitive phase, most become stable oligopolies—markets dominated by a few sellers. The result is that, as Marx predicted, for the last century most industries have been dominated by a few huge multinational firms. Each has substantial market power and vast economies of scale that allow it to make products at relatively low per-unit costs. To compete with a giant firm, as the owners of all small firms know, promises a predictable fate: in general, small fish will be gobbled up by the big ones, or will fail to swim at all in the low-cost world the big firms create. The gargantuan size of these big fish is demonstrated by the following data:

- In 2007, 76 of the largest 150 economic entities in the world were corporations, while 74 were countries.
- ExxonMobil has larger total revenues than the output (GDP) of Belgium or Egypt; Wal-Mart is bigger than Malaysia; Royal Dutch Shell is bigger than Sweden.
- More than 90% of the 200 largest transnational companies are from industrialized countries, mostly Europe, North America and Japan.

When corporations are this huge and this powerful, governments and citizens have limited power to oppose them.

How are these giant firms able to maintain their dominance? When new competitors try to enter an industry, they face significant barriers. Consider, for instance, the formidable costs that would face anyone who wanted to produce automobiles for a profit. How much do you think it would cost to build a modern automobile plant that could compete with existing giants? Depending on the size, the cost could be in the billions of dollars. It simply is not feasible for almost any person or small firm to put up this kind of money. Indeed, Marx saw the increasing complexity and cost of machinery that accompanied the growth of huge corporations as the principal reason that owners of small firms would ultimately be "hurled into the proletariat."

Age, size, and reputation confer other advantages on established firms that become barriers to new ones. Customers of an existing firm are familiar with its products, and often have significant brand loyalty, which makes it difficult for new competitors to vie for business. And established firms may have long-term contracts with large buyers. How much do you think it would cost our new automobile magnate to establish brand name identity, loyalty, and the sales necessary just to pay for the factory? Currently, automobile firms spend in the *billions* of dollars *every year* to persuade you and me that buying their product will lead to adventures, make us cool, and even improve our love lives.

Another source of these firms' power is their ties with government. Whenever new competition appears on the scene, firms do whatever they can to reduce that competition. When U.S. automakers faced competition from Japanese car producers in the 1980s, the U.S. firms did what the big firms always do in a pinch: they went crying to the government for help. Rather than build the smaller, better cars being imported, the firms coerced the government into putting a big import fee on Japanese cars. This move protected the price position of the auto giants, and cost Americans who bought any car during most of the 1980s about $1,000 extra.

In another example, Joseph Stiglitz, an economic advisor to President Clinton and Nobel Prize winner, has written about suspect government measures to boost aluminum prices in the 1990s. These were driven by Paul O'Neill, who, before becoming U.S. Treasury Secretary, was the CEO of Alcoa, the largest aluminum producer in the world. According to Stiglitz, seven years before he became Treasury Secretary, O'Neill

asked for [and got] government help in stopping market forces from operating because they were leading to a worldwide decline in aluminum prices. The aluminum industry concluded that the best way to restore "stability" to the market (meaning high prices and corporate profits) was an international cartel. This cartel put the ordinary workings of competitive markets aside: each member country was assigned a fixed output. (Stiglitz 2002)

This example has all the elements of the monopoly capital drama: big government, big business, an international cartel, all brought together by an industrial-mogul-turned-government-official. These examples, while fairly recent, reflect an old alliance between government officials and well-connected capitalists.

Another key element of the monopoly-capital era is the expansion of government to ensure that businesses remain profitable. As huge firms mechanize and boost productivity, they tend to lay off workers and put downward pressure on wages. To avoid crises of overproduction and to reduce class conflict, increasing levels of government spending are required. As examples, Baran and Sweezy pointed to the development of a social welfare state in the 1930s and 1960s. During these two decades, in response to the worst excesses of capitalism and to quell worker unrest, U.S. politicians created a number of social programs. The Social Security system, minimum-wage and unemployment-compensation laws, the Wagner Act requiring employers to recognize and bargain with unions when workers voted to unionize, tax laws helping the middle and working classes to buy homes—all of these are prominent examples of social-welfare programs that did not exist in Marx's time and that serve to prop up consumer demand. The ever-growing military budget also keeps production humming at the giant firms, and is another way in which government supports huge firms.

Finally, large firms work together to eliminate competition, while government usually looks the other way. For instance, in markets where a handful of firms dominate, they avoid price competition by engaging in such forms of tacit collusion as price leadership, where one industry leader sets prices and the other firms follow suit. Despite the existence of antitrust laws that allow the government prevent actions the reduce competition, the government rarely chooses to invoke these provisions.

Because of all these formidable barriers to the entry of competitors, the giant, dominating firms often behave as if they were a single firm. In other words, they act like monopolies, and that is why Baran and Sweezy used the term "monopoly capitalism" to apply to modern capitalist economies like the U.S. economy.

In general, Baran and Sweezy criticized monopoly capitalism because they thought that the huge firms that dominate it co-opt government, collude, merge and stifle innovation, generating rising profits in the process. But these rising profits cannot always find outlets, leading to waste and even economic crises. And finally, monopoly capitalism, like other forms of capitalism, invariably exploits labor in its pursuit of profit.

For Baran and Sweezy, the giant multinationals that now run the world formed the center of an analysis of capitalism, so that is where we begin. How do these firms exert their power, and what are the consequences?

THE BEHAVIOR OF GIANT FIRMS IN MONOPOLY CAPITALISM

Baran and Sweezy argued that U.S. society is fundamentally organized to maximize the profits of a few vast corporations. To them, this meant that our society is structured to "maintain scarcity in the midst of potential plenty." (Baran and Sweezy 1966, 337) For example, in the United States, one of the wealthiest countries in the world, millions live in abysmal poverty despite the vast wealth that exists for the few. In underdeveloped countries, hundreds of millions of people suffer from disease and starvation even though there is enough food in the world for everyone and enough medicine to cure much existing disease. Baran and Sweezy, and most other political economists, see this inequality as an *inevitable* outcome of monopoly capital.

Baran and Sweezy argued that inequality was an essential result of capitalists' business strategies. Capitalists aimed to lower their production costs, but instead of passing the savings on to workers or consumers, they kept the savings for themselves as increased profits. Considering capitalism's capacity for production, innovation, and cost-cutting, Baran and Sweezy wrote:

> On the face of it this would seem to be an argument for monopoly capitalism's being considered a rational and progressive system. And if its cost-reducing proclivities could somehow be disentangled from monopoly pricing and a way could be found to utilize the fruits of increasing productivity for the benefit of society as a whole, the argument would indeed be a powerful one. But of course this is just what cannot be done. The whole motivation of cost reduction is to increase profits, and the monopolistic structure of markets enables the corporations to appropriate the lion's share of the fruits of increasing productivity directly in the form of higher profits. This means that under monopoly capitalism, declining costs imply continuously widening profit margins. (Baran and Sweezy 1966, 71)

Baran and Sweezy are talking about the long run tendency of the economy because in recessions, for example, profit margins fall. But the tendency of profit margins to increase over longer periods of time is a crucial characteristic of monopoly capital. While Marx believed that the more competitive form of capitalism that existed in his time would generate a declining rate of profit, Baran and Sweezy argued that under conditions of monopoly capitalism, the opposite would often be true.

As an example of their point, Bill Gates boasted during anti-trust hearings that Microsoft had lowered the price of Windows and should not be prosecuted as a monopolist. What he neglected to mention was that costs had fallen so low that in 1997 Microsoft had the highest profit rate in the economy, with gross profit margins reaching 90 percent. (Cassidy 1998a) Similarly, The Gap, like most clothing manufacturers today, has taken to using sweatshop laborers in the Third World to make its clothes. Despite the lower wages The Gap now pays, the prices of its clothes have remained high. Another major retailer, Amazon.com, is known for its low priced books and free shipping. However, Amazon.com demands that publishers sell books at 60% below list price to Amazon.com, and they then offer consumers a 10-30% discount and pocket the difference.

The largest retailer of them all, Wal-Mart, boasts incessantly about its "everyday low prices." What Wal-Mart neglects to point out is that it uses its vast size and market power to demand that suppliers slash the prices of the goods they sell to Wal-Mart. Wal-Mart then keeps a large chunk of the savings, and passes some on to consumers. As a measure of the chunk of savings retained by Wal-Mart, in 2010 four of the richest 10 people in the United States, all billionaires, are from the Walton family that owns Wal-Mart. In every case, we see that firms like Microsoft, The Gap, Amazon.com and Wal-Mart do indeed reduce costs, but they pass as little of the cost savings as possible on to consumers. And, they use their vast size and market power to undercut competition whenever possible. As all small business owners know, the arrival of a Wal-Mart store in their town promises a war on their enterprise, increasing unemployment, and falling prices for its own products.

Why do firms go to such lengths to maximize profits? For one thing, profits are necessary for the "*accumulation of capital*"—the cycle of making profits to reinvest in capital goods in order to make more profits in the future. Accumulation is crucial for firms if they are to dominate markets and find new areas for investment. Capitalists also need profits because they generate the dividends and high stock prices coveted by stockholders. And, CEOs and upper management are only too happy to pursue profits and growth (capital accumulation) on behalf of stockholders because most CEOs receive much of their pay in the form of stock options. Indeed, the incentive of CEOs to inflate stock prices for their own benefit was behind the Enron, WorldCom, and many other corporate scandals in the early 2000s.

Like any gambler, a CEO or investor likes nothing more than a sure thing. Thus a primary goal of multinational corporations is to rig markets in their favor. They collude to avoid price competition, buy out or merge with competitors, and move into new markets, but only once it is clear that the markets are profitable. We will explore the implications of these strategies below.

Tacit Collusion and Price Leadership

In any mature industry with monopoly power, there is virtually no price competition. Big corporations are reluctant to lower prices because that could spark a price war that would cost all the firms in the market. When a firm raises prices, other firms tend to match the price increase because this can result in greater profits for the industry as a whole. If a company increases price because its managers think it is in the interest of the whole industry, it will then wait to see if others follow suit. If they don't the leading firm will rescind the price change. As Baran and Sweezy described this kind of behavior, "it becomes relatively easy for the group as a whole to feel its way toward the price which maximizes the industry's profit." (Baran and Sweezy 1966, 61) In this manner—avoiding price cuts but matching most price increases—an industry can arrive at the price that a monopolist would charge, and that is why so many oligopolies end up pricing like monopolies. Baran and Sweezy noted that this behavior also "introduces a significant upward bias into the general price level," and they (correctly) predicted continuous inflation during the era of monopoly capitalism. (Baran and Sweezy 1966, 62-3) For example, for the three decades prior to the oil price shocks of the 1970s, General Motors was the price leader in the auto industry, setting prices on models that were then matched by Ford and Chrysler. During this period it was not uncommon for automobile price increases to be three times the overall inflation level.

Often, we do see price competition when firms are fending off a foreign competitor or in less mature industries when firms are jockeying for market share. But most industries dominated by big firms settle into a stable, oligopolistic structure with little price competition. William Shepherd, who has been charting the operations of U.S. oligopolies for decades, published a study confirming that in the modern era, "cooperation in price setting is extensive." (Shepherd 1997, 262) To give one recent example (among the many hundreds of instances we know of), from 1954 to 1994, the leading Ivy League colleges conspired to fix the scholarships offered to students who applied to several schools. Admissions officers met to decide exactly what amount to offer each student, thereby preventing students from seeking tuition discounts and preventing colleges from offering more generous scholarships to lure top students away from competing schools.

Buyouts and Mergers

An even better strategy than colluding with competitors is to buy them out or absorb them to lessen competition. There have been regular merger waves of increasing magnitude during the last six decades, and it is now the case that mergers valued in hundreds of billions of dollars take place each and every year. With mergers firms attempted to (a) lessen competition (a horizontal merger), (b) explore profitable new areas by buying into them, or (c) gain greater control over their costs of production by absorbing a supplier (a vertical merger). Mergers that lessen competition, like the one that formed Exxon-Mobil, could be prevented by the government under anti-trust laws, but successive U.S. presidents since 1980—Reagan, the two Bushes, and Clinton—have instructed the anti-trust division of the Justice Department to approve virtually all the mergers that firms have applied to undertake. This policy, which accepts jockeying between a few global giants as sufficient for a "competitive" economy, has allowed corporate behemoths to gain even greater market power. The government's refusal to implement the antitrust laws gives striking evidence of its complicity in the rise of massive corporations.

The Obama administration signaled that it would enforce antitrust laws more vigorously. Though it allowed a merger between Ticketmaster, the world's largest ticket-selling network, and Live Nation, the biggest concert promoter, in 2010, it extracted some major concessions designed to preserve competition in the industry. While such actions are helpful, they will not change an industrial structure which has grown more and more consolidated over the last 30 years via mergers and acquisitions.

Ironically, William Shepherd (1997) notes that mergers often reduce efficiency: most mergers are actually "empire-building" strategies where a firm's main goal is simply to gain greater control over markets. As telecommunications, petrochemical and financial firms expand their empires, one might wonder how the individual consumer will fare in these markets. As our choices diminish, do you think we will be provided with better products at lower prices?

Big Firms and Innovation

A common belief about multinational corporations is that they are innovative, constantly designing new and better products for our consumption. Oligopolies are typically depicted in this way because they alone are supposed to have the funds to put into research and development. Others argue that firms in competitive markets will not undertake the cost of innovating because they know that their results will be stolen by competitors. While oligopolies can be sources of innovation, more often they stifle it. Thorstein Veblen, as we have seen in an earlier chapter, noted this tendency to stifle innovation in the nineteenth century, and called it a form of "industrial sabotage." Today, corporations manipulate patent and copyright laws to prevent the entry of new competitors, and they repackage items as "new and improved" when the product is essentially the same. Furthermore, instead of inventing new products, corporations often simply buy out path-breaking firms. As Baran and Sweezy observed:

> When a new industry or field of operations is being opened up, the big corporation tends to hold back deliberately and to allow individual entrepreneurs or small businesses to do the vital pioneering work. Many fail and drop out of the picture, but those which succeed trace out the most promising lines of development for the future. It is at this stage that the big corporations move to the center of the stage....The record of the giants is one of moving in, buying out and absorbing smaller creators. (Baran and Sweezy 1966, 49)

Meanwhile, the inventors are only too happy to cash out: "Indeed, to be bought out and absorbed is often the ultimate ambition of the small business." (Baran and Sweezy 1966, 74) The Internet boom at the end of the 1990s provided the perfect illustration of this process, as established firms looking to muscle in on the wave of the future snapped up new startups. In fact, as Shepherd documents, most innovations actually come from individuals or small firms, while corporate research labs account for only about one-third of major innovations. The only reason that we associate big companies with new products is that the big corporations buy up innovations and market them.

Monopoly capital's control of markets and relentless cost cutting can produce an increasing rate of profit—or, to use a term from Baran and Sweezy which we will explain shortly, a growing "surplus." While on the surface, this would seem to be a good thing for firms, Baran and Sweezy argued that it was a source of endemic instability in capitalism.

Rising Surpluses, Crises and Waste
In *Monopoly Capital*, Baran and Sweezy developed the concept of "surplus," which was related to, but not the same as, Marx's idea of surplus value. Baran and Sweezy defined the surplus as the difference between what society produces—its Gross Domestic Product—and the costs of producing it:

$$\text{SURPLUS} = \text{GDP} - \text{PRODUCTION COSTS} \qquad (\text{S=GDP-PC})$$

Let's explore the implications of this formula. First, most costs of production are a reflection of the labor costs incurred—either wages or the cost of building machines and making inputs. Second, the "surplus" is a macroeconomic approximation of Marx's concept of surplus value, the part of the total value of output that does not go to workers but becomes profits or is paid to the government.[1] Third, what a society does with its surplus is, to political economists, a key determinant of whether or not an economic system is productive and just. Is the surplus invested in useful activities or is much of it wasted? Do all members of society receive a reasonable share of it or does most of the surplus go to the rich and powerful?

Baran and Sweezy argue that, under monopoly capitalism, firms work tirelessly to lower production costs. In addition, as they grow, they control larger and larger segments of markets, and they can use this market power to increase prices. With downward pressure on costs and upward pressure on prices, Baran and Sweezy held that *there is an inherent tendency for the surplus to rise.* Hence a key economic issue becomes how the economy is able, or not able, to absorb this growing surplus.

These ideas recall the work of John Maynard Keynes, who discussed the circular flow of income among producers, workers, and consumers. In the Keynesian system, firms take in money and pay most of it out in wages and salaries. They pay some to banks that have loaned them money, some to the government in taxes, and they keep some as profits. When the money goes to workers, the workers spend most of it on consumer goods, pay some of it in taxes, and save what's left. In Baran and Sweezy's formulation of the surplus, they are looking at this circular flow of income from a slightly different perspective. In the formula, S=GDP-PC, Baran and Sweezy mean by production costs only those that are truly necessary, not all costs of production. As an example, in the automobile industry, necessary costs would include the wages and salaries paid to production workers, and the wages and salaries paid to those at other firms that supplied materials and machines to the autoworkers. If we subtract these necessary costs from total output, GDP, we get what's left, and what Baran and Sweezy call the "surplus." With that money, firms pay the owners profits, the banks interest, the government taxes, and they also spend enormous sums on such things as advertising, supervisors whose only job is to help drive down costs, officers of the firm, and so on. Thus, the surplus can be divided as follows:

SURPLUS = PROFITS + INTEREST + TAXES + ADVERTISING + MANAGEMENT COSTS

Profits and interest payments are usually used to finance investment (I), and taxes are used to finance government spending (G). Baran and Sweezy see spending on advertising and excess management as waste. So the formula for surplus can also be written as follows:

SURPLUS = I + G + CORPORATE WASTE

We can assume that most of what goes to workers in the form of production costs gets back into the system as consumption spending, but that is not necessarily true in the case of the surplus. Since significant parts of the surplus, particularly that paid to the owners as profits and to the government in taxes, will not automatically get back to the firms in the way of spending, this portion of the surplus becomes a potential source of instability for the entire economy. This is not different, conceptually, from the total "leakages" in the Keynesian system: the surplus leaks out of the circular flow of income, and it must be returned in one form or another. If the entire surplus is not returned, then some income generated from production is not spent, and some goods go unpurchased. The result is stagnation and recession as businesses cut production and lay off workers in response to poor sales.[2]

More concretely, why must profits be reinvested? Why wouldn't corporate executives want to hold onto their profits? Fundamentally, firms must use the profits they keep as retained earnings to invest in new capital and grow; without growth their profits will likely fall below those of other firms. Their stockholders will be displeased, and their competitors will muscle in on their markets. Thus, all profits must find an outlet every year. Or, in other words, the accumulation of capital is an imperative for survival in capitalism: *businesses must grow or die.*

Similarly, profits that firms don't keep, but pay to banks and investors, must also find an outlet. All financial investment firms that earn money one year will want to earn more money next year by buying more stocks, bonds, or other such instruments. Or if the money goes to a bank which pays interest to depositors, the bank must find someone to loan that money to at an even higher rate of interest. Banks therefore need good investment opportunities. The imperative for the financial sector to reinvest is clear when one considers that the wealthy save much of their income: most of the surplus they receive from salaries, stocks, and bonds finds its way back into financial markets seeking a high rate of return. Thus, the generation of profits creates additional demands for future profits, the growth of financial speculation generates more speculation, and economic growth creates the demand for more economic growth.

The problem is that *there are only so many good investment opportunities in an economy.* Firms seek out the surest, most profitable investment options and expand into these areas. But if firms run out of good opportunities, the expansion of investment itself becomes a problem. As Baran and Sweezy put it, "Sooner or later, excess capacity grows so large that it discourages further investment." (Baran and Sweezy 1966, 82) When this happens, as we know from Keynes, the dearth of investment and the excess of leakages over injections can cause a downturn. The only way to avoid a recession is to ensure that spending in other sectors goes up.

Are there enough alternative outlets for investment and spending? Baran and Sweezy didn't think so. Once existing investment outlets in an economy have been exhausted, capitalists must find new outlets, such as new techniques of production, new products, and new markets. However, new technology and products will not always be outlets for investment, because giant corporations frequently slow their introduction when it is more profitable to do so. For example, shoes can now be manufactured, and fast food meals cooked and dispensed, entirely by machine. However, corporations still choose to use exploited labor to make these products because it is more profitable to do so. Companies have no incentive to invest in new technology given low wages.

Similarly, companies are often reluctant to introduce new products into markets that are already profitable. For example, IBM was reluctant to sell networked personal computers as long as its mainframe business was profitable. Microsoft ignored the Internet browser market until Netscape demonstrated its importance. These examples tend to confirm Baran and Sweezy's conclusion that "new products and new processes...tend to be introduced in a controlled fashion." (Baran and Sweezy 1966, 99) This means that monopoly capitalism is "simultaneously characterized by a rapid rate of technical progress and by the retention in use of a large amount of technologically obsolete equipment." (Baran and Sweezy 1966, 96) This is one example of the irrational nature of the U.S. economic system: corporations are desperately searching for opportunities to invest their profits, and in new technology they have a perfect vehicle for profitable investment. But often, companies opt instead to stick with existing, profitable methods and products, even while there are new technological advances and new products that could be explored.

Similarly, Baran and Sweezy noted that overseas investment by U.S. companies cannot be counted on to absorb surplus in the long term. (Baran and Sweezy 1966, 106) If foreign investment is profitable, and collectively it is, then it does not solve the surplus absorption problem because even greater profits from previous investments are coming back at the same time that new investments are being made. International flows of money in and out of the United States since they wrote their book confirm their argument.

The profits from previous investments have been greater than new foreign investments for most years since 1966.

The recessions of 2000-2002 and 2007-2009 both provide examples of what happens when profitable investment outlets dry up. During the mid-1990s, many firms and individuals invested in Internet startups and tele-communications technologies that were profitable or showed promise. These included startups like Netscape, and wireless telephone technology. By the late 1990s, the "sure things" had been exhausted, yet firms and investors continued to pump money into these sectors. Investors fell over each other to get a piece of companies that had never even sold a product, much less made a profit, because they had money to invest and no better place to put it. What was the end result of pumping all this money into the technology sector? In 2000, the sector crashed, slowing the rest of the economy. By 2002, stock prices had fallen to 1997 levels, and dozens of Internet startups and telecommunications companies were bankrupt. Similarly, in the mid-2000s real-estate values were soaring and it seemed like the good times would never end. Banks and speculators invested more and more money from the growing surplus into mortgage-backed securities even as the price of real estate reached unheard-of levels. As we have seen in earlier chapters, the real estate bubble burst, dragging the rest of the economy into the "Great Recession" that started in 2007.

Thus, the rising surplus generated by monopoly capitalism must find an outlet, but the investment opportunities are often insufficient. The ongoing problem of insufficient profitable investment outlets for the ever-increasing surplus means that *corporations must find other ways to dispose of the surplus.* One key way to dispose of the surplus is the sales effort: corporations pull out all the stops to sell more products, and simultaneously spend the expanding surplus.

The Sales Effort

Whether or not corporations find outlets for all their profits, the total investment in capital goods, and thus in capacity, constantly expands. Except in cases of deep recession, U.S. firms' overall capacity to produce output has expanded throughout our history. Therefore, in good times, and even in many bad times, firms continue to add capacity to their production systems. However, a problem looms: as capacity increases, firms must find additional buyers for their products. Consumers buy about two-thirds of all output in U.S. capitalism, and corporations' survival rests largely on the maintenance and growth of consumer spending.

For the sales effort to work, consumers must have enough income to buy their share of the output. But consumers' "purchasing power" is always restricted by the efforts of corporate owners to cut workers' wages and salaries, and get more of the pie for themselves. Most political economists see the recent sluggishness of the U.S. economy partly as a consequence of the redistribution of income since the middle 1970s. Since 1970, incomes at the bottom have been stagnant while incomes of the richest 10% have increased dramatically. The bottom 90% of the population spends a greater percentage of its income than the top 10%, so broad-based income gains that go to the poor as well as the rich would cause larger increases in total spending, and larger increases in economic growth, than income gains that go only to the rich.

Particularly when workers' budgets are restricted, corporations know that consumers must be persuaded ever more emphatically to buy additional new products. Accordingly, corporations must devote increasing funds to the sales effort. No part of the theory of monopoly capital has proven so absolutely on target than the prediction that this sales effort would be ever more deleterious to society at large.

The sales effort has assumed a huge role in monopoly capitalism to provide outlets for the expanding surplus. In the year 2007, U.S. firms spent $280 billion hawking products to consumers here and abroad, filling consumers' attics and basements to capacity (see Figure 1).

One result of this explosion in advertising has been a drop in consumers' personal savings. The U.S. savings rate, which averaged over 9 percent between 1940 and 2000, reached a post-Depression low of 0.4 percent in 2005. The connection between the sales effort in the United States and low savings is direct: as F. M. Scherer has documented, in the United States the savings rate is lower, and advertising spending as a percentage of GDP is higher, than in *any other industrialized nation.* (Scherer 1990)

As Baran and Sweezy observed, the sales effort has evolved over time. "Price competition," they argued, "has largely receded as a means of attracting the public's custom, and has yielded to new ways of sales promotion: advertising, variation of the products' appearance and packaging, planned obsolescence, model changes, credit schemes, and the like." (Baran and Sweezy 1966, 115) All of us are familiar with the marketing of fraudulent newness for repackaged items, goods that are designed to wear out quickly and need replacing, and ads connecting emotional attachments such as sex, love, family and adventure with products that cannot possibly deliver these things. We are discouraged from buying products for their utility value, from driving cars for their entire useful lives of 10 to 15 years, and from spending our money on things other than the latest consumer goods.

Baran and Sweezy added that the sales effort depends on the manipulative practice of branding. Because consumers know little about most of the products they buy, they are susceptible to labels, trademarks, and brand names which offer a sense of security in the product, whether real or imagined. Baran and Sweezy wrote that studies "show conclusively that individuals are influenced by advertising without being aware of that influence," and that "advertising induces the consumer to pay prices markedly higher than those charged for physically identical products which are not backed by suitable advertising techniques." (Baran and Sweezy 1966, 121) In other words, the sales effort is inherently dishonest and manipulative.

Advertising is an integral part of capitalism: it stimulates aggregate demand by creating new desires, it stimulates production, and it employs nonproductive workers in ad agencies and the media. In all these ways, it offsets rising surpluses. Yet while the sales effort props up the system, Baran and Sweezy saw it as "a massive waste of resources, a continual drain on the consumer's income, and a systematic destruction of his freedom of choice between genuine alternatives." (Baran and Sweezy 1966, 122)

Figure 1. U.S. Spending on Advertising, 1935-2007 (billions of $)

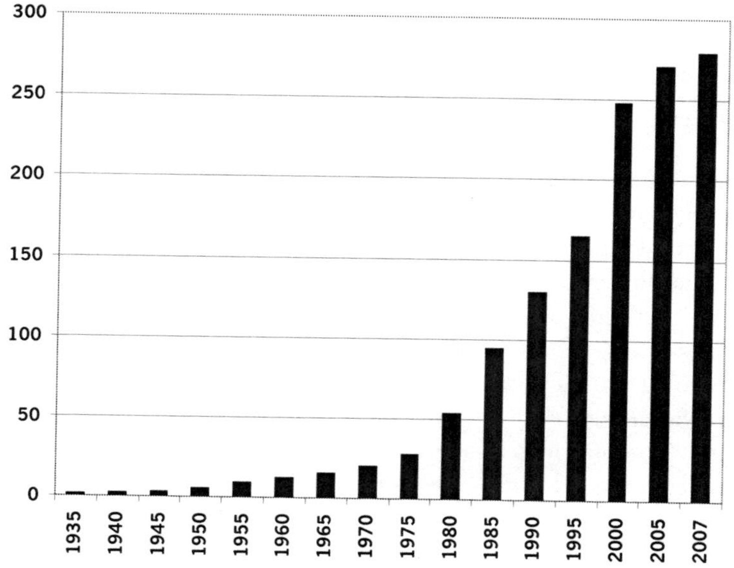

Source: *Statistical Abstract of the United States*, 2001.

As Baran and Sweezy noted after John Kenneth Galbraith, the sales effort is also at war with everything else, which creates a social imbalance. It convinces us to ignore the slums and poverty, crumbling infrastructure and schools, and poisoned air and water. All of our public goods are sacrificed on the altar of products like SUVs—one of the principal culprits in the advance of global warming. Is this truly a rational, optimal outcome that markets are generating—that optimal outcome that mainstream economists extol? Think about your own purchases of consumer goods, and consider some of the following data drawn from the PBS film *Affluenza* and Juliet Schor's book *The Overspent American* (1999):

- On average, Americans now spend more than a year of their lives watching commercials.
- By age 20, the typical American will have seen 1 million commercial messages.
- On average, for every additional hour of television watched in the United States, consumer spending increases by $200.
- Parents average 6 hours per week shopping, but only 40 minutes per week playing with their children. While some shopping is clearly necessary, shopping for recreation now occupies a more prominent role in families than spending quality time with children.

So, do you think Baran and Sweezy themselves were being rational when in 1966 they characterized the sales effort, and its results, as "wasteful" and "irrational"?

Government Absorption of Surplus

If investment falters and consumers don't buy enough to satisfy corporations, there is still one last great user of the surplus: the government. As monopoly capitalism has evolved, the government sector of every developed country, including the United States, has expanded, absorbing more and more of the surplus. U.S. government spending as a percentage of GDP increased steadily from 10 percent in 1929 to 33 percent in 2008. *Laissez-faire* advocates who argue for lower taxes and less government spending miss a fundamental economic fact: if government spending and taxes were reduced, the private sector would have more money to spend, but it would also have more savings. When savings increase, firms must increase investment to prevent a recession. But as we discussed, there are problems with assuming that investment will automatically increase as the economy grows.

Much of the expansion of government spending in the United States has been in the area of military spending, which benefits corporations directly through defense contracts. In 2008, the United States spent $607 billion on national defense. China, the nation with the second largest defense budget, spent $85 billion, less than 1/7 of the amount spent by the United States. The defense spending of all of the countries that the U.S. government views as security risks, Syria, Iran, North Korea, Sudan, Libya and Cuba, was about $23 billion, less than 1/26 of the U.S. budget.

Even given the events of September 11, 2001 (from which our massive expenditures on defense did not protect us), it is not unreasonable to wonder how much of this spending is truly necessary, and how much is politically demanded by what President Dwight Eisenhower called the "military industrial complex." He was referring to the powerful influence that defense contractors like General Electric, General Motors, and AT&T have on government decisions to buy armaments. For decades, politicians have approved spending on weapons that the military has not asked for and does not want, just to stay in the good graces of defense contractors. Thus, some types of government spending, like most of the sales effort, are examples of the "waste" of the surplus. While these funds could refurbish schools—most of which are substandard in urban areas—they are wasted on weapons that even the military does not want.

As examples, in 2009 the United States House of Representatives voted to allocate $2.25 billion for eight C-17 Globemaster aircraft, a plane that for ten years the Pentagon had claimed it did not need. In the same year, the Senate voted to allocate about $1.5 billion to produce a dozen F-22 Raptor fighter planes that the Pentagon also did not need. (*Project on Government Oversight*, www.pogo.org, June 2, 2009) During 2009, Lockheed Martin, which builds the F-22, spent a total of $9.9 million lobbying the members of Congress to keep the program alive. (*Huffington Post*, March 10, 2010) Given that there are about 500 members of Congress, this lobbying effort means that, in effect, Lockheed Martin spent about $20,000 trying to persuade each member of Congress to waste money on this unnecessary program.

On top of defense contracts, our government funnels money to corporations in the form of corporate welfare—subsidies and tax breaks amounting to over $150 billion per year. Anwar Shaikh and Ahmet Tonak observe that these enormous givebacks to corporations leave very little to fund programs for lower and middle-income people:

> By and large, it is the taxes of the working population that essentially pay for...state expenditures on health, education, Social Security, unemployment, public assistance, housing, and a host of other social programs. (Shaikh and Tonak 2000, 254)

Though government officials often suggest that poor "welfare queens" are stealing the money of taxpayers, the truth is that the amount of money transferred from the rich to the poor is negligible, amounting to about one half of one percent of total employee compensation. Baran and Sweezy note that, "[u]ntil the New Deal period of the 1930s, there was not even any pretense that promoting the welfare of the lower classes was a responsibility of government." (Baran and Sweezy 1966, 159) The pretense now exists, but the United States is hardly bankrupting itself with its welfare program. In 2005, the United States ranked 26th out of 29 OECD countries in the amount of GDP devoted to social expenditures like welfare. The United States devoted a smaller percentage of GDP to social spending than *all* OECD countries except Turkey, Mexico and South Korea. Increasingly, the biggest recipients of welfare spending are corporations, which make sure the government they largely control takes good care of their "needs."

In general, large multinational corporations and their owners support greater military outlays, greater spending on highways, corporate welfare, and other measures that lead to higher profits, but they oppose efforts to increase taxes to meet social needs. Baran and Sweezy argue that these spending priorities are at odds with the goal of creating a just society. They note:

> While massive government spending for education and welfare tends to undermine [the oligarchy's] privileged position, the opposite is true of military spending.... [M]ilitarization fosters all the reactionary and irrational forces in society, and inhibits or kills everything progressive and humane. Blind respect is engendered for authority; attitudes of docility and conformity are taught and enforced; dissent is treated as unpatriotic or even treasonable. (Baran and Sweezy 1966, 209)

Hence, while the government is a key absorber of surplus, the way the U.S. government absorbs surplus is typically most favorable to the giant firms, frequently wasteful, and contradictory to social needs.

We are left with an economy facing regular problems of too much surplus and inadequate levels of consumption and investment. The sales effort and government spending can absorb some of the surplus, although in the

United States, these are particularly wasteful forms of spending. And even these efforts often fall short. The problem of surplus absorption under monopoly capital is so severe that in the last 150 years, only epoch-making innovations such as the railroads, automobiles, and information technology (computers), along with the sales effort and militarization, have been able to stave off the depressive effects of monopoly capitalism. Even with these innovations, the economy still regularly falls into recessions as demand fails to sustain the system.

Despite all of these problems with monopoly capitalism—the wasteful squandering of the surplus, the control and manipulation of markets at the expense of consumers—the system might still be justifiable if it produced other benefits. In particular, it might be defensible if it created opportunities for creative work that most political economists see as essential to a healthy, fulfilling life. So before we make a final judgment about this economic system we have, we must ask: What is the nature of wage work in the world of monopoly capital?

LABOR AND MONOPOLY CAPITAL

Baran and Sweezy argued that Marx's theory of alienation aptly described workers' experiences in monopoly capitalism. They wrote that people are:

> being specialized and sorted, imprisoned in the narrow cells prepared for them by the division of labor, their faculties stunted and their minds diminished. And a threat to their security and peace of mind which already loomed large in Marx's day has grown in direct proportion to the spreading incidence and accelerated speed of technological change under monopoly capitalism. (Baran and Sweezy 1966, 343)

Baran and Sweezy went on to show in some detail how Marx's arguments about alienation remained applicable to U.S. capitalism. Not long after their book was published, Harry Braverman, one of their associates at Monthly Review Press, wrote *Labor and Monopoly Capital: The Degradation of Work in the Twentieth Century*. In 1996, David Gordon updated the story in another influential book, *Fat and Mean: The Corporate Squeeze of Working Americans and the Myth of Managerial "Downsizing."* We will focus briefly on the arguments in these two books, and other similar views, that underscore how prescient Marx was about wage labor in capitalism, especially his analysis of what he called "estranged labor." We will also see how these writers strongly confirm Baran and Sweezy's assessment, made half a century ago, about the labor process in American capitalism. As is typical of capitalism, the problems begin with the accumulation process. The drive to accumulate more capital forces firms to invest in ever more productive techniques. One way to increase productivity and profits is to replace a highly skilled, expensive laborer with a machine operated by an unskilled laborer—a process known as *mechanization and deskilling*. When this happens, productivity rises, but workers are often left with mind-numbing jobs and low wages, or no job at all. Another way to increase productivity is by minutely controlling workers' time and motion so that the capitalists, in effect, wring more work out of every hour of labor they pay for. This is known simply as "speed-up." Again, the result is good for capitalists but bad for workers. Workers lose freedom, and their jobs involve less creativity; and these changes frequently lead to worse mental and physical health, as we explained in the chapter on social class. Braverman documents how this process has unfolded for 250 years, and makes this comment:

> [Deskilling means] the incessant breakdown of labor processes into simplified operations taught to workers as tasks. This leads to the conversion of the greatest possible mass of labor into work of the most elementary form, labor from which all conceptual elements have been removed and along with them most of the skill, knowledge, and understanding of production processes.... [T]he more machinery that has been developed as an aid to labor, the more labor becomes a servant of machinery. (Braverman 1974, 319)

One of the profound ironies of capitalism is that machinery, which is particularly good at performing repetitive tasks, has not replaced monotonous labor. Instead, machines become the regulators of human work, forcing people to work faster and more intensely at monotonous tasks. As we pointed out earlier, technology now exists that could allow shoes to be made entirely by machine. This would allow workers to do more creative work in design, programming, and overseeing the operations of machinery. Yet most shoes are made in developing countries by low-wage workers huddling over old machines for long hours every day in unhealthy conditions. The design of production to enhance profit, rather than human creativity, means that most workers are consigned to a work life which denies them the opportunity to use their finest skills.

Braverman spent a good part of his book describing mechanization and deskilling in the half century before he wrote his book. His examples included the following:

- Independent, self-supervising clerks and bookkeepers were converted into specialized workers who could not control or do the whole job.
- Skilled office workers, though once fairly independent, eventually became tied to a computer in a cubicle under the direct watch of a manager.
- Secretaries, doing multiple tasks in support of a manager or a few key employees, were replaced by (a) specialized workers in administrative support doing one or two tasks all day long (e.g., typing, copying, mailing, lay out, etc.), or (b) outsourced workers, hired through firms that specialize in generically structured secretarial tasks. Notably, outsourced workers often work on a contingent basis, and therefore without any job security.
- Skilled butchers were replaced by huge, semi-automated meat processing centers.
- Skilled carpenters were largely supplanted by factories that make machine-made components, and that reduce the craft to nailing and screwing these parts together.

With the advent of the powerful, small computer, there seems to be no limit to the process of replacing skilled jobs with computer-guided machines and less-skilled workers. Unfortunately, as workers have discovered over the last several decades, there is a qualitative difference between a skilled job and less-skilled job involving a computer or machine. A skilled carpentry job involves creativity and craftsmanship, where the worker controls much of the labor process and, because of her skill, is valued by the employer. A worker stapling the same edge of the same type of cabinet using a computer-guided machine has no control over the pace of work, and the work involves no creativity or imagination. Furthermore, this worker is less likely to be valued and treated well because she can be easily replaced.

Even white-collar jobs have been affected negatively by new technologies. In her book *White-Collar Sweatshop: The Deterioration of Work and Its Rewards in Corporate America* (Norton, 2001), Jill Andresky Fraser documents dramatic changes in the quality of white-collar jobs in the last several decades:

Overwork is epidemic, for men and women whose job demands keep increasing, not because of career advances but because of a corporate environment that has depended upon *squeezing*...more and more work out of fewer people with fewer resources. For today's white-collar staffers, the balanced and secure nine-to-five work lives of their parents' generation belongs to a utopian past, as they struggle to fulfill job demands that require them to work after dinner and during lunch hours,...or on Saturdays and Sundays, in between the innings of their children's Little League games, during summer or winter vacations, ...or on countless other occasions as well. (Fraser, 8-9)

Technological changes—especially laptops and cell phones—keep employees at the beck and call of their bosses 24 hours a day, even during vacations. Relentless mergers and downsizing result in each employee doing the work of several people. Meanwhile, the glut of labor as corporations shed workers creates a situation in which many white-collar workers experience stagnant or declining pay and benefits.

In Braverman's view, the drive for greater productivity in monopoly capitalism demands a complete disregard for human beings, the environment, and macroeconomic well-being. As he put it:

[T]he increasing productivity of labor is neither sought nor utilized by capitalism from the point of view of the satisfaction of human needs. Rather, powered by the needs of the capital accumulation process, it becomes a frenzied drive which approaches the level of a generalized social insanity. Never is any level of productivity regarded as sufficient. In the automobile industry, a constantly diminishing number of workers produces, decade by decade, a growing number of increasingly degraded products which, as they are placed upon the streets and highways, poison and disrupt the entire social atmosphere—while at the same time the cities where motor vehicles are produced become centers of degraded labor on the one hand and permanent unemployment on the other. It is a measure of the manner in which capitalist standards have diverged from human standards that this situation is seen as representing a high degree of "economic efficiency." (Braverman 1974, 141)

Automobile firms are content to produce unsafe products subject to rollovers, unexpected acceleration, or other correctable design flaws. They do so in greater and greater quantities while using less and less labor, usually without considering the human and environmental damage they cause. They apparently give no thought, either, to the fact that as they lay off workers and cut wages, they undermine aggregate demand. Finally, U.S. automobile firms are perfectly comfortable moving operations overseas to take advantage of lower production costs, despite the economic devastation they leave behind. Cities such as Flint and Detroit, which depended on automobile jobs, have been economically destroyed by the flight of auto manufacturers.

The destruction of U.S. auto jobs is part of a century-long decline in manufacturing jobs, as machines have replaced workers. Figure 2 indicates that since 1920 the percentage of workers in manufacturing industries (including mining and construction) has declined substantially, and workers have been forced to seek jobs the service sector. Because U.S. unions have not traditionally organized the service sector, wages there tend to be lower; thus, wages stagnate as manufacturing jobs are eliminated and laborers are thrust into services. This in turn sometimes encourages service-sector employers to use old-fashioned, labor-intensive methods.

The shift to a service economy has had devastating effects on U.S. workers. During the first two decades after World War II, as manufacturing expanded, real wages for nonsupervisory workers increased dramatically. However, average hourly real earnings for non-supervisory workers in the United States declined from $20 per hour in 1972 to $18 per hour in 2008, as shown in Figure 3. Moreover, according to the Economic Policy Institute, between 1979 and 2006 the average total compensation (wages and benefits) of manufacturing workers in 17 of 19 developed countries, including our major trading partners, increased more than total compensation for U.S. workers.

In addition to the relentless downward pressure on wages and benefits, and the loss of worker control, independence, and creativity, the U.S. labor

Figure 2. The Decline in Manufacturing Employment in the United States, 1920-2008

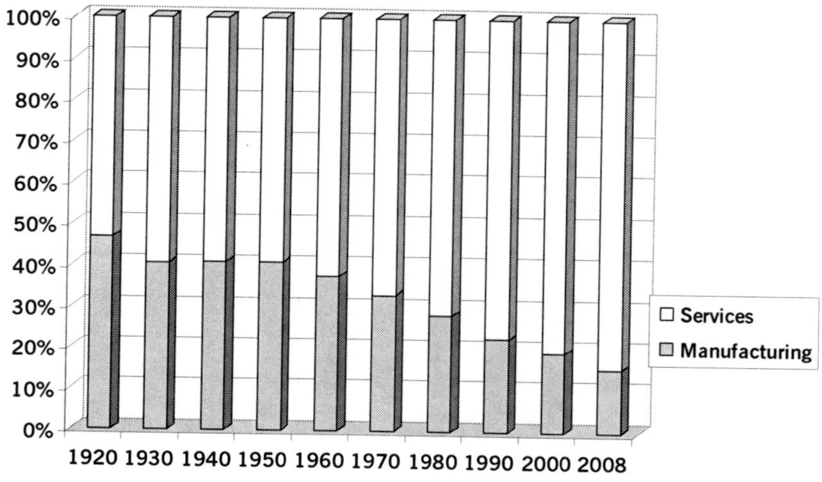

Source: Braverman and *The Economic Report of the President*, 2009..

market has other characteristics that make it bad for workers. In his book *Fat and Mean*, David Gordon demonstrated that U.S. firms are also over-managed and more bureaucratic than firms in other developed countries. According to Gordon, in the early 1970s, U.S. corporations adopted a "stick" strategy to control workers. They broke unions and drove down wages to increase profits. They moved manufacturing operations overseas, outsourced production to low-cost manufacturers (also often overseas), sped up work, and cut wages in their U.S. operations. In order to keep laborers working hard under these conditions, employers added numerous supervisors to monitor employees. This is, according to Gordon, the "dirty little secret" of the U.S. economy. In 1994, 17.3 million supervisors earned $1.3 trillion in compensation, or 20 percent of national income. How is it possible that we have so many people who boss other people around? As Gordon noted in a 1996 article:

> The basic principle is simple. If a labor-management system relies on hierarchical principles for managing and supervising its front-line employees on the shop and office floors, then it needs more than just the front-line supervisors who directly oversee these workers. Who keeps the supervisors honest? What guarantees that those supervisors won't be in cahoots with their charges? In such a hierarchy, you need supervisors to supervise the supervisors...and supervisors above them...and managers to watch the higher-level supervisors ...and higher-level managers to watch the lower-level managers. (Gordon 1996b, 27)

Figure 3. Average Real Hourly Earnings for Production & Nonsupervisory Workers, 1972-2008

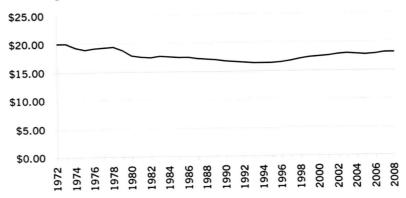

Source: Authors' calculations and data from the Bureau of Labor Statistics (bls.gov).

Clearly, the only way to keep employees working hard under antagonistic, alienating conditions is to hire an army of supervisors to watch them carefully. Of course, as with so many of these aspects of capitalism, Marx was the first to observe that the factory was more analogous to the military, with several layers of hard-fisted sergeants keeping the troops in line.

Today, U.S. companies have more than three times as many supervisors per production worker as Germany and Japan, and five times as many as Sweden. This difference is explained by the more cooperative model of employment in these countries. Germany, Japan and Sweden employ the "carrot" method to increase productivity: workers are given job security, wage incentives, strong union representation, and a role in making important decisions. Such cooperative environments don't require as many bosses because workers are less likely to hate and resent their jobs. Of course, even the "carrot" method of motivating workers is a far cry from the kind of cooperative workplaces that most political economists advocate, where employees would have much more control over all aspects of work. But in the U.S., workers are goaded into working hard via the employment of the "stick": low wages, which might erode morale and productivity, are countered by constant monitoring and the threat of unemployment.

Unfortunately for the United States, cooperative workplaces tend to be much more productive. As Gordon noted in the same article:

> [T]hose economies with more cooperative systems of labor relations also have more rapid productivity growth rates. And with more rapid productivity growth, there is room for financing more productive investments, for affording more rapid wage growth, and for maintaining a competitive edge in the global economy. (Gordon 1996b, 33)

Once again, the U.S. system is efficient at generating profits, but it lags behind other developed countries in terms of other goals, such as productivity and creating a humane workplace.

CONCLUSION

Were Baran and Sweezy reasonable when they ended their book with a chapter called "The Irrational System"—a sustained, mostly negative critique of U.S. capitalism? Their central claims were as follows:

- The U.S. economy is dominated by huge multinational corporations which do everything in their power to stifle competition;

- Stifling competition involves rigging markets through collusion, mergers, and buying protection from the government;
- The drive to accumulate capital is inherent in the system, as past profits require investment opportunities to generate the highest possible return;
- But the very expansion caused by investment and capital accumulation contains within it the seeds of regular recessions as investment opportunities dry up and aggregate demand proves insufficient;
- The U.S. government willingly participates in the system, shoring up firms with billions of dollars in corporate welfare and defense contracts;
- Multinational corporations are sometimes innovative, but they also stifle innovation when it is more profitable to do so;
- Firms work to expand markets as much as possible, wasting hundreds of billions of dollars annually on dishonest attempts to manipulate consumers;
- U.S. corporations relentlessly lower costs via mechanization and attacks on labor, but the cost savings are not generally passed on to consumers;
- The relentless drive to lower costs results in mechanization, deskilling, alienation, and low wages for U.S. workers, culminating in the employment of the "stick" strategy to coerce alienated workers into working hard.

So, what do you think? Are these arguments believable? And, if they are, do they describe an economic system that is fundamentally irrational? It's an interesting question early in the 21st century, a time when Americans are relentlessly told by the media, the sales effort, and their own government, exactly what the economic mainstream has always maintained: that capitalism, though it has a flaw or two, is the best of all possible systems, and a remarkable testament to rational thought and hard work. Maybe so, maybe not.

Perhaps, finally, we should ask another question. Has reading this, and the other chapters, made you wonder if there might be a better way to shape and develop the economy? One that is less unequal—politically and in every other way? One that doesn't systematically destroy its habitat? One that is, well, a bit more rational than our own? We know that after reading material in a book like this one, such questions are as inevitable as the loud honk just after the traffic light turns green. That is why we conclude this book with a description of Sweden's modern welfare state—what they call "social democracy"—and of the worker-owned cooperatives of the Mondragon region in Spain. For decades, the Swedes have been constructing a humane, efficient alternative to our kind of cowboy capitalism where the biggest crooks get the biggest paychecks. We will now see what the Swedes have wrought.

SUGGESTIONS FOR FURTHER READING

Baiman, Ron, Heather Boushey, and Dawn Saunders, editors, *Political Economy and Contemporary Capitalism: Radical Perspectives on Economic Theory and Policy.* Armonk, NY: M. E. Sharpe, 2000.

Baran, Paul and Paul Sweezy, *Monopoly Capital: An Essay on the American Economic and Social Order.* New York: Monthly Review Press, 1966.

Braverman, Harry, *Labor and Monopoly Capital: The Degradation of Work in the Twentieth Century.* New York: Monthly Review Press, 1974.

Gordon, David, *Fat and Mean: The Corporate Squeeze of Working Americans and the Myth of Managerial Downsizing,* New York: Free Press, 1996.

Gordon, David, "Underpaid Workers, Bloated Corporations: Two Pieces in the Puzzle of U.S. Economic Decline," *Dissent,* Vol. 43, Spring 1996, 23-34.

9
The Middle Way: Swedish Social Democracy*

[In Sweden] the state, the consumer, and the producer have intervened to make capitalism "work" in a reasonable way for the greatest good of the whole nation... That this constitutes a...middle course seems to me obvious; it is a course between the absolute socialization of Russia [the USSR] and the end development of capitalism in America. In Russia...the rulers of the state attempted to make all of life conform to an idea, an ideal. In the United States the profit motive was put above every other consideration and it worked to the end of blind self-destruction.
—Marquis Childs, *The Middle Way*, 1936 (143-4)

Think of a bumblebee. With its overly heavy body and little wings, supposedly it should not be able to fly—but it does.... This is how so-called analysts view the Swedish economy. We 'defy gravity.' We have high taxes and a large public sector, and yet, Sweden reaches new heights. We are still flying, so well that many envy us for it today.
—Göran Persson, Swedish Prime Minister, March 10, 2000

INTRODUCTION

What Marquis Childs describes in the passage quoted above are two forms of economic extremism. The Soviet Union developed an economic system based on command-style communism, where the state controlled almost all aspects of the economy, while the United States over the course of its history has always had a market system, where capitalists and individuals made most economic decisions. What we will discuss below is an example of what Childs refers to as the *middle way* between command communism and unregulated capitalism: *social democracy*. Sweden developed an economic sys-

---

* Our thanks to Ellen Campbell, who helped with the research and writing of this chapter.

214 INTRODUCTION TO POLITICAL ECONOMY

tem that successfully incorporated many of the ideas of Marx, Keynes, and Veblen into the economy. As a result, we can see in Sweden's system the practical application of many of the ideas of these influential thinkers. The Swedes created a society that demonstrates impressive levels of equality, stability, and productivity. To use Göran Persson's analogy, quoted above, the Swedish economy can be likened to a bumblebee, with a large, cumbersome public sector that should drag it down, but which actually helps it to soar.

The Social Democratic Labor Party (Socialdemokratiska Arbetarparti, or SAP) that governed Sweden for most of the twentieth century took its cue from Marx, and actively worked to make Sweden an egalitarian society where there was little poverty and where all people had the opportunity to build a good life for themselves. The SAP believed that all Swedish citizens should have the right to a decent job, to security in their old age, to health care, to day care, and to a decent standard of living. These rights evolved over the years through the ongoing implementation of innovative policies, which we will show in our brief sketch of Sweden's economic history.

In Sweden's system we also see the application of the ideas of John Maynard Keynes. Sweden was the first industrialized nation to employ Keynesian policies. Moreover, Swedish economists took Keynes' ideas much further than most. During the 1920s, the Swedish government made some small efforts at stabilizing the economy, such as creating low-wage private-sector jobs for the unemployed. But during the Great Depression of the 1930s, under the direction of the "Stockholm school" of economists, the Swedish government began a large-scale implementation of Keynesian stabilization policies.[1] By 1936, the year Keynes' *General Theory* was published, when other developed countries had only begun to consider Keynes' ideas viable, Sweden had already successfully used these stabilization policies to create jobs and raise wages to their pre-Depression level. Beginning in the 1950s, Sweden took even bolder steps, carefully managing the economy so that *even in recessions*, the unemployment rate remained exceptionally low.

Sweden also incorporated the ideas of Thorstein Veblen into its system. Swedish policymakers sought to limit the predatory and wasteful aspects of capitalism, such as advertising, and instead emphasized the productive side of the economy. For instance, much of the media in Sweden is publicly owned and operated, and high-quality programming is aired without commercials. Likewise, companies in Sweden are allowed to keep their profits as long as they are reinvested in productive activities, but wasteful or destructive practices, such as polluting and downsizing, are penalized.

In short, Sweden has a remarkable economic system that is worthy of careful study, as it provides an interesting counterpart both to the command economies of the former Soviet bloc and the unregulated market economies of the United States and Hong Kong. In what follows below, we will outline what it means to have an economic system described as "social democracy." We then take you through a sketch of Sweden's economic history, which describes the evolution of what came to be called the "Swedish model" or the "Middle Way." Finally, we make the argument that Swedish social democracy is a humane, productive, and civilized economic system that improves upon many aspects of the U.S. economy. We begin by exploring the curious resistance to forms of socialism seen in America.

WHAT IS SOCIAL DEMOCRACY?

The terms used to describe the Swedish economic system, as a rule, do not carry positive connotations for Americans. For example, the term "socialism" often draws a suspicious reaction, as does the idea of a "big government" interfering with the "free" market. Consider your own reaction when you see or hear the word "socialism." Does it conjure images of Communist Russia? Anti-Americanism? A vast and inefficient bureaucracy that limits personal freedom and rights?

But what is the *real* meaning of "socialism"? In a 1967 Webster's dictionary, socialism is defined as "any of various economic and political theories advocating collective or governmental ownership and administration of the means of production and distribution of private property." Yet in a 1923 Webster's dictionary, the definition of socialism is "political and economic theory of social reorganization, the essential feature of which is governmental control of economic activities, to the end that competition shall give way to cooperation and that the opportunities of life and the rewards of labor shall be equitably apportioned..." Consider the difference between these two definitions. What happened to the meaning of this word over a period of 44 years? In the early 1900s, the philosophy of socialism was a response to the philosophy of individualism, a *cultural* philosophy and movement that encouraged self-awareness and personal gain and under which greed is considered a good thing. Therefore, this earlier "socialism" was not strictly political, but social, cultural, and essentially philosophical. However, over time its meaning became more and more politically extreme as the opponents of socialism sought to demonize it. As one can see, we have so politicized the term over the years that our more contemporary dictionaries, our supposedly non-biased sources for meaning, have lost sight of its roots and define it only in political terms.

The word "democratic" has also been politicized over the years. In the United States, we promote democracy as government by and for the people. Yet there are other possible applications of democracy. Democracy in the workplace can mean workers having input into how things are produced and how the workplace is run. (We will see in the final chapter on the Mondragon cooperatives in Spain the details of how worker democracy actually works.) Democracy in a community can mean people deciding how to allocate health care and jobs. The U.S. focus on *political* democracy, especially electoral activity, over and above other arenas for democratic action, demonstrates the extent to which we narrowly define social philosophies in purely political terms.

Similarly, the word "freedom" is heavily politicized in the United States. We are used to referring to "free markets," where the word "free" applies to freedom from a meddling government. But freedom comes in many forms, and historically Sweden's Social Democrats have been more concerned with a broader range of freedoms: freedom from the domination of an employer, from poverty, from the ravages of a recession. Central to this definition of freedom is the idea that access of all to a dignified life is its essential component.

In this chapter we will challenge the traditional definitions of "socialism," "democracy," and "freedom" by moving beyond the simplistic, politicized uses of these terms. Unlike the caricature of socialism as a massive bureaucracy controlling every aspect of our lives, socialism, as practiced in social democracies, is an economic system designed to promote cooperation, equality, and a high standard of living, but not necessarily at the expense of individualism. Social democracy means the freedom for people to control collectively many aspects of their lives, not simply to choose political leaders. As we trace the evolution of the Swedish model below, we will see a genuine example of real social democracy in practice.

THE ORIGINS OF THE SWEDISH "MODEL": 1847-1932

Many books and articles written about Sweden's economic system refer to it as the "Swedish Model." Implied in the word "model" is the idea that this was an experiment, something planned by a centralized group of intellectuals, and then implemented for the world to observe and critique. This was not the case. Sweden's system developed slowly but persistently throughout the twentieth century as a result of many decisions made by many groups striving toward the same goals of equality and quality of life. These groups included the business community, unions, politicians, and scholars. In other words, the majority of Swedish citizens built this socio-economic structure democratically over time.

Sweden's democratically created socioeconomic system is also referred to as a "welfare" state. "Welfare" is another term that has been politically demonized. But the fact that Sweden has a welfare state does not mean that people don't have to work, or that poverty is so pervasive that widespread welfare benefits are required just to keep its citizens in shoes. It means exactly what it says: "welfare" is to "fare well." In other words, the welfare state is designed for the benefit of the whole society.

Historically, Sweden's welfare state evolved from a society that was admirably enlightened long before its Western counterparts, and even before the Social Democrats first came to power in 1920. In 1847 and 1853 Sweden passed "poor relief laws," taking the first step toward implementing its social philosophy of helping those whose impoverished circumstances were beyond their control. In contrast, most of Europe still had debtors' prisons and indentured servitude at this time: people who were too poor to pay their debts were imprisoned, enslaved, or forced into "workhouses" to work for a pittance. As examples, Paris had prisons, such as the Bastille, for many of its impoverished; most of the first colonists in America were indentured servants from Europe; and Australia was a penal colony for Britain's criminals, many of them debtors. Whether it was a mother of three whose husband died, or a worker who was injured and disabled, the cause of indebtedness was irrelevant. The inability to pay one's debts in these countries was treated as a willful, punishable act. But Swedish officials recognized that poverty was usually neither willful nor deserving of punishment. The Swedes saw poverty as a product of economic factors, and began taking responsibility for helping their people out of poverty.

The Social Democratic Labor Party (SAP) was founded in 1889. Around this time, the philosophy that produced the "poor relief laws" began to mature and expand. Instead of assessing the health of their economic system through stock prices and GDP, the Swedes began to develop a system wherein the health and value of the economy was gauged by the quality of life of its entire population. In 1913, Sweden's (non-socialist) Liberal Party government, with the support of the populace, began broadening the range of social benefits. They passed the National Pension Act in 1913 to provide security for the aged, more than twenty years before the United States implemented its own social security system. In 1918 a Liberal-SAP coalition government passed a new poor law, turning the responsibility of assisting anyone in need over to local governments, while the central government contributed administrative support. This law was to remain the cornerstone of Sweden's assistance programs for the next 40 years. It took most other developed countries until the Great Depression of the 1930s to take that path.

THE SAP'S FUNCTIONAL SOCIALISM: 1932-1968
Social and Political Philosophy
The SAP began to influence economic policy immediately after its formation in 1889. At that point, it stated its guiding principles as follows:

1. Legislation to guarantee to every Swedish citizen a simple and decent standard of living...[Social Democrats] hold that it is the duty of society to provide for the needs of the aged, invalids, widows, and those who have lost their income through no fault of their own.
2. Housing and child benefits for needy families so that they should not be forced to lower their standard of living because they have children to raise. [The] idea is to distribute the expense over the entire population as a collective responsibility.
3. Social welfare [is]...the inherent right of every citizen irrespective of his financial status.

In order to implement its philosophy, the SAP was forced to compromise with employers and political opponents. Compromise was possible because although the philosophy behind the SAP's ideas was socialist in nature, the SAP was not dogmatic or rigid. The Social Democrats pursued the goal of a better life for all Swedes, and allowed the economy to operate within a capitalist system as long as it could achieve this goal.

The Social Democrats saw the problems associated with free-market as well as with state-controlled systems. From 1920 to 1932, recessions plagued Sweden's free-market economy as a succession of governments, some including the SAP, failed to stabilize the economy adequately. There was also an unequal distribution of income and wealth, and a significant percentage of the population lived in poverty. But the SAP did not adhere to the idea of state-controlled production in response to these problems, fearing the inefficiency that could come from a command-style economy. Instead, once the SAP was firmly entrenched as Sweden's ruling party in 1932, it allowed the capitalist norm of private ownership to continue, intervening in the economy whenever the needs of labor were not met. As in the U.S. capitalist system, there were wealthy entrepreneurs who owned and controlled much of Swedish industry, but the SAP limited their power and influence. The SAP devised taxes on income and profits so that it was profitable for business owners to reinvest in productive activities and to create jobs. Entrepreneurs were allowed to make a fortune in Sweden, but only if they expanded employment, produced socially useful products, and limited the destruction of the environment. Thus the SAP permitted the private sector to pursue profits as long as firms achieved social goals. In some sectors, the SAP organized consumer and producer cooperatives, and in other sectors, such as health care, dental care and child care, the SAP socialized the provision of services, but overall the SAP preserved private ownership.

The Social Democrats established early on that equality and economic growth were not necessarily incompatible. Conservative Swedish economists who followed the ideas of Adam Smith insisted that some measure of inequality was necessary to stimulate growth: if investors, business owners, and the wealthy in general were not allowed to keep what they earned, they would have no incentive to continue investing and growth would stagnate. Thus they argued that measures to improve equality through high taxation of corporations and wealthy individuals would slow growth. Swedish Social Democrats rejected this argument, and demonstrated that public investment, stability, and careful macroeconomic management could stimulate growth, which would ultimately be very profitable for industry and private individuals, providing incentives for continued investment. The Social Democrats prevailed and were able to win over industry leaders to this approach.

By no means did the Social Democrats have free rein when they came into power. The democratic electoral process remained in place, with political parties (socialist and non-socialist) and special interest groups wielding influence and power, keeping partisan measures from dominating the political arena. Powerful interest groups included both labor unions and employers' associations, and all actors within the economic system were included in the decision-making process for negotiating mutually beneficial policy and legislation. The leaders of the SAP could not have achieved their egalitarian goals without the cooperation of employers, and the fact that employers cooperated indicates the benefits all parties realized in a social democratic economy. Thus through pragmatism and compromise taking, the SAP gradually implemented numerous socialist policies and ideals *without* a revolution or large-scale nationalization. It was the first socialist party in the world to do so.

De-Commodification

One of the primary goals of the SAP was the de-commodification of the things Swedish people needed to live decent lives. This meant improving wages and working conditions and providing essential services to all rather than using markets determine how these things were allocated. People need certain basic goods and services in order to live full lives. In the SAP principles mentioned above, child-care, for example, is treated as a fundamental need because, as is stated, "[Swedish citizens] should not be forced to lower their standard of living because they have children to raise." In many market systems, families that have children must lower their standard of living because, in paying for the costs associated with caring for and raising children, they have less money to spend on other goods. In the United States, child-care is sold as a commodity only to families that can afford the service. From the SAP's perspective, privatizing childcare can be seen as an exploitative practice that has the most dramatic impact on lower wage-earners.

The same can be said for housing, medical care, dental care, and services for the disabled. In an unregulated market system, these fundamental needs are at the mercy of for-profit industries where the bottom line, and not quality of life, is the primary concern, and not everyone can purchase these necessary items. In the United States, those who cannot pay for these basic, life-sustaining services are often forced to go without, and suffer the consequences. But Sweden will not deny these necessities to those without money. All Swedish citizens have the *right* to essential goods and services under the Swedish welfare state.

After the Social Democrats were voted into power in 1932, they introduced legislation that began to fulfill the principles of de-commodification embedded in their social philosophy. Augmenting the Pension Act of 1913 and the Poor Law of 1918, the SAP instituted housing subsidies and a national pension scheme in 1935, and in 1938 added socialized dental care. By the 1950s, the SAP had installed a national health plan and laid the foundation for a comprehensive network of de-commodified rights for all Swedish citizens.

To this point, the provisions mentioned are those needed to survive physically. But the SAP wanted to guarantee a full *quality* of life as well. Their two main goals when they came into power were *equalization* and *integration*. "Equalization" refers to a better distribution of wealth and income, and "integration" refers not to racial or ethnic issues, but to issues of social class. The primary objective in this realm was full employment. Putting everyone to work would reduce the exploitation of labor and reduce income inequality, thereby further reducing class divisions. This would also eliminate what Marx referred to as the "reserve army of the unemployed." As we will describe in more detail below, policies designed to achieve full employment were put into action after World War II, policies that went far beyond simple stabilization of the economy and provision of basic services.

Equalization and integration were also accomplished through investment in *human capital*. This was, and is, primarily accomplished through education. Although the primary reforms in the Swedish educational systems took place between the 1950s and 1970s, education had for a long time been considered vital to the well-being of the nation. Schooling is free at all levels in Sweden; as a result, the inequality seen in the United States, for instance, of personal wealth buying the best education, is much less prevalent. All citizens are entitled to an excellent education, regardless of financial status, giving every person a start from a more level playing field. Sweden's population is one of the most broadly and best educated in the world. This is one of the major reasons why there is greater class mobility in Sweden than in the United States.

As we can see, the "Swedish model" was not a planned experiment, but rather an evolutionary process that resulted from a series of actions over long periods of time. And although the pace of structural change picked up in the 1950s, the groundwork had been in place since 1889.

Economic Stabilization and Full Employment

Most countries instituted Keynesian stabilization policies, designed to boost spending and create jobs during recessions, following the advent of the Great Depression. As noted above, Sweden's stabilization efforts preceded the Depression. The national pension system of 1913 and the comprehensive poor law of 1918 both served to boost spending when times were tough, and the Swedes instituted policies to stabilize employment as early as the 1920s. Stabilization policies in the 1930s were even more aggressive and successful. But because capital was privately owned, there was still a natural dependency on industry to stimulate the economy. The state recognized this, and a pattern of compromise between capital, labor, and the government became the method for ensuring stability, equality and growth within a highly regulated, but still capitalist, system.

The Swedish government implemented an extensive stabilization policy beginning in the 1930s, spending money counter-cyclically. When an economy enters a recession, tax revenues decrease as businesses downsize and workers lose jobs. In such circumstances, sometimes governments decrease spending to counter the reduction in tax revenues, thereby keeping the budget balanced. But cuts in government spending during a recession put even more people out of work, making the recession even worse. Instead, Sweden *increased* spending in recessions by borrowing money to invest in public works projects, to train workers, and to create jobs. This way, the flow of production and income was stabilized, spending didn't decrease dramatically in recessions, industry was encouraged to invest, and the economy was bolstered until industry's investments brought employment back to normal levels.

In addition to using government spending to stave off recessions, the Swedish government instituted a counter-cyclical investment tax credit system called the Investment Reserve in 1938. Firms were allowed to deposit funds with the government which could be invested tax free if invested *in Sweden at specified times*—during a recession, for example. If invested at another time, the firm would have to pay taxes on the funds. Thus the government encouraged the private sector to invest counter-cyclically, stabilizing the economy even further.

In the 1950s, the Rehn-Meidner plan, named after its two economist authors, was implemented to manage the economy more carefully. Included in the plan were two main areas: the solidaristic wage policy, and active labor policies. The primary goal of this plan was to ensure *full employment.*

In the United States, full employment (what economists call the "natural rate of unemployment" or the "non-accelerating inflation rate of unemployment"—NAIRU) is considered to be an unemployment rate of about 5.5%. Many mainstream economists believe that an unemployment rate of less than 5.5% guarantees inflation. Labor becomes more powerful when unemployment is low because there are fewer workers available to fill jobs, and at the same time firms need labor to increase production because more goods are sold when more people are employed. Workers are able to demand wage increases, thereby driving up costs. In theory, a wage-price spiral would result from dramatically low unemployment: labor's demand for higher wages forces business to raise prices to cover the higher cost of labor; the higher prices of goods force workers to demand even higher wages, and so on. But this theory, that low unemployment always causes inflation, does not have to be the case.

With cooperation among unions, employers' associations, and the government, unemployment in Sweden exceeded 3% *only three times* from 1951 to 1991, without causing significant inflation. The agreement was that real wages were increased annually at the rate of one-half percent below the national average rate of labor productivity growth. This meant that if workers increased their productivity by 3%, they would receive a raise of 2.5%, and employers would keep the rest. This formula insured that workers benefited from increases in productivity but also guaranteed that wages did not increase too quickly, thus keeping inflation in check.[2] In other words, wages were voluntarily limited by labor unions so that they wouldn't increase faster than productivity, keeping inflationary pressures down despite full employment and the accompanying power that a tight labor market gives to unions. As a result, workers did not need to strike to force pay increases, and workers and employers were cooperative rather than antagonistic—both labor and capital had a direct incentive to increase productivity since both groups benefited. Following this pattern of compromise, Sweden had full employment without spiraling inflation for 40 years (1951-1991) and laborers received a substantial share of the benefits from economic growth, equalizing incomes to a significant degree. Sweden's experiences call into question both the theory that equality and growth aren't compatible, as well as the assumption that full employment and low inflation aren't possible. Sweden offers a striking contrast to the U.S. system where productivity increases by laborers often do not result in higher wages. For example, from 1973 to 1997, the average productivity of a U.S. worker increased by 34%, but average wages for workers actually declined by 14%. U.S. workers actually lost ground when they increased productivity!

Solidaristic Wage Policy

Another key economic policy was Sweden's *solidaristic wage policy*. This meant equal pay for equal work: all workers at all firms doing the same type of work would be paid the wages that workers in the most efficient, internationally competitive firms were paid. Wages were set nationally in a centralized bargaining process that included employers, labor unions, and the government. The equalization of wages reduced competition between workers, creating a more cooperative environment for labor and removing the inequality of less pay for comparable work. An important byproduct of this policy was that women began receiving pay equal to men. All workers then received the same annual wage increases, based on productivity growth. A provision was later added to the solidaristic wage policy to increase the wages of low-wage workers faster than the rest, to make Sweden even more equal.

Another consequence of the solidaristic wage policy was that firms experiencing rapid growth did not have to raise wages faster than other firms did. Typically, firms in growing industries (such as 1990s high-tech firms in the United States) have to pay laborers a premium in order to keep them. But because of the solidarity wage policy in Sweden, the best, most competitive firms did not have to grant additional wage increases when they were doing well, allowing them to make large profits. Meanwhile, firms experiencing hard times were not able to reduce wages. As an example, in a year with 3% average productivity growth, a firm that increased productivity by 10% would only have to raise wages by the national rate of 2.5% (one-half percent below the average rate of productivity growth). A firm with only 1% productivity growth would still have to increase wages at the same rate of 2.5%. The former firm earns excess profits, while the latter firm loses money. Thus the solidaristic wage policy caused expanding industries to do better, and contracting industries to struggle even more. The result was a reallocation of capital to profitable, expanding industries from contracting industries. The systematic elimination of the least efficient, least profitable firms, and the promotion of the most productive firms, was an explicit goal of the SAP—an attempt to encourage the best businesses with the greatest comparative advantage. And it succeeded: from 1950 to 1970, the golden age of U.S. Keynesian capitalism, Sweden's per capita GDP increased by an average of 4% per year, higher even than the U.S. growth rate of 3.5%. Sweden found that the economy's overall productivity improved as the firms that increased productivity gained excess profits, which were then pumped back into the firm, generating rapid economic growth. The unions, employers' associations, and government, working to energize the economy, supported this reallocation of capital.

An interesting point here is that declining industries were not "bailed out" by the government. If they failed, they were reabsorbed by successful industries. This harsh but pragmatic approach kept the economy growing and competitive. Instead of pouring funds into dying industries, the Swedish government promoted the investment of resources in growth industries, thereby stimulating productivity and improved competitiveness. This is one of the reasons why Sweden's economy performed successfully even with all of the restrictions on corporate behavior imposed by the SAP.

Active Labor Market Policies

Another way of maintaining full employment was via *active labor market policies*. For those who became unemployed, there were generous unemployment benefits with a time limit, training and education with a stipend, and money for relocation costs if needed. If a worker was still unemployed when the benefits ended, employment was available in short term public works projects because the Swedish government established itself as the "employer of last resort" for those workers who could not find work after a certain period of time. Unemployed Swedish workers were given money, time, training, and moving assistance to make sure they could find a good job to replace the one they lost. And if they could not find a job, they were put to work in community projects that needed attention.

Active labor market policies, along with stabilization policies, produced full employment without accelerating inflation in Sweden from 1951 to 1991, as noted above. Full employment is beneficial to any economic system: all workers remain productive, the stream of income and spending supports the economy, industry profits and invests, tax revenues support the government, which in turn supports the full employment system, resulting in a self-sustaining economy in which everyone benefits. The cooperation among labor, capital, and the government in the institution of the "middle way," and the benefits that each group received as a result of it, helps to explain the widespread support in Sweden for a social democratic model of development that is likely inconceivable to most Americans. By 1968, Sweden's system was the envy of much of the world. Swedish firms were internationally competitive, Swedish workers were among the best paid in the world, and poverty and homelessness were eliminated. But labor leaders still thought Sweden could be improved.

SWEDEN BECOMES MORE SOCIALIST:
THE LABOR OFFENSIVE, 1968-1976

Despite the relative generosity of the Swedish welfare state, labor leaders during this period decided that it was time for Sweden to become even more socialist in nature. They were dismayed at the vast profits being earned by Sweden's huge transnational corporations that in part resulted from the solidarity wage policy that controlled wage increases at the most profitable firms. The SAP believed that the vast wealth being generated for a few individuals was unfair and threatened the integrity of the system. Labor wanted to negotiate a fairer distribution of the excess profits that firms were receiving because of union wage restraint.

Furthermore, labor leaders became increasingly concerned with the boring, stressful jobs, typical in Swedish industries, that Marx would have described as alienating in nature. In keeping with the idea that all Swedes have the right to *meaningful* work, labor leaders began to push for greater labor control over the workplace. A series of strikes and work slowdowns led to concessions from employers and workers did in fact gain more control over the workplace. Factories were redesigned to be more flexible, to increase efficiency, and to give workers more control over the work process. Jobs were rotated so that no one laborer was stuck with a particularly dull task for too long a period. The most repetitive jobs were mechanized and workers were retrained for more highly skilled work. Workers also gained more control over job security and promotion. Thus Swedish workers were able to avoid many of the negative consequences of deskilling that Marx saw as an inevitable part of capitalism.

During this period, the SAP also increased the benefits provided to Swedish citizens. Employees were given the right to take educational leaves to upgrade their skills or change professions, health benefits and industrial safety measures were expanded, and the government instituted new programs to promote gender equality. In 1976 the SAP also began to move more explicitly towards traditional socialism during this period through the institution of *wage earner funds*: employee investment funds that were to be funded by taxes on corporate profits. The SAP intended the funds to be used to buy up shares of companies, so workers could gradually gain a voice in all business decisions. Once labor leaders became owners, they would sit on corporate boards and directly influence corporate decision-making. Laborers could then keep firms from moving overseas, or downsizing the workforce unnecessarily. The funds would also inject Swedish firms with new capital for investment, and gradually generate a more equitable distribution of ownership and wealth, as workers became part owners, and eventually majority owners, in all large Swedish firms. The idea was that the workers in each firm would control how it was run, thus differentiating the Swedish approach from that of the Soviet Union, where a centralized government bureaucracy controlled the direction of all firms. Swedish economist G. Adler-Karlsson eloquently stated the ideals behind the push for wage earner funds:

> Let us look upon our capitalists in the same way as we have looked upon our kings in Scandinavia. A hundred years ago a Scandinavian king carried a lot of power. Fifty years ago he still had considerable power. According to our constitutions the king still has equally as much formal power as a hundred years ago, but today he is in fact powerless. We have done this without dangerous and disruptive internal fights. Let us in the same manner avoid the even more dangerous contests that are unavoidable if we enter the road of formal socialization. Let us instead strip and divest our present capitalists of one after another of their ownership functions. Let us give them a new dress, but one similar to that of the famous emperor in Hans Christian Andersen's tale. After a few decades they will then remain, perhaps formally as kings but in reality as naked symbols of a passed and inferior development stage. (Adler-Karlsson 1970, 95-6)

Thus the SAP pushed for the gradual transition from highly regulated private ownership to a socialization of the means of production in the hands of the working class—a peaceful transition to socialism. As one can tell from Adler-Karlsson's statement, the SAP believed that socializing the means of production would lead to a superior society. But it was not to be. Wage earner funds were controversial even within the SAP, and they were never fully instituted. Nevertheless, the SAP was able to extend the welfare state during this period, as noted above.

One reason for the SAP's failure to fully implement wage earner funds was that their campaign came at a time when the world was facing a global recession. The oil crisis of 1973 began a period of worldwide economic instability that would change the economic landscape of many industrialized nations. Sweden in particular suffered, because it was totally dependent on imported oil as its energy source. Inflation reached 10% in 1974, unemployment increased, and capital experienced rapidly rising costs in a highly regulated system that limited the ability of a firm to escape these high costs. This is when profound economic, political and welfare changes began to take place, resulting in what some have termed "the decline of the Swedish model."

CAPITAL'S OFFENSIVE, 1976-1994

The economic difficulties of the early 1970s caused Swedish voters to oust the SAP and elect a center-right government that was more conservative, and more sympathetic to industry. This ushered in an era in which big corporations successfully fought to roll back taxes and the welfare state. The rise of Sweden's business interests and the subsequent decline of the power of labor unions parallels the experiences of the United States as well as other developed nations with the advent of globalization. In essence, globalization erodes the power of labor, because instead of paying organized laborers higher wages at home, businesses can move to countries where wages are low and where labor unions are suppressed. As a result we see employers worldwide pursuing a race to the bottom, seeking out the lowest wages and the least organized labor, just as Marx predicted would occur under unregulated capitalism.

The erosion of the Swedish system began in the early 1980s when employers, with the support of the conservative government, abandoned the practice of centralized bargaining with labor that had been in existence since 1938. Instead, they turned to bargaining individually with their labor unions, undermining the solidaristic wage policy that had been a cornerstone of Swedish social democracy. The "divide and conquer" strategy was somewhat successful. With such a vital element of the system disempowered, corporations excluded workers more and more from the decision-making process, and increasingly moved operations overseas.

The center-right government also worked to cut taxes and decrease government spending and control over the economy. For example, the investment tax credit system, which gave businesses incentives to invest during recessions, was abolished. Corporations were now free to invest whenever they wished without tax penalties. But an even more significant change was the deregulation of capital markets in the 1980s, as Swedish firms were allowed to invest abroad instead of just at home, and funds could be moved freely internationally for the first time in many years. The chief result of the new-found ability of capital to invest wherever it wanted, along with tax cuts that increased the amount of money at capital's disposal, was to create a boom in the assets market. Money flowed rapidly into real estate, art, and other speculative, non-productive assets, resulting in huge price increases for these assets—a speculative boom. Unfortunately, as spending increased but productivity did not, an overheated economy resulted, generating inflation as high as 10.5% in 1990. Gregg Olsen describes the debacle that followed:

> The Swedish credit market…was rapidly deregulated throughout the 1980s. By the end of the decade, Sweden's long-standing system of controls over foreign investment and exchange and the financial sector were effectively eliminated. Finance houses proliferated during this period, and money flooded into office buildings and real estate, both in Sweden and abroad. However, the speculative boom ended in short order. The Swedish credit system foundered by the end of 1991, forcing the government to divert tax revenues to bail out several of its major banks at a cost of 3% of GDP. The near collapse of the key banks and insurance companies that comprise the financial industry helped to bring the international recession to Sweden. (Olsen 1999, 241ff)

Readers may note the uncanny similarity to the U.S. financial crisis of 2007-2009.

As a result of the collapse of the speculative boom, many assets became worthless, leading to large financial losses for many banks and businesses. Sweden's central bank responded to the inflation of the late 1980s with tight money policies, generating huge increases in interest rates to rein it in. Real interest rates reached an incredible 14% in 1992, leading to significantly higher unemployment, as consumer spending dropped and business investment collapsed. The combination of high interest rates, the bursting of the speculative bubble of the 1980s, and an international recession all during the same period proved devastating. In 1991, the Swedish economy entered its deepest recession since the Great Depression, with unemployment reaching 8%.

However, despite the rise of corporate power, some aspects of the government's solution to the financial crisis of the early 1990s proved that social democratic principles were still alive. Like U.S. banks during the financial crisis of 2007-2009, Swedish banks had large amounts of worthless, toxic assets. To shore up the financial system and to prevent the crisis from worsening, the Swedish government had no choice but to bail out banks. Nevertheless, the Swedish government demanded that taxpayers be granted something in return for the bailout: an ownership stake in the banks receiving government money. This imposed direct costs on the bank owners and insured that banks had strong incentives to insure that such failures never happened again. The Swedish government poured an amount equal to 3% of GDP into the financial system (roughly the same percentage of GDP the United States government used to bail out banks in 2008-9) in exchange for equity. At one point, the government controlled more than 20% of the banking system. No such conditions were imposed on U.S. banks. Once the economy recovered, the Swedish government recouped the bailout funds when it sold off the equity.

A major goal of the conservatives who ruled Sweden from 1976-1982 and 1991-1994 was to reduce the size of the Swedish welfare state, by reducing taxes and cutting government spending on social programs. They reduced the top tax rate from 85% to 50%, extended sales taxes to make up revenue, and reduced but did not eliminate benefits for parental leave, health and dental care, housing, unemployment, retirement, and sick leave. These policy changes helped to produce a doubling of the poverty rate in Sweden from 1978 to 1992, although the Swedish poverty rate remained the lowest in the world. Sweden also experienced the inevitable decrease in equality in all areas—the rich grew richer while the poor grew poorer, wage inequality between men and women increased, and opportunities were no longer as equal. The "fare well" state was under attack.

Even more drastic changes in the welfare state were enacted during the 1991-1993 recession. The new center-right government, elected in 1991, instituted corporate welfare programs (subsidies and tax breaks for corporations), and privatized education, child-care, and health care in some cases. Prior to this time, Swedes had widely accepted the idea that benefits should be universal, and not subject to the inequities of the market (in other words, they should not be treated like commodities), so these changes marked a significant departure in the nature of Sweden's welfare state. Nevertheless, much of the Swedish welfare state remained in place and the system still guaranteed a high degree of equality. For example, the voucher system in education gave all Swedish citizens enough funding to attend excellent public schools, though wealthier citizens were able to use vouchers and their own money to purchase a more expensive private education. The allowance of private health care spending worked in a similar fashion: all citizens were guaranteed excellent public care, but the wealthy were able to purchase more expensive private health care if they wished.

In 1994 voters rejected the conservative government because of its failure to improve Sweden's economic performance and returned the SAP to power, signaling a renewed commitment to social democracy. The partial erosion of the welfare state in Sweden led some conservative commentators to talk about the "end of the Swedish model." However, as we will see below, Sweden retains a vast government sector that still safeguards the social and economic rights of its citizens. And overall, Sweden's recent experiences are not unique: the Swedes faced the same hardships that all developed countries faced beginning in the early 1970s.

Sweden's Economic Performance Since 1970

In general, the economic performance of Sweden deteriorated after 1970 due to a number of factors, including globalization, industrial decline, and the aging of the population. With the advent of increased global competition, traditional manufacturing industries that Sweden specialized in, such as cars and household durable goods, faced more competitive markets. Furthermore, Sweden's huge industrial giants were unable to adjust and move out of declining sectors and into rising sectors of the global economy, much as the rust belt industries in the United States had trouble adjusting. Some industries even gave up producing in Sweden and moved operations to less costly locations in the Third World.

Sweden also faced an aging population, which meant fewer working people supporting more and more elderly retirees. By the end of the 1990s, Sweden had the largest proportion of seniors in the world. (Olsen 1999) A natural byproduct of these demographic changes was a less productive economy. The United States will soon be facing a similar problem in the years ahead as the baby boomers—those born between 1946 and 1964—retire in larger and larger numbers.

These forces—global competition in traditional manufacturing, the flight of transnational corporations to the developing world, and the aging of the population—have presented problems throughout the developed world. For instance, both Sweden and the United States experienced slower economic growth and a more unequal distribution of income since 1970. Although Sweden faced higher levels of unemployment and stagnation in the 1990s, while the U.S. economy experienced relatively more economic growth, Sweden's average real economic growth rate from 1967 to 1996 was 2.1%, while the real growth rate in the United States was 2.5%.

Conservative commentators argue that the generous benefits of the Swedish welfare state may have also contributed to the difficulties in staying competitive in the global marketplace, although the evidence on this issue is mixed. Sweden's welfare state expanded dramatically after World War II, yet as noted above, Sweden's average real economic growth rate from 1950 to 1970 was 4%, a half a percentage point higher than the U.S. average real rate of growth over the same period. Given this fact, there is clearly no reason to think that the welfare state is inherently inefficient or that it constrains economic growth. In actuality, it was when the welfare state was eroded and markets deregulated that Sweden's economic performance began to decline significantly, a trend we also saw in the United States in the 1970s and 1980s.

Sweden's economy has rebounded since 1993, and now features one of the most dynamic technology sectors in the world. This rebound can be attributed to some modest tinkering of the Swedish approach to economic policy to "mend it, not end it." The Swedish government adjusted labor laws, business regulations, and tax policies, and it reduced federal budget deficits, freeing up funds for investment. These reforms, when combined with a highly educated, hard-working, tech-savvy work force, and extensive, modernized infrastructure, attracted numerous information technology firms beginning in the mid-1990s. Even with its extensive welfare state and high taxes, Sweden's business environment was ranked 3rd or 4th most competitive in the world from 2004 to 2010 by the decidedly pro-capitalist World Economic Forum, meaning that it was one of the best places in the world in which to do business. In fact, Sweden's extensive welfare state proved instrumental in helping Sweden adjust to global realities. Workers and entrepreneurs were willing to take risks, trying new jobs and forming new businesses because they knew that the welfare state would support them if they failed. Extensive training and education programs meant that Sweden's workers had the latest skills. Family-friendly policies freed more people for work, especially women, allowing businesses to tap a larger pool of productive people. Most importantly, the welfare state provided security and stability, helping the economy to weather shocks and promoting a safe environment for long term business investment. Thus, it appears that Sweden has weathered the storm and adapted into a nimble, internationally competitive country specializing in high tech and biotechnology.

The Swedish Welfare State Since 1994

Since 1994, Swedish governments have pursued a less regulated form of capitalism. Even when the SAP has been in power, as recently as 2006, it too largely pursued a market-based agenda. The pursuit of these policies on the part of all political parties in Sweden is strikingly similar to political developments in England and the United States, where conservative groups pushed the economy in a free-market direction, formerly liberal groups (Democrats in the United States, the Labor Party in England, the SAP in Sweden) turned to a moderate market-based approach, and organized labor ceased to be as powerful a voice in national politics.

As in the United States, Sweden is dominated by huge transnational corporations (TNCs). Industrial concentration in Sweden is extremely high (a small number of large firms dominate the economy), in part because of the solidaristic wage policy that created more profitable conditions for large, efficient, export-oriented companies. As these companies increased in size and power, they pushed for a deregulated market approach to the economy, along with membership in the European Union so that they would have even more mobility and more markets in which to operate. Swedish TNCs now attack any form of government regulation in the popular press, criticizing the "public sector," the "welfare state," and "collectivism," while supporting the market economy, which supposedly generates a "free and good society." Sweden's CEOs now regularly threaten to relocate outside of Sweden unless the government creates a more business-friendly environment for them. And many businesses are carrying out these threats. Despite being profitable, Volvo closed its taxpayer-financed plants that experimented with worker autonomy and a more humane workplace, moved some operations overseas, and then sold out to Ford (after which it was sold to a Chinese company).

Meanwhile, as TNCs offer a united front in favor of unregulated markets, Swedish labor unions fight amongst themselves, and the SAP is no longer directly associated with the labor movement. The welfare state is largely intact, shored up by the return of the SAP to power from 1994 to 2006, but industrial relations between employers and unions have been dramatically altered, and the new government's ability to pursue equality and stability is, in the words of Gregg Olsen, "severely circumscribed in a neo-liberal (*laissez-faire*) environment dominated by TNCs and global financial markets." (Olsen, 1996, 16) But Sweden remains committed to a high degree of equality and to collective decision-making, with the participation of labor, capital, and the government in major decisions.

Is the Swedish version of social democracy in danger of being replaced finally by another bustling, increasingly unequal capitalist state? This is not at all likely. The SAP, and its coalition partner, the Greens, were only narrowly defeated in 2006 by a center-right coalition led by the Moderate Party, but the SAP continues to be the largest political party in Sweden. Even out of power, with the SAP enjoying broad-based support and with labor unions still relatively powerful, the "Swedish model" will be in place for the foreseeable future, albeit in a somewhat less progressive form than its 1970s incarnation.

CONCLUSION: THE CASE FOR SWEDISH SOCIAL DEMOCRACY

Despite the recent erosion in some areas of the welfare state, Swedish social democracy remains intact, and there is no denying the effectiveness of the Swedish model over the last 70 years. Ultimately, Sweden's system for most of the past century has been, and still is, based on the following general goals and principles:

1. **Economic development and efficiency.** In order to have a prosperous society, the economy must function efficiently, and in a worker-friendly manner. This means cooperative management of the economy to serve the needs of society, but not necessarily government control of the entire economy. Cooperation between labor and capital can increase efficiency and productivity, resulting in fewer strikes, less litigation, more rapid technological change, and innovative forms of work organization.

2. **Economic well-being and security for all.** The benefits of prosperity should be shared with all citizens. This can only be accomplished with the de-commodification of all basic necessities. Those who fall on hard times should be given support and opportunities.

3. **Solidarity.** Individuals are members of a community, not only with rights but with obligations to that community as well. A society based on mutual cooperation is preferable to one based on unmitigated competition.

4. **Universality and equality.** Most Swedes rely on the same network of services and participate in deciding how the local government

234 INTRODUCTION TO POLITICAL ECONOMY

operates these services. This network gives everyone a stake in the system as well as a voice. The provision of a wide range of services is a buffer against the predatory nature of an unregulated market system, while local control over services is a buffer against an overly controlling or inefficient national bureaucracy. This builds both equality and community.

5. **Democracy and cooperation.** Every society needs rules, which should be determined by the people themselves, and not unduly influenced by money. True democracy means that workers should have input into management decisions as well as political decisions, otherwise society degenerates into a barbaric system in which only the wealthiest and most aggressive prosper, and where workers are exploited. Firms influence the direction of the economy, as do labor unions and community groups. These groups must work together and compromise for the economy to work effectively.

6. **Education and access to information.** In order for a democratic society to work, all citizens need to be well educated and informed. One measure taken by the Swedes is public control of some of the media in order to insure an unbiased flow of information. A number of Swedish radio and television stations are run by the Swedish Broadcasting Corporation and contain no commercials. Programming emphasizes education and information in addition to entertainment.

7. **Pragmatism.** The SAP is remarkably free of dogmatism, and has shown itself to be quite flexible. The goal is to establish a society that benefits all people, and if this can be achieved without worker control of the means of production, then the SAP accepts that. On the other hand, the SAP refuses to accept the social costs associated with unregulated capitalism.

In Sweden, social democracy has resulted in an economy that is remarkably prosperous, and one that has the least poverty, the most equitable income distribution, and, proportionally, the highest levels of spending on health and education in the developed world.

Further, Sweden succeeded in Keynesian stabilization policy and the pursuit of full employment far better than any other developed country. From 1950 to 1991, a period of 42 years, Sweden's unemployment rate only exceeded 3% a total of three times, whereas U.S. unemployment exceeded that level 38 times. Sweden's average rate of unemployment, even including the deep recession of 1991-1993, was kept relatively low when compared with other European and developed (OECD) countries, as Table 1 indicates. Table 1 also indicates that Sweden had a somewhat higher unemployment rate than the U.S. from 1995-2008, although many economists note that this is misleading due to the extremely high rate of underemployment (people working fewer hours than they want to and performing work below their skill level) in the United States.

Table 1. Average Unemployment Rates for Sweden, the U.S. and OECD Countries, 1960-1994 and 1995-2008.

Country or Group of Countries	Average Rate of Unemployment 1960-1994	Average Rate of Unemployment 1995-2008
Sweden	2.4%	7.2%
All OECD countries	5.2%	6.6%
United States	6.0%	5.1%

Source: Olsen 1999 and OECD Stat, http://stats.oecd.org/Index.aspx.

Sweden was able to maintain full employment between 1960 and 1991 because of the following factors: 1) wage restraint on the part of labor, as part of the nationwide collective bargaining agreement; 2) an unemployment benefit system with a fixed duration of benefits, a wide range of labor-market programs to promote the acquisition of skills, and strict work requirements; 3) an active labor-market policy in which the government creates jobs through public works and employment subsidies, provides training, assists people in finding jobs and moves them to areas where there are jobs (there is a nationwide labor-market exchange which matches job seekers with jobs).

During this period, Sweden demonstrated conclusively that there is no reason for a country to live with a high "natural" rate of unemployment in order to have price stability. As Swedish economist Rudolf Meidner stated, "There is no such thing as a natural rate of unemployment. The level of employment and unemployment is significantly influenced by what the government does. It is a result of economic policies...Price stability and full employment are not incompatible goals." (Quoted in Silverman 1998, 86) Sweden's inflation rate averaged 6.4% from 1961 to 1994, 33% higher than the U.S. average inflation rate of 4.8% over the same period, but the average unemployment rate in

Table 2. Rights of a Swedish Citizen vs. Rights of a U.S. Citizen

	SWEDEN	UNITED STATES
PARENTAL LEAVE	All parents have the right to stay home and care for an infant for up to one full year per child at 90% of normal salary. All parents also receive a child allowance to cover the costs of raising children.	All parents have the right to six weeks of unpaid leave to care for a newborn child. Some parents receive monetary assistance for a limited period of time if they are very poor.
VACATIONS	*All* workers get at least five weeks of paid vacation per year plus extensive sick leave benefits.	U.S. workers *may* get at least two weeks of unpaid vacation per year *if* they are permanent employees; there are no mandatory vacations for temporary employees, and no one is guaranteed sick leave. Permanent employees at good firms usually get 2 weeks of paid vacation.
HEALTH CARE	All citizens receive high-quality health and dental care, with modest co-payments up to a maximum yearly payment. Care is generally so good that many of the wealthy use public health care.	Medicare and Medicaid provide health insurance to the elderly and very poor. Many workers receive health insurance through their employer, but in 2009 over 46 million Americans, including over 8 million children and many of the working poor, had no health insurance.
EMPLOYMENT	The Swedish government believes that every citizen has the right to meaningful work. Unemployed workers receive unemployment benefits, retraining, or a job in a public works project.	*Some* of the unemployed receive up to 6 months of unemployment benefits and job search assistance. After six months, benefits are usually cut off.

	SWEDEN	UNITED STATES
JOB TRAINING	Free training is provided to all citizens who desire it. Those undergoing training receive a stipend from the government.	Some training programs exist, but they are limited in nature, and usually only for the poor. Trainees do not usually receive a stipend.
EDUCATION	Free education is provided (via vouchers) for everyone at all levels, including college, vocational and adult education (for those people who want to explore new careers). Adult students receive time off from work and a stipend. The quality of education is so universally high, that it is not uncommon for the children of the wealthy to attend public schools.	Free primary and secondary education is available to all, with the quality varying widely depending on where one lives. People living in a poorer school district generally receive an inferior education. Some limited funding is available for college students, but college is often beyond the reach of the poor and the lower middle class. What funding is available is usually in the form of loans, creating a long-term debt for most.
SOCIAL SECURITY	All Swedish citizens receive a pension from the state, which pays people at least 75% of what they earned when they were working, or a guaranteed minimum amount if they did not work.	Most U.S. citizens receive social security benefits, but often the payments are not enough to live on.
HOUSING	If Swedish citizens cannot afford a house, they are given a housing subsidy. Sweden does not have a problem with homelessness due to the success of their housing and anti-poverty programs, and they have no slums.	Some U.S. citizens receive housing subsidies or a spot in public housing. But many citizens do not qualify for these benefits, and the U.S. has a significant number of homeless people. Every major U.S. city has slums.

the United States was *150%* higher than Sweden's unemployment rate.

Despite the existence of extensive benefits for those who do not work, Sweden has the highest labor participation rate in the world. Whereas mainstream economists predict that generous welfare benefits provide a disincentive to work, the Swedish experience demonstrates that people *want* to be productive (recall Veblen's idea of the instinct of workmanship), and that if work is not drudgery, people will work willingly and enthusiastically.

Sweden's experiences with economic growth are similar to those of the United States, with relatively high rates of growth for much of the 1870-1970 period and slower growth since 1970. The build-up of the welfare state in Sweden was quite compatible with economic growth. The benefits of social peace and stability along with public investment in infrastructure and human capital more than offset the high taxes and the restraints on businesses. The cooperative nature of economic decision-making, with businesses, labor unions, and the government all participating, insured that economic growth could occur in a socially responsible context.

Meanwhile, Sweden also succeeded in creating one of the most peaceful, crime-free, egalitarian societies in the world. It de-commodified many aspects of the market system, thereby insuring that all citizens have the right to a good education, housing, health care, and a job. As Table 2 indicates, the rights of a Swedish citizen are much more extensive than the rights of an American citizen. If you came from an average family, which society do you think would be the most pleasant one to live in?

Figure 1. Social Expenditure and Taxes as % of GDP, 2005 and 2007-8

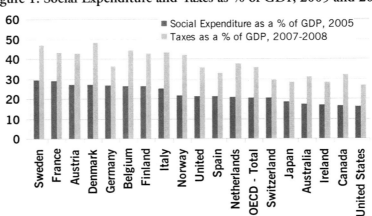

Source: OECD Social Expenditure Database, stats.oecd.org.

Because of its extensive system of benefits and rights, proportionally Sweden has the largest government sector in the world. The Swedes believe this to be necessary to control aspects of life that should not be left to the market. As Figure 1 indicates, Sweden devotes the largest percentage of GDP in the world to social expenditures (poverty, inequality, health, social security, family, unemployment, labor, housing, and other programs), which it pays for with the world's second-highest tax rate. Sweden and the other social democracies of Europe have the largest proportional governments, while the United States, United Kingdom, and Japan have among the smallest governments. This is a clear indication of the economic philosophies of the different countries. Sweden, Denmark, France and the Netherlands, to name a few, use government programs to insure that all citizens have the right to a decent standard of living and real opportunities. The United States, the United Kingdom, and Japan do

Figure 2. Percentage of People and Children Living in Poverty, mid-2000s

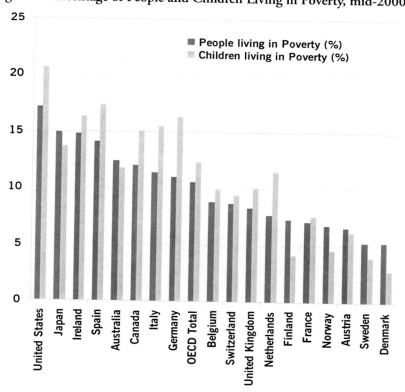

Source: OECD Social Expenditure Database, stats.oecd.org.

have substantial governments, but these countries leave much more up to the market than does Sweden.

As Figure 2 shows, through extensive spending on education, labor, and social programs, Sweden has almost eliminated poverty. Sweden's large government is accompanied by the 2nd lowest poverty rate in the world, a byproduct of its highly regulated economy and generous allocation of rights. Meanwhile, the United States has one of the smallest governments in the world, but also the highest poverty rate and highest child poverty rate of all developed countries. Many, if not most, poor people in the United States are not able to lift themselves out of poverty through their own efforts, and often those who are more privileged characterize them as lazy or incompetent. The reality is that most poor people want to work, but do not have the necessary resources (education, training, a car, work clothes, child care, or opportunities) available to them that would allow them to find self-sustaining employment. Together, Figures 1 and 2 conclusively demonstrate that a country can eliminate poverty if it is willing to spend the money, but without such intervention, many people will remain poor.

In addition to eliminating more poverty than any other country, Sweden has one of the most egalitarian societies in terms of income distribution. Its highly progressive tax and transfer system insures that those who have the most contribute the most, and those who have the least are guaranteed a decent income. Figure 3 shows how much more equal Sweden is than the United States as a result of its different tax and transfer system. The bottom 80% of

Figure 3. Inequality (Gini Coefficient), Mid-2000s

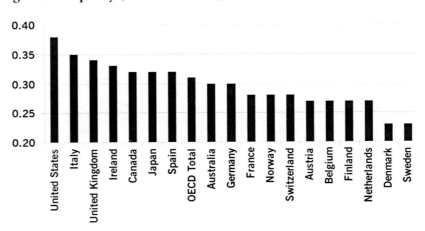

Source: OECD Social Expenditure Database, stats.oecd.org.

the population does much better in Sweden than in the United States. Sweden's highly progressive tax system contains within it a value judgment about different kinds of consumption based on the ideas of Thorstein Veblen. It is assumed that the consumption of basic necessities by all people is more important than the consumption of additional conspicuous luxury goods by the wealthy. In contrast, most U.S. politicians argue that the wealthy have the right to spend all their money as they see fit. Many conservative politicians in the United States even want to create a flat tax, where the rich and the poor would pay the same marginal tax rate. In the United States, with the central position given to individual choice in consumption decisions, there is no stigma attached to a rich person spending $10 million for a yacht, but politicians who propose that society has a responsibility to spend an equivalent amount on health insurance for 2,000 uninsured children are criticized for advocating big government. Most political economists find this U.S. method of allocating resources immoral and barbaric.

Sweden's center-right government eliminated the country's high inheritance tax in 2005, but the tax code is still highly redistributive. The government levies an annual wealth tax of 1.5% on the net worth of any sin-

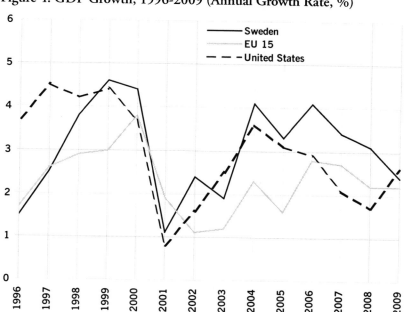

Figure 4. GDP Growth, 1996-2009 (Annual Growth Rate, %)

Source: OECD Social Expenditure Database, stats.oecd.org.

gle-person household above 1.5 million kroner (or about $200,000), and above 3 million kroner for couples. Explicit in such tax policies, which help reduce incomes at the top, is the egalitarian idea that everyone should start life at a reasonably similar level. Most Swedes agree that people with money should not be able to live on the dividends coming from an inheritance simply because their ancestors made a fortune. True equality of opportunity means that all people have equal access to education and that even the children of the rich should have work. Furthermore, in order to avoid alienation, that work should be meaningful and workers must have some control over the workplace.

Another Swedish practice that coincides with Veblen's ideas is their policy of restricting advertising while simultaneously channeling funds into productive areas such as research and development. As noted above, the Swedish Broadcasting Corporation runs much of the television and radio programming, which it airs commercial-free. Newspapers receive state subsidies so they are not entirely dependent on ads. Again, Swedes make a value judgment about economic activity: advertising is wasteful and commercial impulses distort the content of television and newspapers. While the U.S. media resists "restrictions" on programming, most Swedes believe the commercial nature of the media in the United States is much more restrictive, and not in society's best interests. Can we really depend on the huge corporations that own the media to present a balanced version of the news? If so, then why haven't we all heard more about the success of Sweden's economic system?

It is often said that the United States is the land of opportunity; yet most working people do not have an equal opportunity to succeed because they lack access to equal education and training. In Sweden, all citizens have access to a high quality education. The United States is spoken of as the land of the free because we have few government regulations over the marketplace. This gives us the freedom to succeed and to keep most of the money we make. We also have the freedom to work wherever we want—but for millions this means working at jobs that don't pay a living wage. This is, of course, a freedom much admired by some Swedes: the corporate bosses.

Swedish economists also question whether the United States is truly prosperous in any meaningful sense. Despite a very large GDP, should the United States be boasting about a level of prosperity that fails to provide crucial necessities like health insurance for over 30 million people, that is benefiting only a small percentage of the population, and that was built on the low wages of workers with declining, or no benefits?

Shouldn't U.S. citizens be concerned that despite this supposed prosperity, millions of people in the United States, including many children, are condemned to poverty, and over two million mostly poor people are in prison or jail? The debtors' prisons of the 1800s are reviled in history books, but is imprisoning poor, desperate people who resort to crime really so different? Is the purpose of an economy to generate billions for Bill Gates or to generate the greatest standard of living for all that belong to that society? In all of these ways and more, the social democracy of Sweden serves most people better than the (largely) unregulated capitalism of the United States.

And, in perhaps the ultimate irony, the United States doesn't always generate better economic growth than Sweden with its relatively unregulated market system. As Figure 4 demonstrates, once Sweden adjusted its policies after its economic crisis of the early 1990s, it experienced more rapid GDP growth than the United States and other European countries.

Thus the experiences of Sweden demonstrate the possibility of a "Middle Way" between unregulated capitalism and command communism: social democracy. Sweden may not be a paradise on Earth. Sweden has problems just like all other countries. Swedish citizens sometimes complain about their high taxes and their sometimes-inefficient government. But building on the ideas of Marx, Keynes and Veblen, Sweden proved that a country can maintain full employment, be efficient and productive, and give every citizen the right to decent levels of food, clothing, health care, to a job, and to some control over their lives. Ultimately, each country must decide what things to leave up to the market and what things should be determined by the collective decisions of all citizens. In the United States, most things are allocated based on how much money a person has, which gives unprecedented levels of freedom and choice to the very wealthy, but leaves much of the population without the basic necessities of life.

Perhaps, as most Americans tend to believe, the United States is the land of the free. But this might not be the case if your definition of a "free people" is one that includes everyone. To us, based on what we have argued in this chapter, because their nation's social democracy provides everyone with such benefits as free education, excellent, low-cost health care, and civilized working conditions, the Swedes have a much stronger claim than do Americans that they are a truly free people.

SUGGESTIONS FOR FURTHER READING

Childs, Marquis. 1936. *The Middle Way.* New Haven: Yale University Press.

Korpi, Walter. 2000. "Welfare States, Economic Growth, and Scholarly Objectivity." *Challenge*, vol. 43, no. 2, pp. 49-66.

Kuhnle, Stein. 1998. "The Nordic Approach to General Welfare." http://www.nnn.se/intro/approach.htm.

Rosser, J. Barkley and Marina V. Rosser. 2004. "Sweden: Crisis and Reform of the Social Market Welfare State." Chapter 8 in *Comparative Economics in a Transforming World Economy*. Cambridge, Mass.: MIT Press.

10
The Mondragón Cooperative: A Path to Worker Democracy

The middle road taken in Sweden and in other parts of Northern Europe exemplifies one way that people have used the ideas of political economists to civilize the roughest edges of modern capitalism. In these cases, nation-wide efforts were possible because of the long-term support of the majority of the population. Yet the need to modify the most egregious consequences of capitalism has not always produced national responses. In fact, one of the best known and most successful of such efforts emerged in the 1940s in a province in the Basque Country in northern Spain. As it grew and began to gain attention, it became known as the "Mondragón Cooperative," or simply as "Mondragón." In 1991, reflecting changes in Mondragón's structure and operations, its worker members gave it the name "*Mondragón Corporación Cooperativa*" (Mondragón Cooperative Corporation, or MCC). As an integrated system of over 250 companies, about half of which are cooperatives, MCC is the seventh largest firm in Spain and currently employs over 90,000 people, almost double the number from just a decade ago. This remarkable growth reflects most directly the growth in MCC's international operations, a matter we describe in greater detail below.

In the United States, outside of the agricultural sector and small urban food co-ops, cooperatives have never gained much popularity. However, they have played a larger role in many European societies since the early 1800s. Robert Owen, one of the early "utopian socialists" who influenced

---

*   This chapter began as an essay written by a Bucknell student, Alan Snyder ('07), under the direction of Geoffrey Schneider. Since then it has been revised, updated and expanded. We appreciate Alan's permission to use his work in this edition.

Marx and many others, launched the cooperative movement in 1811 in New Lanark, Scotland, with his first "Village of Cooperation." That experiment, aimed at relieving the burden of the growing legion of wage slaves in Britain, had some successes but failed after two decades. The great majority of communes and cooperatives established in the United States and in Europe by "Owenites" and others sympathetic to such ideas suffered similar fates. Nevertheless, the cooperative movement in Europe never completely died, and today many different kinds of co-ops are thriving and becoming increasingly important to the modern European economy. According to Ricardo Lotti, et al.:

> Although co-ops tend to operate with little fanfare and are often unrecognized by the financial press, they account for 83 percent of Dutch agricultural production, 55 percent of agricultural production in Italy, more than 50 percent of banking services in France, and 21 percent of Spanish health care. In 2004, sales figures included 9 billion Dutch guilders ($11 billion) each for Coop and Coop Norden (consumer cooperatives in Switzerland and Scandinavia), more than 30 billion Dutch guilders ($36 billion) each for Edeka and ITM Enterprises (retailer co-ops in Germany and France, respectively) and 40 billion Dutch guilders ($48.5 billion) for the German retailer REWE Group. (Lotti 2006, 2)

There are many different kinds of co-ops. The most common are mutual life insurance societies, building societies, credit unions, and consumer co-ops. In consumer co-ops, such as the popular food co-ops in the United States, people create an organization and use their numbers to procure better prices for better products than they could afford as individuals. Producer co-ops, such as the agricultural ones in the Netherlands and Italy, and MCC, are altogether different animals. Their goal is to use the power of a large number of producers, rather than consumers, to buy inputs more cheaply than they could on their own, to coordinate their production and distribution, and to get the best price for their output. They are typically larger integrated operations, sometimes a loose affiliation of firms over a large region, sometimes more tightly coordinated firms in a particular location, or some mix of the two. José María Arizmendiarrieta, MCC's principal founder, described the MCC as the "only example of credit unions, producer co-ops and research centers that operate as one integrated functional unit." (Arizmendiarrieta 2002, 78) This characteristic of Mondragón is a principal reason for the widespread attention it has received.

In this chapter, we will take a close look at MCC because of its unique history and because of its ability—as a democratic workers' co-op—to expand dramatically in a capitalist world order while providing competitive wages, good working conditions, and extensive contributions to the local community. We will also discuss why in recent years MCC has gradually relaxed some of the cooperative ideals and principles declared by its founders almost half a century ago. It has done this in the face of the frenzied pressures of globalization, and we will want to assess the likelihood of its maintaining its historical commitment to worker democracy in the face of a capitalist free-for-all that is concerned only with the interests of its owners and managers.

ESSENTIAL PRACTICES OF A PRODUCER COOPERATIVE

By far the most fundamental difference between producer cooperatives and capitalist firms is that in the former—sometimes called "democratic firms"—workers, rather than stockholders, own the company. That is, workers and their representatives ultimately have the power to determine key decisions about the firm's operations. As an example, consider the behavior of managers of a capitalist firm experiencing increasing productivity. They will, if they can get away with it (as they have in the United States for the past two decades), distribute the consequent gains to themselves, to shareholders, or to investment projects rather than paying higher wages. In democratic firms, on the other hand, a management elected by the workers themselves would decide how to distribute such productivity gains with the single overall goal of enhancing the short- and long-term welfare of the worker-owners. In capitalist firms, workers are seen as labor power, merely one more factor of production, and will benefit from productivity gains, if at all, only as a by-product of a corporate strategy concerned ultimately with the welfare of shareholders and management. Wage-earners in almost all capitalist firms have a very limited role in shaping the firm's operating practices, whether wages, working conditions, or any other aspect of corporate decision-making, and even this role has eroded steadily for the past three decades in the face of declining union membership.

The power of workers in cooperatives most typically emerges both from open elections to choose officials and from the right to vote about how to construct and modify the essential processes and operations of their co-op. Democratic election of officials is especially important because it produces less cronyism and nepotism and tends to lead to the election of more competent officials than in traditional firms. This does not mean, of course, that

elect managers who are efficient leaders. However, coopera-
ually have the power to engage in "democratic firing" of of-
..., assuring that the majority of leadership positions are filled by
competent people. This interdependence of workers and managers tends to
create a high degree of trust between the two groups. This trust in turn reduces the need for managers to monitor employees and fosters information
exchange, thereby improving productivity.

Cooperatives typically have a compressed wage scale compared to capitalist firms, due in large measure to the fact that worker-members in cooperatives get to vote on the distribution of wages. For example, in the Mondragón
cooperatives, the lowest-paid workers receive more than comparable local
workers, while managers and more highly skilled workers receive about half
of what they could earn elsewhere. (Dow 2003, 60) Wage compression encourages higher productivity because workers receive a higher share of profits than is typical for capitalist firms. It also encourages high morale by reducing the kind of resentment and the envy that contaminates all firms to
some degree. Cooperative pay scales can also lead non-cooperative firms in
the area to compress their own wage scales in order to attract employees and
enhance their social standing. Tax authorities in the Basque region of Alto
Deba, where co-op activity is the most intense, describe the region as having
"an outstanding model of fairer economic development." (MCC,
"Cooperativas")

THE HISTORICAL ROOTS OF THE MONDRAGÓN COOPERATIVE

What is the setting in which the story of the MCC takes place? Mondragón
is a small city in the Basque Country of northern Spain—the region is called
País Vasco in Spanish, or *Euskadi* in the Basque language—with a population
of about 23,000. The Basque Country is known for its movement to separate from Spain in order to preserve the region's unique culture and language, *Euskara* (in English, simply "Basque"). Basque nationalism, coupled
with a long history of labor union activity which fostered socialist ideas,
combined to form a powerful force for an independent, locally-based cooperative form of economic development. However, since 1959, this desire for
independence has often taken violent form in the actions of ETA (in English,
"Basque Homeland and Freedom"). ETA is classified as a terrorist organization by the European Union and the United States, and has often engaged
in violent actions, including bombings. In 2006, ETA signed a peace accord
with Spain that has not altogether stopped the violence, and it remains a potential destabilizing prospect for the Basque Country and thus for MCC.

Another reminder of the area's turbulent history is the city of Guernica, made famous by Pablo Picasso's mural depicting its bombing by Nazi pilots during the Spanish Civil War (1936-39). The Nazis had joined an alliance with the fascist military rebel, Francisco Franco, whose forces overthrew the elected "Republican" government of Spain in 1939. One of the members of the Republican forces defending the elected government was the future founder of the Mondragón cooperatives, José María Arizmendiarrieta. During the war, José María, as he is typically referred to in the literature, was imprisoned; he joined the Catholic clergy upon his release. He was strongly influenced by the encyclicals of Pope Leo XIII, which stressed the importance of better working conditions, a living wage, a fairer distribution of wealth, and the amelioration of the excesses of capitalism. (Schultze 2002, 13)

In 1943, José María, assigned as a missionary to Mondragón and responding to these new ideas, opened a technical training school with the support of the townspeople. He taught his students the importance of changing the capitalist system, and that successful economic transformation would more likely emerge from the teachings of the Catholic Church than from another of his influences, Karl Marx. This mix of experience and influences led José María to the idea of cooperativism and to the conclusion that cooperatives could foster democracy more effectively than the dictatorial regimes in such self-proclaimed Marxist states as the Soviet Union. José María was no doubt aware that central to Marx's writing was a powerful advocacy of the sort of worker democracy that developed in MCC, and that Marx would have had as much contempt for bureaucratic tyrants as he had for capitalist ones.

José María also concluded that a blue-collar middle class acculturated in cooperative production would be able to bring communities together better than traditional capitalist companies. This belief is amply demonstrated in his writings, for example:

Nobody shall be slave or master of anyone, everyone shall simply work for the benefit of everyone else, and we shall have to behave differently in the way we work. (Arizmendiarrieta 2002, 10)

Cooperators should converge together on this final aim with all those who hunger and thirst for justice in the labor world. The only thing capitalist companies can offer you is more money.... An honorable person should be ashamed of being, and living like, a rich person in a world with 2,000 million undernourished people. (Arizmendiarrieta 2002, 11)

Let us consider that the enterprise ought to be a human community of activities and interests, based in private property and initiative (except in the cases where the state intervenes for the common good) instituted to provide to the society a necessary service or useful production, for which it will receive an economic payment according to the services rendered, which is distributed to its members in a just manner. (quoted in MacLeod 1997, 82-83)

In 1956, five of the students from the first graduating class of José María's technical school formed Mondragón's first cooperative. The shop, named ULGOR (an acronym of the first letters of the students' last names), specialized in the production of oil stoves. (Whyte 1999, 1) The direct connection between the technical school and the Mondragón cooperatives was one of the first innovations in the Mondragón story. The school provided an ideological grounding in cooperative principles for its graduates, nurturing values which would foster a cooperative ethos in the workplace. In addition, the school provided ingredients crucial to industrial success—managerial skills as well as training in the most updated technologies—that would serve the cooperatives well.

ULGOR attempted to make real José María's vision, and based its structure on principles that would endure in the Mondragón cooperatives: democratic decision-making, profit-sharing, wage solidarity, and community responsibility. All workers were expected to invest their own money into the cooperative enterprise in order to encourage a personal interest in the enterprise as well as provide crucial capital for the cooperative. Workers were allowed to borrow the initial investment amount so that they could join the co-op without having to wait to save for it. Some profits would be invested in the local community and some would be set aside for contingencies, but most profits would be used to expand cooperative capital. Cooperative members could only withdraw their own funds, plus accumulated profits, when they retired. This practice assured the cooperative access to a pool of capital for a long period of time while it encouraged a high level of motivation among the workers. Wage differences between highest- and lowest-paid employees were limited to emphasize solidarity and equality.

The co-op was an immediate success and was soon ready to expand. But expansion demanded additional financing, and existing banks were reluctant to lend to a cooperative enterprise. This need prompted another of José María's major innovations, the creation of a bank (*Caja Laboral Popular*, or "People's Worker Bank"), that would channel local savings directly into local economic development efforts and into new co-operatives. Over time, Caja Laboral was highly successful in these functions and thus became a key resource, both financial and managerial, for the expansion of the Mondragón cooperatives into a broad array of industries. A growing host of cooperative enterprises grew up centered around José María's technical school and Caja Laboral.

In addition to José María's ideas and innovations, and the support of Mondragón's townspeople, the cooperative had several other advantages that pushed it forward. During the years of the Franco government (1939 to 1975), the existing tariff barriers protected the cooperative from foreign competition. In its early years, the cooperative also benefited from the steady growth the Spanish economy enjoyed as a whole. Further, according to Manfred Davidmann (2):

> The Spanish government provided a good deal of support, providing from 12.5 to 20 percent of the capital required by a new cooperative, at a fixed low rate of interest….Cooperatives paid no corporation tax for the first ten years, and half the standard rate after that.

As P.L. Taylor points out, another contributing factor was that "Franco's Falangists appreciated [cooperatives'] commitment to classless production and their decision to exclude unions." (Taylor 1997, 433) Despite this crucial support in getting co-ops off the ground, the government decided not to pay pension and health benefits to co-op members, a move that members deeply resented at the time. In a twist, this ruling ultimately served MCC well because it forced the cooperatives to develop pension and health-care plans that would become, to its members, among its most attractive features. It is worth noting that, despite the government's refusal to pay pension and health benefits, the early success of MCC provides a clear example of the usefulness of protectionism and government support in nurturing an infant industry in the early stages of economic development.

With these factors working to their advantage, José María's students and others created a growing number of cooperatives throughout the Basque Country. In 1965, they formed ULARCO (which became Fagor in 1980), the first time a group of cooperatives in the region began to coordinate at least some parts of their operations among themselves. In 1969, the Eroski supermarket chain was established to assist with marketing and selling Mondragón products. Then, in the early 1970s, the cooperatives founded centers for research and for management that tapped the expertise of the technical school and the bank to foster the development of advanced technology. Over the years, these two centers have supplied skilled management staff who also valued community responsibility and cooperative principles.

Thus, by the mid-1970s, the Mondragón cooperatives had evolved into a collection of factories with a unique organizational structure, all of them run democratically. Workers invested in a cooperative when they joined it (described below), and their stake was managed by their own co-op and swelled over time with profit-sharing. The cooperative bank provided funds for investment projects and used emergency funding to help insulate the firms against downturns. The technical institute provided skilled labor and the research center worked to keep abreast of the latest technologies. The Mondragón co-ops invested in local education and infrastructure with some of their profits, but most of the funds were used to expand existing firms or construct new ones. Profit -pooling also allowed specific enterprises to survive temporary downturns. However, if a cooperative proved to be untenable in the longer term, overall employment levels were maintained by reallocating its workers to other more successful cooperatives. In short, Mondragón had created a microcosm of an entire economy, run entirely on cooperative principles and grounded in the local community.

Throughout the 1980s, the Mondragón system of cooperatives continued to grow, in the number of firms and employees and in the diversity of products. During the same period, as a direct consequence of the growing pressure of globalization, the members of the Mondragón co-ops created the *Mondragón Corporación Cooperativa*, or MCC, whose offices became the movement's central headquarters. Jesús Cantinia Cobo, until recently the MCC board chairman, succinctly ties this history to the corporation's current operations and its overall mission:

Mondragón Corporación Cooperativa is the fruit of the sound vision of a young priest, Don José María Arizmendiarrieta, as well as the solidarity and efforts of all our worker-members. Together we have been able to transform a humble factory, which in 1956 manufactured oil stoves and paraffin heaters, into the leading industrial group in the Basque Country and 7th in the ranking in Spain. MCC's mission combines the basic objectives of a business organisation competing in international markets with the use of democratic methods in its organisation and with special emphasis on job creation, the promotion of its workers in human and professional terms and a commitment to the development of its social environment. (MCC, "Who we are.")

THE "FORMATION" PROCESS

Not surprisingly, as MCC grew in complexity and size, so did its management and decision-making structure, which evolved into a complicated system of checks-and-balances, operating at two levels. One of these is the governance of the individual firms, the other the control center of the whole system. Yet, before we present the key details of that system, we need to emphasize that underlying MCC's commitment to building industrial democracy is a complex and universal socialization process—"formation"—that is perhaps the principal reason for MCC's longevity. We will quote at length from Jacquelyn Yates's (2001, 3) detailed description:

> One of the most fascinating aspects of Mondragón's story is its flexibility. The organization has almost always managed to avoid rigidity, splinter groups and intra-organizational warfare. Much depends on the *process of formation*, which socializes managers and members into the Mondragón style. Formation is a term that encompasses both formal cognitive education and moral and affective development. In addition to traditional business education, Mondragón formation helps its people to be open to change and criticism, to engage in mutual support and to balance values. The methods of instruction include traditional lectures, seminars and laboratories, but extend to experiential learning, mentoring and supportive monitoring beyond formal schooling. All associates and managers can receive formation according to their interests and talents.

And, Yates argues, this leads to a management style that is:

> [F]undamentally and philosophically unique to Mondragón, and certainly has no corresponding model in East or West. Decisions take place after intense discussion at all levels and fine-tuning of management ideas. The necessity to make profits in a free and competitive market is never far from the center of any decision, but concern with profit must be balanced by respect for the basic principles. The goal of discussion is the development of sound business decisions that are understood and supported by all members.

GOVERNANCE OF INDIVIDUAL FIRMS

A worker's day-to-day existence depends most on the *atmosphere* of the firm, and that atmosphere is shaped fundamentally by the firm's governance structure. In a Mondragón cooperative, the reigning control of an individual firm resides in the General Assembly, whose annual meetings are open to all members of the cooperative. At these meetings, members participate in a collective examination and assessment of the management of the firm during the previous year. Most importantly, members will assess the managers' decisions regarding financial matters, especially the allocation of profits, losses, and share capital, and how well they are direct-ing the remainder of the firm's operations. The counterpart in capitalist firms is, of course, the annual stockholders meeting, where all but a few major stockholders are effectively disenfranchised from having any say in what happens in the firm.

In between the annual meetings of the General Assembly, the firm's op-erations are directed by a Governing Council and a Social Council. The Governing Council is a group of up to twelve members elected at the General Assembly. Its principal functions are to select the firm's managers and over-see their activities, to carry out the admission and withdrawal of members into the cooperative, and to discipline or sanction workers if it deems doing so is important to the firm's profitable operations. The principal obligation of the Social Council, which has members from each kind of activity in the cooperative and answers to the Governing Council, is the overall welfare of the workers. The Social Council draws up proposals and makes reports on such matters as the pay scale and working conditions, often responding to members' initiatives. It thereby serves the functions of a labor union, solicit-ing input directly from workers of every type and striving to make the work environment as favorable as possible.

The power structure of an MCC cooperative can be seen in Figure 1. It shows that a worker exercises her say over the organization by electing Governing Council and Social Council members sympathetic to her inter-ests. These two councils work directly with the Management Team to make sure that the cooperative works in the best interests of its members. Workers do not vote on every decision their managers make, as that would be too un-wieldy. But because they elect the council members that hire and fire man-agers, workers' voices are crucial in determining the direction of the firm.

GOVERNANCE OF THE ENTIRE MCC SYSTEM

The MCC Congress is the equivalent of the General Assembly at the indi-vidual firms, with the important difference that Congress decisions affect the MCC as a whole. Since there are too many MCC members for all to at-tend, the individual co-ops elect about 6,000 representatives. The Congress has a plenary meeting every four years and an annual Delegates Assembly with only advisory powers. At the plenary meetings, the Congress elects a twenty-person Standing Committee that roughly parallels the Governing Council of individual cooperatives. This committee's central function is to promote and monitor the implementation of MCC policies and agreements adopted by the Congress, and to monitor and oversee ongoing operations.

Most of the members of the Standing Committee are elected by the Governing Councils of the individual co-ops, but the committee can elect up to 25% of its own members. It can also include people from outside the MCC system if they have particularly useful expertise.

The General Council is the executive branch of MCC, and it parallels the board of directors in a large, integrated capitalist firm—with the critical difference that its members are also members of individual cooperatives and are elected by the workers. The General Council selects the top management, and it plans and coordinates long-term strategies to maintain MCC as a single integrated and internationally competitive unit. As MCC has increased its foreign operations, the General Council has found it necessary to choose a group of managers with functions, and expectations for compensation, increasingly like those at the huge capitalist firms with which it competes. This particular transition at MCC has not been without conflict, as some members, and outside critics, see a higher-paid and more distant man-

Figure 1. Typical Organization of a Mondragón Cooperative

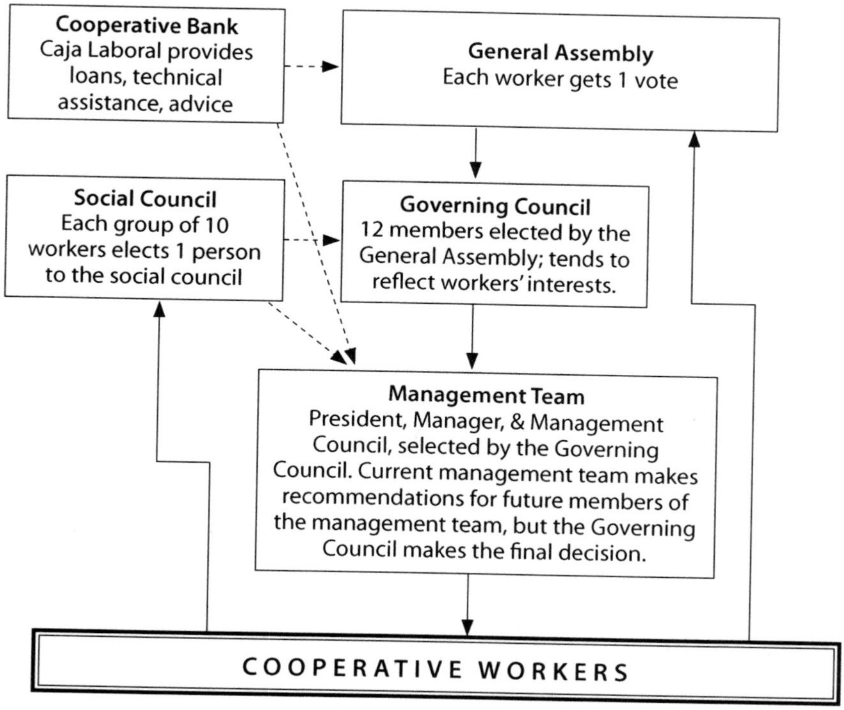

Cooperative Bank
Caja Laboral provides loans, technical assistance, advice

General Assembly
Each worker gets 1 vote

Social Council
Each group of 10 workers elects 1 person to the social council

Governing Council
12 members elected by the General Assembly; tends to reflect workers' interests.

Management Team
President, Manager, & Management Council, selected by the Governing Council. Current management team makes recommendations for future members of the management team, but the Governing Council makes the final decision.

COOPERATIVE WORKERS

agement as contradictory to cooperative principles. Nevertheless, manage-rial behavior in MCC remains decisively different from that in capitalist firms in several ways. MCC managers are running a business rather than wielding a stick for its board, and therefore expend less energy monitoring and disciplining workers. In other words, these managers and the workers are genuinely on the same side, have participated in the same formation pro-cess, and will share in the firm's success. The managers also serve at the will of the majority of the workers, in contrast to the managers of capitalist firms who, by law, must serve the bests interests of stockholders. Further, because MCC builds education and training of all employees into its structure, its line workers are more likely than their counterparts in capitalist firms to find their way into management positions.

We recognize that it is a matter of degree that defines the differences be-tween control mechanisms in cooperatives and capitalist firms, and that managers in all firms are human beings who make mistakes, who often hun-ger for authority, status, and riches, and whose principal commitments might be to loved ones, a sports team, the church, or a political party, rather than to their firm or fellow workers. Yet, the environment in an MCC co-operative stems from the collective imagination of people who believe in the possibility of an alternative to the dictatorial functioning of capitalist firms. That means that MCC workers, managers, hired experts, and all the mem-bers of the governing committees and councils are on a thoroughly different wave-length than people who run capitalist firms, or the people that work under them.

PRODUCTION AND DISTRIBUTION AT MCC

The most compelling aspect of MCC's current production and distribution is the explosive growth in its operations as it has adapted to globalized capi-talism. MCC's employment growth between 1980 and 2008 reflects the enormous growth in every part of the system. Of the current work force, 44% are based in the Basque Country, 40% in the rest of Spain, and 16% in foreign countries. Reflecting globalization, the largest increases have been in these last two areas.

This dramatic growth in MCC employment has outstripped its ability to have all new employees go through the formation process on the way to be-coming full worker-members. In fact, the proportion of its workforce that are members has declined rapidly in the past decade, and now about two-thirds are non-members, concentrated in industrial plants outside the Basque country in Spain and overseas. (Below, we will provide more details about this issue.) In the mid-1980s, the growing influence of the global economy generated a discussion at all levels of MCC about how to respond. The result was the thorough restructuring in 1991 of all enterprises into four groups: Industrial, Distribution, Research and Training, and Financial. The table below presents the current employment level in each group, and we follow with key details about each of them.

The Industrial Group. Industrial production began as, and remains, the heart of MCC. The group's 48,000 workers currently operate in seven subdivisions, and the largest three—household goods and appliances, automotive parts, and equipment and capital goods—account for about 90% of the total. MCC cooperatives often function as suppliers of components and tools for large, non-cooperative corporations, such as car and appliance manufacturers. As a major example, Batz, an MCC cooperative in the Basque region, recently set up subsidiaries in Mexico and the Czech Republic that will help it to make parts to be distributed to most automobile manufacturers around the world. Batz also plans within five years to open a plant in China to supply pedal sets and parking-brake levers for General Motors automobiles. MCC's finished products range from bicycles, fitness equipment, washing machines, and industrial dryers to office furniture and milling machines. The industrial group also carries out numerous large-scale construction projects, most notably the Sant Jordi Sports Arena, built for

Figure 2. MCC Employment, 1980-2006

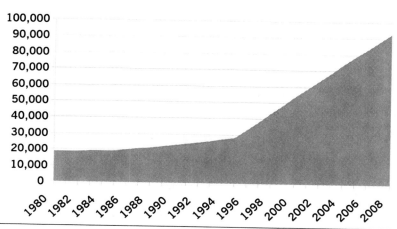

the 1992 Olympic Games in Barcelona, Spain. The following chart describes the industrial group's dramatic growth in recent years.

The decline in the industrial group's output in 2008, compared to 2006, derives from the substantial decline in orders in the last half of the year as a consequence of the international economic crisis. However, we will see that this decline was more than offset by an expanding distribution sector, especially from its acquisition of another firm.

Financial Companies within MCC. Describing the operations of the two most important financial firms, Caja Laboral and Lagun Aro, as well as firms in other sectors, underscores the core differences between their functions and those of capitalist financial firms. Caja Laboral is the largest cooperative credit union in Spain. It provides loans to MCC as well as loans at favorable rates to cooperatives outside of MCC. Of course, this bank must make a profit like any other firm, but those profits remain *inside the MCC.* As Davidmann (1996, 5) put it, "The bank backs the co-ops and the co-ops back the bank. Each needs the other for success and growth." According to Errasti et al. (2003, 550), Caja Laboral is one of the 150 most solvent financial entities in the world.

MCC, like many cooperatives, requires its employees to create individual capital accounts—a joining fee—when they become worker-members. In 2007, this fee was approximately €13,000, or $17,771, a significant amount

Figure 3. Distribution of Employment According to Activity, 2008

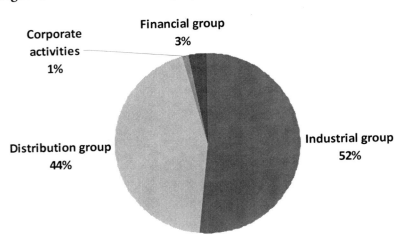

Corporate
activities
1%

Financial group
3%

Industrial group
52%

Distribution group
44%

of money, especially for those entering low-skill jobs. However, MCC will loan the fee to new members at a favorable interest rate with the member's agreement to repay it within two years. A member's capital account is essentially his or her private fund, kept in the Caja Laboral, and used by MCC as a source of capital for new projects and acquisitions. This joining fee helps to weed out potential employees unlikely to take their jobs seriously, and assures that the great majority of worker-members stay with their co-ops throughout their careers. Moreover, before paying the joining fee, potential members work for a period of time in a cooperative in order to see whether they, and existing members in the firm, agree that it is a good fit. MCC allots 75% of the joining fee to open a member's capital account and puts the rest into the co-op's reserves. The members can redeem their capital accounts upon retirement or when they leave the cooperative.

An individual's capital account, aside from earning interest, also gains from the general profits of the MCC. The MCC leadership allocates profits each year as follows: a minimum of 10% to the co-op social fund, to be used for betterment of the community; a minimum of 20% to the collective reserve fund; and the rest to member capital accounts. The members of individual cooperatives receive profit payments to their capital accounts based in large part on their cooperative's profits, and a firm must make a profit for its members to be eligible for such payments. Members also receive interest on their capital accounts at a rate determined by the General Council and consistent with Spanish laws. It is common for workers to accumulate more

Figure 4. Industrial Group: Sales and International Sales, 1986-2008

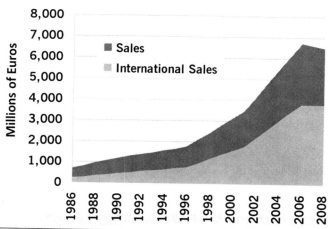

than $100,000 in their capital accounts during their working careers; they receive these funds in addition to their regular pensions once they retire.

Typically, according to Davidmann, "the greater the co-op's success and profit, the smaller is the proportion of the profit allocated to members. Greater success is increasingly channeled into the co-op's collective reserves instead of members' own capital accounts." (Mondragón, 1996, 4) MCC's policy of favoring long-term saving over short-term worker benefits, however crucial to the cooperative's longevity, has often been resisted by the workers but has nevertheless endured. Figure 5 demonstrates the growth of Caja Laboral, and the accelerating expansion since the mid-1990s.

Lagun Aro, the second most important MCC financial firm, provides social security for co-op members, including medical insurance, sickness and disability benefits, and pensions. These pensions are set at 75% of the worker-member's final salary, which is quite high when compared to the retirement benefits paid in the United States by the Social Security Administration. MCC contributes to the fund and it deducts the bulk of such costs from the workers' paychecks. These deductions are another source of capital for MCC. In 2008, Lagun Aro had about €4 billion in its reserve fund, roughly double the amount available in 2000.

The financial group has been a most crucial contributor to MCC's growth over the years. Ready access to capital and financial expertise gives the cooperatives a key advantage over many capitalist firms. MCC cooperatives are less likely to fail from a short-term downturn, and a cooperative that spots a new business opportunity has access to funds for investment and expansion. Cooperatives that do prove to be unprofitable over the long term can be closed with less harm to workers and their families than would occur at capitalist firms, given that MCC will retain the workers with pay, retrain them, and eventually place them in a growing co-op. This gives MCC a nimble character, allowing it to adjust to external shocks while protecting workers and their communities. Its approach compares favorably to the typical alternative: a dying industry gets propped up for decades with government subsidies because there is no mechanism to save the workers or their communities from the inevitable decline in income and jobs.

Research and Training Groups. Because producer cooperatives are worker-owned and operated, education and training of the work force is a central undertaking, both for improving work skills and for cultivation of cooperative attitudes. MCC carries out its education and training with multiple research and development centers, technical training schools, and a university.

In 1997, it founded Mondragón Unibersitatea (MU), basing it on the extensive experience of its three key centers, a technical institute (the best in Spain, according to Macleod 1997, 18), a faculty of business studies, and a faculty of humanities and education. The university is a co-operative organization open to the public. Its educational model combines real-world experience with classroom training, and it utilizes a trilingual teaching system in Spanish, Basque, and English. Training facilities outside the university focus on professional and vocational training and work together to ensure that MCC employs qualified and well-trained employees sympathetic to the cooperative's ideals of social change.

A particularly important aspect of these training centers is how they aid in the mobility of labor throughout the Mondragón cooperatives. For instance, if a particular cooperative can no longer afford to fully pay its salaries, some of its workers will be sent to training centers while still earning wages. After the workers are retrained, MCC relocates them to a firm with a labor shortage. This process of allocating labor spurs productivity; and it also contributes to the morale and the overall humanity of the entire system. In comparing labor allocation in the MCC and in capitalist firms, Marie-Anne Saive (1980, 238) writes that:

> … unlike the majority of capitalist firms, the Mondragón group seems to have dealt with the problem of structural unemployment by recourse to a system of vocational training which not only provides skilled manpower but also ensures the latter's occupational mobility.

Figure 5. Resources Administered by Caja Laboral 1986-2008

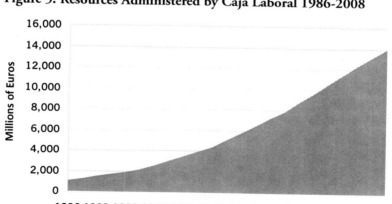

MCC has eleven research and development centers that encourage higher product quality and greater productivity. Many of these centers are linked to individual cooperatives while some, such as Ikerlan, Mondragón's largest research facility, are utilized by the MCC as a whole. In 2008, MCC's research centers had 1,022 employees.

The Distribution Group. This group includes retail outlets, cash-and-carry establishments, and specialized shops, and is under the control of Eroski, a huge consumer cooperative. These shops and outlets have become the buying public's most typical contact with MCC, and with the growing scope of its direct sales to consumers, more and more people around the world are being introduced to the cooperative alternative. The major and fastest growing firm in Eroski is CONSUM, now Spain's leading supermarket chain. The distribution group's income from sales has almost tripled in the past decade, from about €3,188 million to €9,073 million.

THE INTERNATIONALIZATION OF MCC

The doubling of MCC's labor force since 1998 is, in large part, due to MCC's expansion into operations outside the Basque region, including foreign operations. When Spain entered the European Economic Union in 1986, competition with the rest of Europe became an established fact. MCC could have decided to seek out niche markets typically associated with cooperative production and distribution operations. Instead, its leaders decided that, in order to protect extensive investments in its products that were now part of an international market, it would itself need to become a competitor in the global economy.

Several long-standing elements of MCC operations facilitated its move to expand foreign operations. Its university and training centers provided it with the latest in production and marketing technologies. Its management, though elected by the members, exercised its power to restrict wages to enable the reinvestment of a relatively high percentage of the company's profits. Some of the worker-members objected to these restrictions, but this unrest largely evaporated as the rapid growth expanded everyone's income and options. MCC also holds an advantage over capitalist firms in that its shares are not available on the open market. This means MCC's operations cannot be destabilized by outsiders buying a profitable MCC firm, sacking a few thousand people, and then selling it off to the highest capitalist bidder.

Presently, firms applying to join MCC, whether Spanish or foreign, must: (1) be, or become, a cooperative; (2) agree to abide by all MCC regulations; (3) have a "feasible" development plan; (4) be approved by the cooperatives within the sector the new firm would belong to, and then by the General Council and Standing Committee. MCC has also increased its size on its own by acquiring companies and joint ventures both in Spain and, increasingly, abroad. All of its current 57 (in 2006) foreign firms are corporations, rather than co-ops, and are either joint ventures or wholly owned MCC subsidiaries.

Most MCC companies are in Europe, but others are in, for example, Morocco, India, China, Brazil, and Thailand. In some of these factories, such as a household goods firm in Morocco, MCC sells the product exclusively in the country that produces it in order to avoid duties and shipping costs. However, in most cases, especially outside of continental Europe, MCC exports the products for sale in Spain. The following report exemplifies well the type of foreign project that MCC currently is developing:

> [MCC] has begun operations at its industrial estate in Kunshan, around 50km south of Shanghai. It is aiming to concentrate its production centres in China at one site in order to boost its corporate image and allow it a greater weight in negotiations with local suppliers and authorities. The estate covers a total surface area of 300,000 sq m, with the first phase (85,000 sq m) representing investment of €15 million. (*Financial Times Information*, March 7, 2007)

MCC's need to expand and internationalize its operations has also led it to modify some of its central operating practices. Because MCC now em-

Figure 6. Distribution Sales (1979 to 2008)

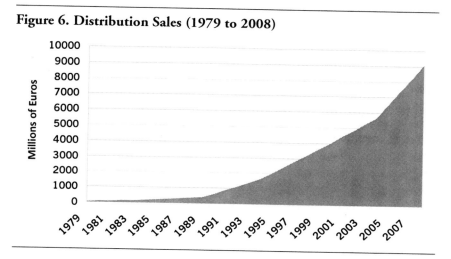

ploys many workers outside of the Basque region who are unfamiliar with cooperative practices, it often runs these firms in a more traditional capitalist manner. MCC describes the problems with developing cooperatives outside of the Basque region as follows:

> … Outside the Basque Country, either in Spain or abroad, thousands of new jobs have been created in accordance with the non-co-operative system. This is due to: the lack of adequate co-operative laws in the areas into which we have expanded; the fact that many new companies have been set up as part of a joint venture with other partners; and, above all, the fact that the creation of co-operatives requires the existence of co-operative members who understand and are committed to the co-operative culture, something which is impossible to obtain over a short period of time and in such a wide variety of locations. (MCC)

As we mentioned earlier, the rapid expansion of MCC abroad has meant that in 2008 only about one third of all MCC employees and only 10-15% of employees outside the Basque region are co-op members. Many MCC members have been uneasy with these changes. In the Social Council in Fagor, MCC's first and largest co-op, a common complaint was that, "Bringing the cooperatives up-to-date in competitiveness is one thing … . The unnecessary loss of their fundamental character—economic democracy and member participation—is another." (Huet 1997)

This percentage of worker-members will, according to MCC, increase to over 75% by 2012 after Grupo Eroski has completed its cooperativisation process for all its non-member employees, who work mainly outside the Basque Country and Navarra. Eroski can have this effect because it is the largest sector in MCC, generating about a third of its total outcome by operating a chain of food supermarkets, perfume stores, service stations, travel agencies, and other such retail outlets. It is now one of the largest fifty retail outlets in Europe. Eroski started its move to increase membership among its employees with a firm Sociedad Gespa, in the typical experimental fashion. It gradually assimilated workers into the formation process, allowing them by stages to evolve into the responsibilities and benefits of membership. The success of the process at Gespa provided a formula now being used throughout the Eroski Group as it adds new employees from expansion of existing firms and new acquisitions. A majority of non-members who have been offered an opportunity to go through this process has opted to do so.

Regarding MCC's rapid expansion abroad, Christina Clamp (2000, 562) argues that MCC took the path described above in order to achieve four principal goals:

> (1) preserve MCC jobs; (2) sustain profitability of MCC firms; (3) comply with local labor practices in overseas operation; and (4) develop substitute technologies, when possible, that enable the MCC to return manufacturing operations from overseas to the Basque region.

It is clear that the first of these goals, to preserve the members' jobs, is central, and to achieve it MCC in some respects must act like a traditional capitalist firm. In particular, MCC managers argued that if they did not achieve sufficient economies of scale in certain industries, they would not be able to compete with the giant multinational corporations that dominate those industries. This has meant expanding into regions of the world without a legacy of cooperative businesses, while keeping costs as low as possible. In Spain and elsewhere, this strategy was also driven in part because MCC gradually ran out of cooperatives to take on that appeared both cost-efficient and able to make needed products.

A critical consequence of the changing nature of its acquisition strategy, despite its efforts to make more of its employees members, is that MCC now employs a growing number of different categories of workers, each receiving different wages and benefits:

- Traditional workers are [now one-third] of all MCC workers who are members and who have ownership and voting rights within the individual coops and MCC.
- Limited period workers share the same rights as traditional members, but are only hired for fixed terms.
- Contract workers are usually short-term workers who cannot vote or have ownership in the MCC, but may share in the MCC's profits. Their presence allows MCC to lower labor costs in the same way that capitalist firms do.
- Employees on contract from affiliated companies are mostly workers outside Spain who have none of the privileges of MCC members. These workers receive payment at the going wage for the area, subject only to the legal framework of that particular country.
- Subcontracted workers, such as electrical workers and others, are hired by MCC when the firm has a shortage of such employees or does not typically keep them in its workforce. (Errasti et al. 2003, 561)

The General Council sets the wage scale for these different categories and, as MCC's rules dictate, "in accordance with each person's individual contribution, based on equality, internal solidarity, and external competitiveness." This external competitiveness is, presumably, one loophole that allows MCC to justify to its members and to the rest of the world its reversion to a more capitalist distribution of wages and salaries. However, as has been the case throughout its history, MCC continues to offer more and better opportunities to workers than is typical under capitalist firms.

Originally, MCC set a maximum pay ratio of 1:3 between the lowest paid worker-member and the highest. At one point, this ratio was raised to 1:4.5 to reflect that MCC managers were assessed a tax other employees could avoid. Recently, the General Council raised the ratio to 1:6, essentially in order to pay competitive salaries for the types of managers MCC considers necessary to compete in a rapidly growing global company. This is still remarkably egalitarian in comparison to capitalist firms. In its defense of the widening inequality within the corporation, MCC points to the considerably greater ratios between the pay of average workers and that of CEOs in big capitalist firms, which often exceed 500:1. However, in excluding nonmembers from this calculation, given the enormous increase in their numbers and because they are increasingly low-skilled workers in developing countries, the 1:6 ratio is understated.

To stay competitive, MCC has also been forced to alter working conditions to more closely resemble those of profit-driven companies. (Kasmir 1996) Thomas and Logan (1982, 70) explain the difficulty of adhering to cooperative ideals while immersed in a capitalist economic system:

> While it may be true that upward mobility is slightly higher than in capitalist enterprises, this does not mean that Mondragón cooperatives are able to offer on a huge scale less monotonous and more interesting work than elsewhere. The cooperative group is aware of this and at times explores other ways of distributing work, but existing technologies severely restrict the experiments that can be undertaken in this respect. The necessity to compete in national and international markets leaves insufficient space to implement alternative manners of work organization on a large scale.

Shift work, the assembly line, repetitive work, and a sped-up pace are common in the MCC today, even within some of its cooperatives. Of course, teamwork and brainstorming still play a major role in the MCC system, and have received greater emphasis recently. Most members apparently have accepted that midnight shifts and some degree of assembly-line work are necessary to compete in the global economy and thus are crucial to their, and the co-ops', long-term well-being. There seems to be no question that globalization has forced an increasing emphasis on this kind of nimble managerial decision and has put into flux the democratic character of the Mondragón cooperatives.

MCC has also responded to these pressures of global competition with two promising initiatives designed to reinvigorate cooperativism, along lines that are thoroughly different from the sprawling, grasping multinational firms now remaking the world economy. The first is based at the Mundukide Foundation, established by MCC in 1999 at the urging of a group of retired managers. MCC created the foundation after an extended discussion among its members, and with representatives from other cooperatives and NGOs in the southern hemisphere, about how the cooperative movement might be useful to poor, developing countries in the age of globalization. The discussions led to a commitment to work towards cooperation for development in poor countries through the creation of an organization and specific system designed for this purpose. The resulting foundation declared itself in solidarity with all the workers in the entire developing world, and laid out two programs to put that solidarity into action.

The first of these plans is known as "Inter-Cooperation," described by MCC as "collaborating with communities seeking to achieve comprehensive self-management." Inter-Cooperation encompasses such projects as regular meetings with MCC representatives and members of "popular economy cooperatives," as MCC describes those in developing countries; a rapidly expanding central information system between MCC and these cooperatives; and other efforts that utilize the knowledge and experience of students and retired workers from MCC schools and co-ops in order to increase the management capacity of the newer cooperatives.

The second element of the practical work of the Mundukide Foundation is comprised of several "Comprehensive Regional Development" efforts, broad-based programs designed for low-income developing countries. One of the most extensive programs, in Mozambique, involves MCC support for comprehensive community development that includes supporting educational, health, and transportation initiatives, as well as basic manufacturing and services operations.

Other projects include working with agricultural firms in Colombia to form integrated cooperatives, and helping Ecuadorians in Alto Napo province establish a cooperative to build an animal feed production plant, and then diversify its activities into breeding and slaughtering chickens. Additional projects in Zimbabwe and Chile are currently in the planning stages.

Aside from these recent initiatives, MCC has always engaged in what it calls "social action." That is, central to its mission from the start has been "solidarity with, and continuing commitment to, the wellbeing and quality of life of the communities where our companies are located." (MCC) Currently, MCC spends over €35 million annually on social-action programs, most of it going to finance education, training, and research, and to subsidize "welfare initiatives" that include NGO activities and projects in developing countries. MCC spends the remainder of the funds on the promotion of cultural activities, including the teaching of the Basque language.

MCC EXPANDS TO THE UNITED STATES

MCC's expansion around the globe found its way to the United States most publicly in October 2009 in Cleveland, when Evergreen Cooperative Laundry began operations. It is a worker owned co-op, with membership rules designed structurally to be about the same as those at MCC. Further, the ECL is only the first of ten such co-ops that its developers and others are planning for Cleveland, all of them bound by an agreement to provide a living wage, affordable health insurance, and the possibility of asset accumulations from sharing in the firms' profits. These co-ops will manufacture such products as solar panels, weatherizing services, a local newspaper, and food grown by hydroponics, and are combining private fund raising, bank loans, and government grants to finance their capital and operating costs. The Cleveland co-ops are aimed especially to reinvigorate low-income areas in a city with declining population, economic activity and employment.

Also, in October, 2009 the potential for a substantial increase in the size and scope of co-ops in the North America emerged in an agreement between the United Steelworkers union and MCC to move in the direction of building manufacturing co-ops in the United States and in Canada. Nancy Folbre, an economist with the Center for Popular Economics, and at the University of Massachusetts at Amherst, wrote this about the announcement on the *New York Times'* Economix blog:

> It certainly represents a new direction for the American labor movement. The United Steelworkers is the largest industrial union in the United States, with 1.2 million workers. Its ranks have been devastated by the decline in domestic steel production, and it now represents workers in a variety of industries, including health and education....The proposed Mondragón collaboration grew out of a United

Steelworkers partnership with a Spanish wind turbine firm, Gamesa, to refit steel plants in Pennsylvania for wind-turbine manufacture. Mondragón could provide the organizational expertise and help raise the venture capital necessary to expand such initiatives. Expansion of worker-owned enterprises could potentially increase the demand for skilled manufacturing workers in so-called "green jobs."

MCC's expansion to the United States is going to be enhanced by its having been able to weather the storm of the economic crises that started in 2007 in the United States and spread around the world. Despite the decline in the level of employment in 2008 of 1.1%, and the substantial decline in demand for its industrial products beginning in mid-2008, MCC retained its solid foundation. Though its investments were down, along with stake-holder funds for its workers and its allocation to community projects, its total sales increased by 3.5%. This increase was largely due to the final assimilation of 500 supermarkets, employing 15,000 workers, that MCC had acquired when it purchased 75% of the total assets of a major competitor, Comprado.

The corporation also retained its share of output in all its major markets, and the assets of its bank Caja Laboral grew at a rate greater than the average for all European banks. The success of the MCC bank makes a notable comparison to most of the rest of the banking system in Spain. In early 2010, two of Spain's major international banks, Santander and BBVA, faced downgraded bond ratings because of a combination of Spain's deep recession and because of reckless speculation: in the middle of the crisis they began buying up foreign banks rather than taking care of bad loans of the same kind that brought down some of the big U.S. investment banks. As *AOL Daily Finance* put it, "Instead of buckling down to face an inevitable spike in loan losses on existing business, the banks expanded their balance sheets through acquisitions and became more leveraged." (2-09-10)

The existence of MCC's bank is a major reason that the cooperative has long championed its model as being far more crisis-proof than the typical capitalist firm. Cajal Laboral strongly complements its built-in antidote to structural unemployment and the great flexibility it has in shifting production throughout the firm. As MCC's current chairman, José María Aldecoa, put it in 2009, "I am sure that our values of participation and business commitment will continue to be a major competitive advantage in this globalized market, helping us to the turn the crisis into new business opportunities." No doubt the new co-ops in Cleveland, and the eagerness of the United Steelworkers to agree to work with MCC, are the kinds of "new business opportunities" that Aldecoa has in mind.

CONCLUSION

Without question, MCC in recent years has become something quite different from how Fr. José María Arizmendiarrieta imagined it at the beginning. The new global economy has forced MCC, and all firms that engage in foreign trade, to reconstruct their methods of doing business. Had it remained an essentially insular company producing and marketing its goods mostly in Spain, it might eventually have lost even its local customers to global firms producing goods in low-wage countries with little or no environmental regulation. As Marx and others have long noted, unregulated capitalism will necessarily force the capitalists to emulate the behavior of those who achieve the lowest costs. That is, in cowboy capitalism, the wage level, working conditions, and thus the moral imperatives of the whole system, will ultimately descend to the lowest common denominator.

These developments have led critics to conclude that MCC is selling out its ideals. We understand the critics' arguments and their remorse at what they see as the weakening of one of the most successful alternatives to the capitalist firm. Yet our view is that MCC should be allowed more time to discover whether "market forces" will ultimately force it to abandon more of its cooperative roots or whether, after establishing itself firmly in the global economy, it will fulfill its promise to have 75% of its employees as members.

Whatever the outcome of the corporation's current changes, Mondragón will have provided the modern world with an example of a highly successful firm competing in the hard-knocks world of global capitalism while maintaining an essentially democratic form of control. There are, to be sure, traditional capitalist-style managers at MCC, and they make more money than workers do; yet they and all the operations they oversee are ultimately subject to the control of the worker-members. This is the crucial characteristic to keep in mind because it represents the great divide between MCC and traditional capitalist firms; that is, were you to visit MCC and then, for example, the executive offices of General Motors, you would get utterly different responses if you were to ask: "Who's in control, here?"

What a vision for the modern world! A giant firm prospering in an increasingly barbaric, global free-for-all, where the workers—the real producers—are freed from the overhanging sword of capitalist managers and absentee owners who necessarily see employees as cash cows from whom to milk surplus value. In short, in its long and resourceful struggle to try to humanize work and its consequences in the modern capitalist world, the Mondragón Cooperative, as they say, is the real deal.

SUGGESTIONS FOR FURTHER READING

Arizmendiarreta, Fr José María. "Special feature: Mondragón Cooperatives—Core Ideas from Mondragón's Founder." *Social Policy,* v32, n2 (2002): 10-11.

Bakaikoa, Baleran et al. "Governance of the Mondragón Corporación Cooperativa." *Annals of Public and Cooperative Economics,* v75, n1 (March 2004): 61-87.

Bowles, Samuel et al. *Understanding Capitalism; Competition, Command, and Change* (Third Edition). New York. Oxford University Press, 2005.

Bradley, Keith and Alan Gelb. *Cooperation at Work: The Mondragón Experience.* London: Heinemann, 1983.

Cheney, George. *Values at Work: Employee Participation Meets Market Pressure at Mondragón,* updated edition. Ithaca: Cornell University Press, 2002.

Clamp, Christina A. "The Internationalization of Mondragón." *Annals of Public and Cooperative Economics,* v71, n4 (December 2000): 557-77.

Davidmann, Manfred. "Co-operatives and Co-operation: Causes of Failure, Guidelines for Success." 1996. 1/26/2006. http://www.solbaram.org/articles/coops.html.

Davidmann, Manfred. "Mondragón Cooperatives." 1996. 1/26/2006. http://www.solbaram.org/articles/mondra.html

Dow, Gregory K. *Governing the Firm: Workers' Control in Theory and Practice.* New York: Cambridge University Press, 2003.

Errasti, Anjel Mari, et al. "The Internationalisation of Cooperatives: The Case of the Mondragón Cooperative Corporation." *Annals of Public and Cooperative Economics,* v74, n4 (December 2003): 553-84.

Financial Times Information. Europe Intelligence Wire Service, January 7, 2007.

Financial Times Information. Europe Intelligence Wire Service, March 7, 2007.

Financial Times Information Limited. Indian Express Online Media Ltd Source. November 10, 2006. A200611111-12ECB-GNW.

Nancy Folbre, *New York Times* Economix blog, "Workers of the World, Incorporate," November 16, 2009.

Gunn, Christopher. "Markets Against Economic Democracy." *Review of Radical Political Economics*, v32, n3 (September 2000): 448-60.

Huet, Tim. "Can Co-ops Go Global? Mondragón is Trying." *Dollars & Sense*, November/December, 1997.

Kasmir, Sharryn. *The Myth of Mondragón: Cooperatives, Politics, and Working-Class Life in a Basque Town.* Albany: State University of New York Press, 1996.

Lotti, Riccardo, Peter Mensing, and Davide Valenti. "A Cooperative Solution," *Strategy + Business*, July 17, 2006.

MacLeod, Greg. *From Mondragón to America: Experiments in Community Economic Development.* Sydney, N.S. University College of Cape Breton Press, 1997.

MCC, *The History of an Experience.* To access this document, go to *Who We Are*, and click on this title.

Miller, Mike. "Special feature: Mondragón Cooperatives—Mondragón: Lessons for Our Times." *Social Policy,* v32, n2, (2002): 17-20.

Mondragón Corporación Cooperativave Website. (MCC). www. Mondragón.mcc

Saive, Marie-Anne. "Mondragón: An Experiment with Co-operative Development in the Industrial Sector." *Annals of Public and Cooperative Economics,* v51, n3 (Sept. 1980): 223-55.

Schultze, George. "Special feature: Mondragón Cooperatives—Worker Ownership & Catholic Social Thought." *Social Policy,* v32, n2 (2002): 12-16.

Taylor, P. L. "The Rhetorical Construction of Efficiency: Restructuring and Industrial Democracy in Mondragón, Spain." *Sociological Forum,* v9, n3 (1994): 459-489.

Taylor, P. L. "The Myth of Mondragón: Cooperatives, Politics, and Working-Class Life in a Basque Town (Review)." *American Anthropologist, New Series,* v99, n2 (Jun. 1997): 433-434.

Thomas, Henk and Chris Logan. *Mondragón: An Economic Analysis.* London: George Allen & Unwin, 1982.

Whyte, William F. "Learning from the Mondragón Cooperative Experience." *Studies in Comparative International Development*, v30, n2, (1995): 58-67.

Whyte, Willam F. "The Mondragón Cooperatives in 1976 and 1998." *Industrial & Labor Relations Review*, v52, n3, (1999): 478-481.

Whyte, William Foote and Kathleen King Whyte, *Making Mondragón: The Growth and Dynamics of the Worker Cooperative Complex*, 2nd ed. Cornell University Press, 1991.

Yates, Jacquelyn. "Values at Work: Employee Participation Meets Market Pressure at Mondragón & Making Mondragón: The Growth and Dynamics of the Worker Cooperative Complex." (Review essay). *International Journal of Politics and Ethics*, March 22, 2001.

Endnotes

Ch. 1: The Political Economy Challenge to Mainstream Economics

1 On this matter of what to call the various schools of economics that we have discussed above, there are several possibilities. John Kenneth Galbraith has called the dominating school of economics, from Adam Smith until our own time, the "central tradition." We will use that term on occasion. Typically, we will draw from a fusion of terms used by Marx, Keynes, and Samuelson, as follows: we will refer to the central tradition in economics from Adam Smith until Keynes' *General Theory*, in 1936, as "classical" economics. For economists in the central tradition after 1936, we will continue to use the term "mainstream" or "neoclassical."

Ch. 2: Adam Smith and the Philosophy of Limited Laissez-Faire

1 George J. Stigler in Ronald L. Meek, *Smith, Marx, & After* (London: Chapman and Hall, 1977), p. 30.

2 Chapter VII is titled "Of the natural and market Price of Commodities." Adam Smith, *An Inquiry Into the Nature and Causes of the Wealth of Nations*, edited by R. H. Campbell and A. S. Skinner (Indianapolis: Liberty Press/Liberty Classics, 1981), Vol. I, p. 72.

3 Karl Marx, *Capital*, edited by Frederick Engels and translated by Samuel Moore and Edward Aveling (New York: International Publishers, 1947), Vol. I, pp. 52n, 53n).

4 The term is derived from the Greek word *holos*, which means "whole." See Allan G. Gruchy, *Modern Economic Thought: The American Contribution* (New York: Prentice-Hall, 1947), pp. 4, 5, 26, 553-581.

5 Horst Claus Recktenwald, "An Adam Smith Renaissance *anno* 1976? The Bicentenary Output—A Reappraisal of His Scholarship," *The Journal of Economic Literature*, March 1978, pp. 56, 65. Emphasis in original.

6 Smith, *Wealth of Nations*, Vol. I, pp. 422, 96.

7 Samual Hollander, *Classical Economics* (Oxford: Basil Blackwell, 1987), p. 12.

8 Smith, *Wealth of Nations*, Vol. I, pp. 99, 97.

9 Adam Smith, *Lectures on Jurisprudence*, edited by R. L. Meek, D. D. Raphael, and P. G. Stein (Indianapolis: Liberty Press/Liberty Classics, 1982), p. 193.

10 Joseph A. Schumpeter, "Science and Ideology," *The American Economic Review*, March 1949, p. 353.

11 Dugald Stewart, "Account of the Life and Writings of Adam Smith, LL. D.," 1794, ed-

ited by I. S. Ross. In Adam Smith, *Essays on Philosophical Subjects*, edited by W. P. D. Wightman and J. C. Bryce (Indianapolis: Liberty Press/Liberty Classics, 1982), p. 271.

12 Smith, *Wealth of Nations*, Vol. I, p. 22.

13 Adam Smith, "Early Draft of Part of *The Wealth of Nations*." In Adam Smith, *Lectures on Jurisprudence*, edited by R. L. Meek, D. D. Raphael and P. G. Stein (Indianapolis: Liberty Press/Liberty Classics, 1982), p. 566.

14 Smith, *Wealth of Nations*, Vol. I, p. 10.

15 Adam Smith, *An Inquiry Into the Nature and Causes of the Wealth of Nations*, edited by R. H. Campbell and A. S. Skinner (Indianapolis: Liberty Press/Liberty Classics, 1981), Vol. II, pp. 678-679.

16 Smith, *Wealth of Nations*, Vol. I, p. 428.

17 Smith, *Wealth of Nations*, Vol. I, p. 13.

18 Smith, *Wealth of Nations*, Vol. 1, p. 17.

19 Smith, *Wealth of Nations*, Vol. 1, pp. 15, 23, 22.

20 Smith, *Wealth of Nations*, Vol. 1, p. 104.

21 Smith, *Wealth of Nations*, Vol. 1, p. 308.

22 Smith, *Lectures on Jurisprudence*, p. 492.

23 Smith, *Wealth of Nations*, Vol. I, p. 20.

24 Smith, *Wealth of Nations*, Vol. I, p. 21,

25 C. E. Ayres, *The Theory of Economic Progress* (Chapel Hill: The University of North Carolina Press, 1944), p. 56.

26 Smith, *Lectures on Jurisprudence*, p. 492. Smith goes into considerable detail on this topic in describing the evolution of the steam engine. He states, "When an artist makes any such discovery he shows himself to be not a mere artist but a real philosopher, whatever may be his nominal profession. It was a real philosopher only who could invent the fire engine [i. e., the steam engine], and first form the idea of producing so great an effort by a power in nature which had never before been thought of" (Smith, "Early Draft of ... the *Wealth of Nations*," p. 570). It is most likely that Smith was referring to James Watt. Smith had known Watt since 1757, when Smith was on the faculty of the University of Glasgow and Watt was employed by the university as a mathematical instrument maker. It was in his workshop there that Watt repaired and improved the Newcomen steam engine (Ernest Campbell Mossner and Ian Simpson Ross, editors of *The Correspondence of Adam Smith* (Indianapolis: Liberty Press/Liberty Classics, 1987), p. 248n.). It may therefore be hypothesized that Smith formulated his concept of exogenous invention, at least partly, on the basis of conversations with Watt and his familiarity with the latter's inventive activities.

27 Smith, *Wealth of Nations*, Vol. I, pp, 29, 152, 119; "Early Draft of ... the *Wealth of Nations*," p. 570; and *Wealth of Nations*, Vol. I, p. 22.

28 Smith, *Wealth of Nations*, Vol. II, pp. 781-782. Emphasis added.

29 Smith, *Lectures on Jurisprudence*, pp. 539-540; *Wealth of Nations*, Vol. II, p. 784; *Lectures on Jurisprudence*, p. 539; and *Wealth of Nations*, Vol. II, pp. 784-785.

30 Smith, *Wealth of Nations*, Vol. II, p. 784.

31 Smith, *Wealth of Nations*, Vol. I, pp. 104, 277, 104.

32 Cf. William L. Baldwin, *Market Power, Competition and Antitrust Policy* (Homewood, IL: Irwin, 1987).

33 Smith, *Lectures on Jurisprudence*, pp. 331, 521; and *Wealth of Nations*, Vol. II, p. 643.

34 Smith, *Wealth of Nations*, Vol. II, p. 429.

35 Smith, *Wealth of Nations*, Vol. II, p. 438.

36 That is, repayment to exporters by the government of duties levied either on imported raw materials that went into the production of exported goods or imposed on goods that were imported from one country for the purpose of its profitable export to another country.

37 Smith, *Wealth of Nations*, Vol. I, p. 450.

38 Smith, *Wealth of Nations*, Vol. I, pp. 79, 145, 11, 145.

39 Smith, *Wealth of Nations*, Vol. I, p. 145.

40 Smith, *Wealth of Nations*, Vol. I, p. 145.

41 Economists use the term monopsony for a market in which one firm or group controls the entire demand for a product— in this case the demand for labor.

42 Smith, *Wealth of Nations*, Vol. I, pp. 145, 79, 84.

43 Smith, *Wealth of Nations*, quoted in William K. Tabb, *Reconstructing Political Economy* (New York: Routledge, 1999), pp. 40-41.

44 Smith, *Wealth of Nations*, Vol. I, pp. 79, 156, 137, 470.

45 Smith, *Wealth of Nations*, Vol. I, pp. 79, 470.

46 Smith, *Wealth of Nations*, Vol. I, p. 78.

47 Smith, *Wealth of Nations*, Vol. I, p. 471.

48 Smith, Wealth of Nations, Vol. I, p. 267.

49 Smith, *Wealth of Nations*, Vol. I, pp. 493, 472.

50 The word "monopoly" appears 175 times in the *Wealth of Nations*. Fred A. Glahe (ed.) *Adam Smith's An Inquiry into the Nature and Causes of the Wealth of Nations: A Concordance* (Lanham, MD: Rowman and Littlefield, 1993), pp. 334-335.

51 Smith, *Wealth of Nations*, Vol. I, pp. 470, 79; and Vol. II, p. 687.

52 Smith, *Wealth of Nations*, Vol. II, p. 687.

53 Smith, *Wealth of Nations*, Vol. II, pp. 687-688.

54 Adam Smith, *The Theory of Moral Sentiments*, edited by D. D. Raphael and A. L. Macfie (Indianapolis: Liberty Press/Liberty Classics, 1982), pp. 389, 86.

55 Smith, *Wealth of Nations*, Vol. II, 723.

56 Smith, *Wealth of Nations*, Vol. II, pp. 724, 731.

57 To Smith, one class deserving of government assistance was composed of British exporters and businessmen who owned enterprises in foreign countries. Smith approved of the British government's practice of appointing resident "ambassadors or ministers" in the capitals of those countries in which British citizens had substantial economic and "commercial interests." The frequent "interference with those interests" by govern-

ments and businessmen in the pertinent countries necessitated the presence of resident British ambassadors to protect their countrymen's investments and commercial activities. As Smith saw it, "extensive [international] commerce renders it impossible to preserve peace a month, unless grievances be redressed by a man of authority [i.e., the British ambassador] who knows the customs of the country [in which he is stationed] and is capable of explaining what injuries are really done" (Smith, *Wealth of Nations*, Vol. II, p. 732; and *Lectures on Jurisprudence*, p. 552). Additionally, British firms that did business "with barbarous and uncivilized nations, require[d] extraordinary protection," observed Smith. He viewed it therefore as proper for the British government to finance the construction and operation of those "forts" which the "Turkey" and "East India Companies" had erected at their foreign bases (Smith, *Wealth of Nations*, Vol. II, p. 732). Here, it seems Smith sides with British imperialism and against the natural liberty of those in British colonies, a blind spot that afflicted many of Smith's era.

58 Milton Friedman understood this all too well! Thus he said: "It pains me" to call attention to the "mischief … done" by Smith when he declared it the government's "'duty of erecting and maintaining certain public works and certain public institutions'." Friedman censured Smith for having "provide[d] arguments for the interventionist and the statist." Milton Friedman, *Adam Smith's Relevance for 1976*. Ottawa, IL: Green Hill Publishers for the International Institute for Economic Research, 1976), pp. 10, 11.

59 Smith, *Wealth of Nations*, Vol. II, p. 733.

60 Smith, *Wealth of Nations*, Vol. I, p. 46; Vol. II, p. 687; and Vol. I, p. 469.

61 Smith, *Wealth of Nations*, Vol. I, p. 118.

62 Smith, *Wealth of Nations*, Vol. I, p. 282. Emphasis added.

63 Smith, *Wealth of Nations*, Vol. II, pp. 782, 781.

64 Smith, *Wealth of Nations*, Vol. II, pp. 785, 787.

65 In accordance with the prevailing norms of his time, Smith could not conceive of education of the female youth on a par with education of the male youth. Thus it seems that he did not object to the fact that there were "no public institutions for the education of women…. They are taught what their parents or guardians judge is necessary or useful for them to learn; and they are taught nothing else. Every part of their education tends evidently to some useful purpose; either to improve the natural attraction of their person, or to form their mind to reserve, to modesty, to chastity, and to oeconomy: to render them both likely to become the mistress of a family, and to behave properly when they have become such." Smith, *Wealth of Nations*, Vol. II, p. 781.

66 Smith, *Wealth of Nations*, Vol. I, p. 20.

67 Smith, *Wealth of Nations*, Vol. I, p. 10.

68 Smith, *Wealth of Nations*, Vol. I, p. 330.

69 John Maynard Keynes, *The General Theory of Employment, Interest and Money* (New York: Harcourt, Brace and Company, 1936), pp. 213-214. Emphasis in original.

70 Smith, *Wealth of Nations*, Vol. I, pp. 47-48, 46.

71 Smith, *Wealth of Nations*, Vol. I, pp. 51, 49. Below, the chapter briefly takes up the manner in which Smith viewed the competitive processes that ensured this equality in the system of bridled *laissez-faire*.

72 Smith, *Wealth of Nations*, Vol. II, p. 815.

73 Smith, *Wealth of Nations*, Vol. II, p. 687; Vol. I , pp. 73, 78; and Vol. II, p. 759.

74 Smith, *Wealth of Nations*, Vol. I, pp. 471, 315, 494.

75 Smith, *Wealth of Nations*, Vol. I, pp. 456, 27.

76 Smith, *Theory of Moral Sentiments*, I, i, p. 1.

77 Quoted in William K. Tabb, *Reconstructing Political Economy* (New York: Routledge, 1999), p. 39.

78 Indeed, because of the characteristics ascribed to such a system, it has been suggested by advocates of *laissez-faire* that "the system of political economy which Smith designates 'natural liberty' is virtually synonymous with justice"(Jeffrey T. Young, *Economics as a Moral Science: The Political Economy of Adam Smith*, Cheltenham, UK: Edward Elgar, 1997, p. 125).

79 Smith, *Wealth of Nations*, Vol. I, p. 456.

80 Smith, *Wealth of Nations*, Vol. I, p. 422; *Lectures on Jurisprudence*, p. 497; and *Wealth of Nations*, Vol. I, pp. 411, 432, 33, 277.

81 Smith, *Wealth of Nations*, Vol. I, pp. 277, 74.

82 Smith, *Wealth of Nations*, Vol. I, pp. 279, 31, 337, 83.

83 Smith, *Wealth of Nations*, Vol. I, p. 83.

84 Smith, *Wealth of Nations*, Vol. I, p. 337.

85 Smith, *Wealth of Nations*, Vol. I, p. 337.

86 Smith, *Wealth of Nations*, Vol. I, pp. 17, 277. Later political economists such as Veblen point out that increasing production is one method of increasing profits, but there are other, more destructive methods as well.

87 Smith, *Wealth of Nations*, Vol. I, pp. 266, 68. Emphasis added.

88 Smith, *Wealth of Nations*, Vol. I, p. 77.

89 Smith, *Wealth of Nations*, Vol. I, p. 411.

90 Smith, *Wealth of Nations*, Vol. I, pp. 74, 104, 77, 111, 75.

91 Smith, *Wealth of Nations*, Vol. I, pp. 75, 73, 99.

92 Smith, *Wealth of Nations*, Vol. I, p. 66.

93 The relationship between market structure and innovation has been widely studied. The consensus is that innovative activity does increase as market concentration increases, but beyond moderate levels of concentration, markets are observed to have lower rates of innovative activity. Cf., Shepherd, *The Economics of Industrial Organization* (Long Grove, Waveland Press, 2004), Baldwin, op cit, 283. We take this issue up in more detail below in the chapter on monopoly capitalism.

94 Smith, *Wealth of Nations*, Vol. I, p. 456; and *The Theory of Moral Sentiments*, pp. 184-185.

95 D. D. Raphael, *"A master for many schools."* In D. D. Raphael, Donald Winch, and Lord Skidelsky, *Three Great Economists: Smith, Malthus, Keynes* (New York: Oxford University Press, 1997), pp. 66, 66-67. Emphasis added.

Ch. 3: Karl Marx and the Contradictions of Capitalism

1   In talking about modes of production, Marxists use a few terms that one should know. The *forces of production* include all things needed to produce output: machinery, tools, natural resources, and human effort and human capital (skills and knowledge). By themselves, the machinery, tools, and resources are the means of production. Those who own them are the *bourgeoisie*, or *capitalists*. Those who don't own such capital goods, who must live by wage labor, are *proletarians* (members of the *proletariat*). The *social relations of production* in capitalism are the ongoing interactions between capitalists and laborers in the workplace, in particular the conditions by which workers will produce enough output to guarantee a profit to capitalists.

2   Adam Smith had also noticed the negative effects of the division of labor on workers. In *Capital*, Marx quotes from Smith's *Wealth of Nations* (1776) that divided labor can "make the worker as stupid and as ignorant as it is possible for a human creature to become." To appreciate the argument that both make, one only has to imagine performing the same mind-numbing task hundreds, or thousands, of times per day for decades.

3   As our consulting example shows, in terms of the extraction of surplus value in a particular firm, it makes no difference whether the output is an intangible service or a can of beans. However, in considering how surplus value flows through the economy, Marx did distinguish between services which are "necessary" costs of production and those that aren't. A consultant, Marx might have noted, does not produce any value at all but simply allows her employer to obtain surplus value produced elsewhere. This matter goes beyond the level of our introduction, but for those interested, it is discussed clearly in Wolff and Resnick 1987.

4   This "enclosure movement" in England meant that land in villages traditionally set aside in "commons"—groups of plots farmed by individual families—were by Parliamentary acts taken over by large landowners or by the British Crown. In eliminating the commons, these enclosures made it impossible for most rural families to sustain themselves on the land. This was, of course, the first step in the process by which rural families found themselves headed to cities and into the factories of the emerging class of capitalist owners.

Ch. 4: Veblen and the Predatory Nature of Contemporary Capitalism

1   Smith devoted considerable effort in *Wealth of Nations* to a critique of monopolies, so much so that many interpreters of the book see it as a polemical attack on the existing government policies as well as an exposition of classical economic theory. See Canterbery 1995, 49, as well as the *Wealth of Nations* itself.

2   Cumulative causation is contrasted to simple cause and effect, where action a results in reaction b, end of story. Cumulative causation suggests that reaction b may become a cause of reaction c, and in turn reaction c may be a cause of reaction d, and on and on ad infinitum.

3   In an example of his irony Veblen notes that "it may even be that the men's work contributes as much to the food supply and the other necessary consumption of the group" (Veblen 1973, 23).

4   Mainstream economists argue that in a competitive market economy, the wage rate for different occupations will equal the value of the marginal product produced by the last

worker hired. In other words, the wage rate is considered to be set at a level equivalent to the productivity of the worker, rather than being set on the basis of the power relations within the workplace or in the overall economy.

5   Ron Chernow discusses this in depth in his biography of Rockefeller. The opportunity for railroads to get large and steady shipments of oil lowered their own costs, so the rebates were a way of sharing those benefits with the shippers; as Rockefeller himself said, "It was a large, regular volume of business such as had not hitherto been given to the roads in question" (Chernow 1999, 113). Rockefeller was further aided by the fact that railroads like the Erie and the New York Central were very interested in promoting Cleveland as an oil-refining center, in order to boost the shipments through their own railway networks.

6   Rockefeller also used less brutal tactics to compete. He was the first oil refiner to build his own pipelines for shipping oil, to set up his own marketing operations, and to reduce his costs further and further. At the same time, by owning his own pipelines and setting up marketing operations, he closed off the distribution markets from the wholesalers and railroads in favor of his own divisions, thus centralizing even more power over the national oil refining market in the hands of the Standard Oil Trust (Chandler 1977, Ch. 10).

7   He is often accused of moving into an activist stance with his book *Engineers and the Price System*. In this book, he advocated for engineers and others of an industrial state of mind to take over the nation's industrial apparatus and reorganize it to provision the entire economy.

Chapter 5: John Maynard Keynes and the Turbulent Birth of Macroeconomics

1   There are many ways to classify the different schools of economics, and we will use the following one: the "classical school" refers to the mainstream of economics from Adam Smith to John Maynard Keynes; the "neoclassical school" refers to the mainstream of economics since the 1930s, with its two broad branches of microeconomics and macroeconomics. The "central tradition" refers to both the classical and neo-classical schools, thus the mainstream from the time of Adam Smith to our time. "Political economy" refers to schools of thought outside the mainstream, particularly those that emerged in the thinking of Karl Marx and Thorstein Veblen, and in the works of critics such as Keynes who worked inside the mainstream school but were highly critical of it.

2   In our brief discussion of Say's Law we must leave out two important additions by later economists that made the macroeconomics of the classical more sophisticated than his simple law. These additions are an explanation of how interest rates equilibrate the market for loans, and a theory of the role of money in capitalist societies. Omitting these two, we are thus presenting an oversimplified version of classical macroeconomic theory, yet the parts that we are discussing—Say's Law and its theory of unemployment—were its central tenants and can reasonably be discussed on their own.

3   These savings come from two sources: retained earnings, which is the part of total profits the capitalists keep for the firm rather than paying them as dividends to the stockholders; and depreciation allowances, funds they also retain out of sales revenue that are used for replacing used-up capital goods and for buying new capital goods.

4   All economic majors must pay their dues in part by taking a course in intermediate

282 INTRODUCTION TO POLITICAL ECONOMY

macroeconomics. In such a course, if it is a thorough one, the principal critics of Keynes, as well as the post-Keynesians, will be given the necessary coverage.

5   The practices of the IMF, World Bank, and the WTO, have in recent years been given wide coverage in academic and popular presses, in other media, and from all points of view. Thus, one can easily add the details and perspectives we are necessarily ignoring here. For a sustained, readable, and highly critical analysis of the practices of the IMF and the World Bank (and of many other aspects of international capitalism), one should see: Korten 1996. Korten is a former professor at Harvard's Business School and was an official with a U.S. international development agency; his book has gotten wide attention.

Ch. 6: Social Class in American Capitalism

1   Dennis Gilbert, whose work we will discuss, reports that studies on children's attitudes about social class show that 3rd graders have begun to recognize different social classes, that 70% of 6th graders see about the same class alignments as their parents, and that most 12th graders will see such alignments the same as do their parents (Gilbert 1998, 116-7).

2   One reviewer of this essay, John Boylan, wrote us these wise words of warning about the narrow focus we were taking. "While economics and class structure play a signifi-cant role in the creation of culture, they must be factored in with a whole pattern of other elements....Individuals also develop their individual personalities from countless influences, forces, and circumstances, including, of course, class background, many of which they are only dimly aware....[We] live in [and are shaped by] a culture that is a tremendous ever-shifting web of words, images, rules, lies, taboos, prejudices, fears, hopes, and dreams. It pervades laws, norms, rules both stated and unspoken....[Once] you start examining it, it shifts, changes, camouflages itself, and envelopes the observer. I think of it as a huge tinker toy in which the pieces are constantly being reassembled ....We tend to understand it the same way that the blind men know the elephant by describing only the part of the animal that each is actually touching."

3   In addition to Vincente Navarro, mentioned in the text, two other scholars have been making these arguments for a long time. One, Leonard Sagan, covered much the same territory as Navarro in *The Health of Nations* (1987), particularly in Chapter 8 on "Mortality Gradients Among Social Classes." Another, Harvey Brenner, has for twenty years produced a long series of books and articles about the relationship between socio-economic variables and health, with a particular focus on unemployment.

4   Since 1990, structural changes in the U.S. economy, such as more and more people be-ing shoved into low-paying service jobs and—related to it—increasing income inequal-ity in the United States, have almost certainly increased the rigidity of class barriers. Thus, given these changes, our argument about the difficulty of upward mobility may ac-tually be understated.

5   In this research we based our conclusion on the most influential study of the time: Coleman and Rainwater 1978.

6   A good discussion of the theoretical complexities of looking at social mobility data is presented in Grimes and Morris 1997.

7   In our analysis we have dropped the last category of farm workers because they represent less than 3% of all workers, and because they are such a mix—ranging from migrant

workers to more highly paid workers in corporate farms—that their average circumstances do not give us useful information.

8 Concerning this 61%, how do these people arrange to stay in the social classes of their privileged parents? We have used the idea of "cultural capital" to provide an abstract, structural answer to the question. For much greater detail on this intriguing question, but one that is too broad to take up here in an adequate fashion, we think the best book is Domhoff 2002. Since 1967, when he wrote the first edition, Domhoff has studied the upper classes in the U.S., who they are, how they behave, and how they got there. We very highly recommend his work.

9 We should emphasize a point we mentioned briefly before, that all these barriers to upward mobility are greater for most women than for men with similar circumstances and in particular if they have children along the way. Tokarczyk and Fay 1993, a book we mentioned above, has a number of essays making this point, particularly the one by Donna Langston. Another book that focuses on the relatively greater barriers to upward mobility for black women is Benjamin 1997.

Ch. 7: John Kenneth Galbraith and the Theory of Social Balance

1 We have focused in this chapter on Galbraith's theory of social balance rather than on a larger slice of his work because we believe it is his most important contribution to modern social analysis.

2 This estimate was given by Sut Jhally, who narrates a documentary film, *Advertising and the End of the World*, by the Media Education Foundation. This film provides compelling evidence that Galbraith's 1958 theory of social balance was genuinely prophetic.

3 Some of Galbraith's critics have argued that he overestimated the power of the technostructure to direct the operations of the giant firms and that globalization has shifted some of its power to high-profile CEOs and, especially, investment banking firms. While no doubt there is merit to these criticisms, they are actually not particularly relevant to the theory of social balance. Suffice it say that the world economy is under the sway of giant firms, thoroughly committed to maximizing profits, and their effects on social balance are the same whether they are themselves dominated by owners, the technostructure, financial interests, or all three.

4 *The Anatomy of Power*, like so many of Galbraith's works, is highly recommended for those who seek to understand our economic order. We can only mention its argument in passing because to give it the credit its many insights merit we would need to go considerably beyond the limits of a short chapter. The bright side of this situation is that *The Anatomy of Power* is another of Galbraith's most clearly written books.

5 This newsletter is an exceptionally valuable resource for research on environmental pollution, and is written for the general public. Each issue lists ample source material for those interested in more information on a subject. The newsletter is typically referred to as *Rachel's*.

Ch. 8: U.S. Monopoly Capitalism: An Irrational System?

1 Baran and Sweezy's idea of surplus derives from Marx's idea of surplus value, but it is not the same. For example, Marx's measure of surplus value would not have included

all taxes, but taxes are a key component of Baran and Sweezy's definition of surplus. Baran and Sweezy's development of the idea of surplus was the first of many efforts by contemporary Marxists to refine the concept of surplus value.

2   For a more detailed explanation of this idea of the surplus as it relates to the aggregate economy, the best source is Wolff and Resnick 1987.

Ch. 9: The Middle Way: Swedish Social Democracy

1   Although Swedish economists were writing about and implementing stabilization policies at the same time Keynes was advocating them, these ideas came to be known as "Keynesian" policies because of the widespread influence of Keynes' masterwork, *The General Theory*.

2   The key point here is that if workers increase their productivity by 3%, this lowers firms' costs by 3%, since the same work force is now producing 3% more than before. Because firms' costs have decreased by 3%, firms can increase wages by as much as 3% without having to increase prices at all. Ultimately, wage increases only cause inflation if wages increase faster than productivity increases.

Ch. 10: The Mondragon Cooperative: A Path to Worker Democracy

1   There is a growing literature on the MCC because of its pioneering history and because of its recent rapid growth and the consequent changes in its governing structure. We have composed our description and analysis from a variety of sources, but readers wanting to dig deeper should visit the MCC website: www.mondragon.mcc (and in the text, we have cited this site as "MCC"). The information there is broadly informative and includes considerable detail we have excluded in order to keep this chapter from being too unwieldy. Because MCC has been experiencing its most rapid growth ever during the past decade, we have found its website to be the best source of information to help researchers from publishing findings that are quickly outdated. Additionally, the most informative short history of MCC is "The History of an Experience," accessible on its website in the "Who are we?" section.

Works Cited

Adams, Walter, and James Brock, eds. 1995. *The Structure of American Industry.* New York: Prentice-Hall, Inc.

Adams, Walter, and Hans Mueller. 1986. "The Steel Industry." *The Structure of American Industry.* Edited by Walter Adams and James Brock. New York: MacMillan Publishing Co.

Adler-Karlsson, Gunnar. 1970. *Reclaiming the Canadian Economy: A Swedish Approach Through Functional Socialism.* Toronto: Anansi.

Amott, Teresa. 1996. "Class." *A Dictionary of Cultural and Critical Theory.* Edited by Michael Payne, et al. Lewisburg, Penn.: Bucknell University Press.

Amsden, Alice H. 2002. "Gilded Age II," review of Kevin Phillips, *Wealth and Democracy. The Nation*, September 2.

Andrews, Edmund. 2001. "Bush Angers Europe by Eroding Pact on Warming." *New York Times*, April 1.

Arizmendiarrieta, Fr Jose Maria. 2002 "Special feature: Mondragon Cooperatives—Core Ideas from Mondragon's Founder." *Social Policy*, v32, n2: 10-11.

Ayres, C. E. 1944. *The Theory of Economic Progress.* Chapel Hill: The University of North Carolina Press.

Bakaikoa, Baleran et al. 2004. "Governance of the Mondragon Corporación Cooperativa." *Annals of Public and Cooperative Economics*, v75, n1: 61-87.

Baran, Paul, and Paul Sweezy. 1966. *Monopoly Capital: An Essay on the American Economic and Social Order.* New York: Monthly Review.

Bartlett, Donald, and James Steele. 1994. *America: Who Really Pays the Taxes?* New York: Simon and Schuster.

Benjamin, Lois, ed. 1997. *Black Women in the Academy.* Gainesville: University of Florida Press.

Bourdieu, Pierre. 1984. *Distinction: A Social Critique of the Judgment of Taste.* Cambridge, Mass.: Harvard University Press.

Bowden, Elbert, and Judith Bowden. 1995. *Economics: The Science of Common Sense.* 8th Edition. Cincinnati: Southwestern Publishing Company.

Bowles, Samuel et al. 2005. *Understanding Capitalism; Competition, Command, and Change* (Third Edition). New York: Oxford University Press.

Bradley, Keith and Alan Gelb. 1983. *Cooperation at Work: The Mondragon Experience.* London: Heinemann.

Braverman, Harry. 1974. *Labor and Monopoly Capital: The Degradation of Work in the Twentieth Century.* New York: Monthly Review.

Brown, Paul. 1998. "Greenhouse Effect Worse than Feared." *Manchester Guardian Weekly*, November 9.

Burros, Marian. 1999. "High Pesticide Levels Seen in U.S. Food." *New York Times*, February 19.

Canterbury, E. Ray. 1995. *The Literate Economist.* New York: Harper Collins College Publishers.

Cassidy, John. 1996. "The Decline of Economics." *The New Yorker*, December.

——. 1998a. "Rich Man, Richer Man." *The New Yorker*, May 11.

——. 1998b. "The New World Disorder." *The New Yorker*, October 22.

——. 1999. "No Satisfaction." *The New Yorker*, January 25.

Chandler, Alfred D., Jr. 1977. *Visible Hand.* Cambridge, Mass.: The Belknap Press of Harvard University Press.

Cheney, George. 2002. *Values at Work: Employee Participation Meets Market Pressure at Mondragon,* updated edition. Ithaca: Cornell University Press.

Cohen, Patricia. 2009. "Ivory Tower Unswayed by Crashing Economy?" *New York Times*, March 5.

Chernow, Ron. 1999. *Titan*. New York: Random House.

Childs, Marquis. 1936. *The Middle Way*. New Haven: Yale University Press.

Clamp, Christina A. 2000. "The Internationalization of Mondragon." *Annals of Public and Cooperative Economics*, v71, n4: 557-77.

Coleman, Richard, and Lee Rainwater. 1978. *Social Standing in the United States*. New York: Basic Books.

Collander, David, and Alfred W. Coates, eds. 1998. *The Spread of Economic Ideas*. New York: Cambridge University Press.

Cushman, John H. 1997. "U.S. Reshaping Cancer Strategy as Incidence in Children Rises." *New York Times*, September 29.

Dahrendorf, Ralf. 1979. *Life Chances*. Chicago: University of Chicago Press.

Davidmann, Manfred. 1996. "Co-operatives and Co-operation: Causes of Failure, Guidelines for Success." www.solbaram.org/articles/coops.html, January 26.

Davidmann, Manfred. 1996. "Mondragon Cooperatives." www.solbaram.org/articles/mondra.html, January 26.

Dews, C. L. B., and Carolyn Law. 1995. *This Fine Place So Far From Home: Voices of Academics from the Working Class*. Philadelphia: Temple University Press.

Dillard, Dudley. 1967. *The Economic Development of the North Atlantic Community*. Englewood Cliffs: Prentice-Hall.

Domhoff, G. William. 2002. *Who Rules America?* 4th Edition. New York: McGraw-Hill.

Dorfman, Joseph. 1961. *Thorstein Veblen and His America*. New York: August M. Kelly.

——. 1973. *Essays, Reviews, and Reports*. New York: August M. Kelly.

Dow, Gregory K. 2003. *Governing the Firm: Workers' Control in Theory and Practice*. New York: Cambridge University Press.

Du Boff, Richard, and Edward Herman. 2001. "Mergers, Concentration, and the Erosion of Democracy." *Monthly Review*, May.

Engels, Frederick. 1975. *Socialism: Utopian and Scientific.* Peking: Foreign Language Press.

Errasti, Anjel Mari, et al. 2003. "The Internationalisation of Cooperatives: The Case of the Mondragon Cooperative Corporation." *Annals of Public and Cooperative Economics,* v74, n4: 553-84.

Anthony Faiola, Ellen Nakashima and Jill Drew. 2008. "What Went Wrong?" *Washington Post,* October 15.

Financial Times Information. 2007. Europe Intelligence Wire Service, January 7.

Financial Times Information. 2007. Europe Intelligence Wire Service, March 7.

Financial Times Information Limited. Indian Express Online Media Ltd Source. 2006. A200611111-12ECB-GNW, November 10.

Nancy Folbre. 2009. "Workers of the World, Incorporate." *New York Times* Economix blog, November 16.

Frank, Robert. 2000. *Luxury Fever: Money and Happiness in an Era of Excess.* Princeton: Princeton University Press.

Fraser, Jill Andresky. 2001. *White-Collar Sweatshop: The Deterioration of Work and Its Rewards in Corporate America.* New York: Norton.

Friedman, Milton. 1963. *Capitalism and Freedom.* Chicago: University of Chicago Press.

——. (1976) *Adam Smith's Relevance for 1976.* Ottawa, IL: Green Hill Publishers for the International Institute for Economic Research.

Fussell, Paul. 1983. *Class.* New York: Ballantine.

Galbraith, John Kenneth. 1958. *The Affluent Society.* Boston: Houghton-Mifflin.

——. 1967. *The New Industrial State.* Boston: Houghton-Mifflin.

——. 1972. Introduction to *The Theory of the Leisure Class* by Thorstein Veblen. Boston: Houghton-Mifflin.

——. 1977. *The Age of Uncertainty.* Boston: Houghton-Mifflin.

——. 1982. *The Anatomy of Power.* Boston: Houghton-Mifflin.

——. 1987. *Economics in Perspective: A Critical Analysis.* Boston: Houghton-Mifflin.

——. 1998. *The Affluent Society.* Boston: Houghton-Mifflin.

Gallup Organization, Inc. 1999. *Giving and Volunteering in the United States.* Washington, D.C.: Gallup Organization.

Gerth, H. H., and C. Wright Mills, eds. 1946. *From Max Weber: Essays in Sociology.* New York: Oxford University Press.

Gilbert, Dennis. 1998, 2010. *The American Class Structure in An Age of Growing Inequality.* 5th Edition, 8th Edition. Belmont, Calif.: Wadsworth (5th); Pine Forge Press (8th).

Glahe, Fred A. (ed.) 1992. *Adam Smith's An Inquiry into the Nature and Causes of the Wealth of Nations: A Concordance.* Lanham, MD: Rowman and Littlefield.

Goode, Erica. 1999. "For Good Health, It Helps to be Rich and Important." *New York Times,* June 1.

Gordon, David. 1996a. *Fat and Mean: The Corporate Squeeze of Working Americans and the Myth of Managerial Downsizing.* New York: Free Press.

——. 1996b. "Underpaid Workers, Bloated Corporations: Two Pieces in the Puzzle of U.S. Economic Decline." *Dissent,* Vol. 43, Spring.

Grimes, Michael D., and Joan M. Morris. 1997. *Caught in the Middle: Contradictions in the Lives of Sociologists from Working-Class Backgrounds.* Westport, Conn.: Praeger.

Gruchy, Allan G. 1947. *Modern Economic Thought: The American Contribution.* New York: Prentice-Hall.

Gunn, Christopher. 2001. "Markets Against Economic Democracy." *Review of Radical Political Economics,* v32, n3. September: 448-60.

Hamilton, David. 1991. *Evolutionary Economics.* New Brunswick, New Jersey: Transaction.

Heilbroner, Robert. 1999. *The Worldly Philosophers.* New York: Touchstone Books.

Henwood, Doug. 1997. *Wall Street.* New York: Verso.

Herbert, Bob. 1997. *Bad Air Day. New York Times,* February 10.

Hertz, Tom. 2006. *Understanding Mobility in America.* www.amaricanprogress.org/kf/hertz_mobility_analysis.pdf.

Hollingshead, August, and Fredrick Redlich. 1957. *Social Class and Mental Illness: A Community Study.* New York: Wiley.

Hollander, Samuel (1987) *Classical Economics.* Oxford: Basil Blackwell.

Holt, Douglas. 1999. "Does Cultural Capital Structure American Consumption?" *Journal of Consumer Research*, June.

Huet, Tim. 1997. "Can Co-ops Go Global? Mondragon is Trying." *Dollars and Sense*, November/December.

Kadi, Joanna. 1996. *Thinking Class: Sketches from a Cultural Worker.* Boston: South End Press.

Karasek, Robert and Tores Theorell. 1990. *Healthy Work: Stress, Productivity, and the Reconstruction of Working Life.* New York: Basic Books.

Kasmir, Sharryn. 1996. *The Myth of Mondragon: Cooperatives, Politics, and Working-Class Life in a Basque Town.* Albany: State University of New York Press..

Keynes, John Maynard. 1933. *Essays in Biography.* New York: Harcourt-Brace.

——. 1936. *General Theory of Employment, Interest, and Money.* New York: Harcourt, Brace, and World.

——. 1963. *Essays in Biography.* New York: W. W. Norton and Co.

Kong, Delores. 1999. "Jobs Don't Kill People, But Stress in the Workplace Can." *Boston Globe*, August 30.

Korten, David. 1996. *When Corporations Rule the World.* West Hartford, Conn.: Kumerian Press.

Lerner, Max, ed. 1976. *Portable Veblen.* New York: Penguin Books.

Leonhardt, David. 2008, "Economix: Greenspan's Mea Culpa," *New York Times*, October 23.

Leonhardt, David, and Kathleen Kerwin. 1997. "Hey Kid, Buy This!" *Business Week*, June 30.

Lotti, Riccardo, Peter Mensing, and Davide Valenti. 2006. "A Cooperative Solution," *Strategy + Business*, July 17.

MacLeod, Greg. 1997. *From Mondragon to America: Experiments in Community Economic Development.* Sydney, N.S. University College of Cape Breton Press.

Mankiw, N. Gregory. *Essentials of Economics.* 4th edition. 2004. Cincinatti: Southwest Publishing Company.

Marx, Karl. 1967. *Capital.* Vol. 1. New York: International Publishers.

——. 1981. *Capital.* Vol. 2. New York: Vintage.

——. 1947 *Capital,* Vol. I, trans. Samuel Moore and Edward Aveling (eds.) New York: International Publishers.

Marx, Karl, and Frederick Engels. 1978. *The Marx-Engels Reader.* Edited by Robert Tucker. New York: Princeton University Press.

——. 1998. *The Communist Manifesto.* New York: Verso.

Mayer, Caroline E. 2000. "It's Becoming a Mad Ad World." *Manchester Guardian Weekly,* June 1-7.

Miller, Mike. 2002. "Special feature: Mondragon Cooperatives— Mondragon: Lessons for Our Times." *Social Policy,* v32, n2.

Miller, Roger Leroy. 1997. *Economics Today: The Micro View.* New York: McGraw-Hill.

Mills, C. Wright. 1962. *The Marxists.* New York: Dell.

Mirowski, John, and Catherine Ross. 1989. *Social Causes of Psychological Distress.* New York: deGruyter.

Mishel, Lawrence, Jared Bersnsein, and Sylivia Allegretto. 2005. *The State of Working America* 2004/2005. Ithaca: Cornell University Press.

Mondragon Corporación Cooperativave. (MCC). Website. www.mondragon-corporation.com.

Mondragon Corporación Cooperativave. 2010. "The MONDRAGON Co-operative Experiencie" (formerly, "The History of an Experience"). www.mondragon-corporation.com

Mossner, Ernest Campbell and Simpson Ross, Ian (eds.). 1987. *The Correspondence of Adam Smith,* the Glasgow Edition. Indianapolis: Liberty Press/Liberty Classics.

Myrdal, Gunnar. 1965. *The Political Element in the Development of Economic Theory.* Cambridge, Mass.: Harvard University Press.

Navarro, Vincente. 1991. "Class and Race: Life and Death Situations." *Monthly Review,* September.

Olsen, Gregg. 1999. "Half Empty or Half Full?" *Canadian Review of Sociology and Anthropology*, May.

Polanyi, Karl. 1944. *The Great Transformation*. New York: Farrar and Rinehart.

Porter, Glenn. 1973. *The Rise of Big Business*. Arlington Heights, Illinois: Harlan Davidson, Inc.

Rachel's Environmental and Health Weekly. Edited by Peter Montague. Annapolis, Maryland: Environmental Research Foundation.

Raphael, D. D. 1997. "A master for many schools." In D. D. Raphael, Donald Winch, and Lord Skidelsky, *Three Great Economists: Smith, Malthus, Keynes*, New York: Oxford University Press: 7-104.

Ratner, Sidney, James Soltow, and Richard Sylla. 1993. *The Evolution of the American Economy*. New York: MacMillan Publishing Co.

Recktenwald, Horst Claus. 1978. "An Adam Smith Renaissance 1976? The Bicentenary Output–A Reappraisal of his Scholarship," *The Journal of Economic Literature* 16(1) (March): 56-83.

Reich, Robert. 1999. "Galbraith in the New Gilded Age." *Between Friends: Perspectives on John Kenneth Galbraith*. Edited by Helen Sasson. Boston: Houghton-Mifflin.

Riddell, Tom, Jean Shackelford, and Steve Stamos. 1998. *Economics: A Tool for Critically Understanding Society*. 5th Edition. Boston: Addison-Wesley.

Rohlf, William. 1997. *Economic Reasoning*. 4th Edition. Reading, Mass.: Addison-Wesley.

Routh, Guy. 1977. *The Origin of Economic Ideas*. New York: Vintage Books.

——. 1986. *Unemployment: Economic Perspectives*. London: MacMillan.

Ryan, Jake, and Charles Sackrey. 1984. *Strangers in Paradise: Academics from the Working Class*. Boston: South End Press.

——. 1996. *Strangers in Paradise: Academics from the Working Class*. Rev. ed. New York: University Press of America.

Saive, Marie-Anne. 1980. "Mondragon: An Experiment with Co-operative Development in the Industrial Sector." *Annals of Public and Cooperative Economics*, v51, n3, September: 223-55.

Samuelson, Paul. 1964. *Economics: An Introductory Analysis.* 6th Edition. New York: McGraw-Hill.

____. 1980. *Economics: An Introductory Analysis.* 11th Edition. New York: McGraw-Hill.

Scherer, F. M. 1990. *Industrial Market Structure and Economic Performance.* Boston: Houghton-Mifflin.

Schor, Juliet. 1999. *The Overspent American.* New York: Basic Books.

Schultze, George. 2002. Special feature: Mondragon Cooperatives—Worker Ownership & Catholic Social Thought." *Social Policy,* v32, n2: 12-16.

Schumpeter, Joseph. 1954. *History of Economic Analysis.* New York: Oxford University Press.

——. 1949 "Science and Ideology," *The American Economic Review* 39(2), March: 345- 359.

Scott, Janny. 2005. "Life at the Top in America is Not Just Better, It's Longer." *The New York Times*, May 16.

Shaikh, Anwar, and Ahmet Tonak. 2000. "The Rise and Fall of the U.S. Welfare State." In *Political Economy and Contemporary Capitalism.* Edited by Ron Baiman, Heather Boushey, and Dawn Saunders. New York: M. E. Sharpe.

Shepherd, William. 1997. *The Economics of Industrial Organization.* Upper Saddle River, New Jersey: Prentice-Hall.

Silverman, Bertram. 1998. "The Rise and Fall of the Swedish Model." *Challenge,* Vol. 41, No.1.

Smith, Adam. 1763. "Early Draft of Part of *The Wealth of Nations.*" In Adam Smith, *Lectures on Jurisprudence,* Glasgow Edition, eds. R. L. Meek, D. D. Raphael and P.G. Stein. Indianapolis: Liberty Press/Liberty Classics, 1982: 562-581.

——. 1981. *An Inquiry into the Nature and Causes of the Wealth of Nations,* 2 Vols. Glasgow Edition, eds. R. H. Campbell and A. S. Skinner. Indianapolis: Liberty Press/Liberty Classics 1776.

——. 1982a. *Lectures on Jurisprudence,* Glasgow Edition, eds. R. L. Meek, D. D. Raphael and P. G. Stein. Indianapolis: Liberty Press/Liberty Classics (1762-1763 and 1766).

——. 1982b. *The Theory of Moral Sentiments*, Glasgow Edition, eds. D. D. Raphael and A.L. Macfie. Indianapolis: Liberty Press/Liberty Classics (1759).

Stanfield, James Ron. 1996. *John Kenneth Galbraith*. New York: St. Martin's Press.

Stigler, George J. 1977. In Ronald L. Meek, *Smith, Marx, & After: Ten Essays in the Development of Economic Thought*. London: Chapman and Hall.

Stiglitz, Joseph. 2002. "The Roaring Nineties." *Atlantic Monthly*, October.

Stockman, Alan. 1999. *Introduction to Economics*. 2nd Edition. Chicago: Dryden Press.

Stewart, Dugald. 1794. "Account of the Life and Writings of Adam Smith, LL.D." ed. I. S. Ross. In Adam Smith, *Essays on Philosophical Subjects*, Glasgow Edition, eds. W. P. D. Wightman and J. C. Bryce. Indianapolis: Liberty Press/Liberty Classics, 1982 (1795): 269-351.

Tabb, William K. 1999. *Reconstructing Political Economy*. New York: Routledge.

Taylor, P. L. 1994. "The Rhetorical Construction of Efficiency: Restructuring and Industrial Democracy in Mondragon, Spain." *Sociological Forum*, v9, n3: 459-489.

Taylor, P. L. 1997. "The Myth of Mondragon: Cooperatives, Politics, and Working-Class Life in a Basque Town (Review)." *American Anthropologist, New Series*, v99, n2, June: 433-434.

Thomas, Henk and Chris Logan. 1982. *Mondragon: An Economic Analysis*. London: George Allen & Unwin.

Tilman, Rick. 1993. *Veblen Treasury*. Armonk, New York: M. E. Sharpe.

Tokarczyk, Michelle, and Elizabeth Fay, eds. 1993. *Working Class Women in the Academy*. Amherst: University of Massachusetts Press.

Uchitelle, Louis. 1999. "Reviving the Economics of Fear: In Bad Times, Consumers Might Simply Refuse to Spend." *New York Times*, June 2.

University of Pennsylvania. 1997. *Almanac* . November 25.

Vanneman, Reeve, and Lynn Weber Cannon. 1983. *The American Perception of Class*. Philadelphia: Temple University Press.

Veblen, Thorstein. 1919. *The Place of Science in Modern Civilization.* New York: B. W. Huebsch.

——. 1973. *The Theory of the Leisure Class.* Boston: Houghton-Mifflin.

——. 1978. *The Theory of Business Enterprise.* New Brunswick, New Jersey: Transaction.

——. 1990. *Engineers and the Price System.* New Brunswick, New Jersey: Transaction.

——. 1997. *Absentee Ownership.* New Brunswick, New Jersey: Transaction.

——. 1998. *The Nature of the Peace.* New Brunswick, New Jersey: Transaction.

Weinstein, Michael. 1999. "Students Seek Reality Amid the Math of Economics." *New York Times,* September 18.

Whyte, William F. 1995. "Learning from the Mondragon Cooperative Experience." *Studies in Comparative International Development,* v30, n2, 58-67.

Whyte, Willam F. 1999. "The Mondragon Cooperatives in 1976 and 1998." *Industrial & Labor Relations Review,* v52, n3: 478-481.

Whyte, William Foote and Kathleen King Whyte. 1991. *Making Mondragon: The Growth and Dynamics of the Worker Cooperative Complex,* 2nd ed. Cornell University Press.

Winter, Greg. 2001. "Contaminated Food Makes Millions Ill Despite Advances." *New York Times,* March 18.

Wolff, Richard, and Stephen Resnick. 1987. *Economics: Marxian vs. Neoclassical.* Baltimore: Johns Hopkins University Press.

Yates, Jacquelyn. 2001. "Values at Work: Employee Participation Meets Market Pressure at Mondragon & Making Mondragon: The Growth and Dynamics of the Worker Cooperative Complex." (Review essay). *International Journal of Politics and Ethics,* March 22.

Young, Jeffrey T. 1997. *Economics as a Moral Science: The Political Economy of Adam Smith.* Cheltenham, UK: Edward Elgar.

Zinn, Howard. 2005. *A People's History of the United States.* New York: Harper/Collins.

Index

global warming (see climate change)
Gordon, David 203, 208-9
government 5-9, 15-18, 33-9, 41, 43,
    49, 54, 106, 108, 111, 114-21,
    124-31, 143-4, 146, 152, 168, 171-
    2, 176-7, 187-8, 192, 194-5, 200-3,
    210, 215-8, 221-43, 251
    and absorption of surplus 200
Great Recession 17, 106, 197
Great Transformation, The (Polanyi) 14
Green Student U 178
Greenspan, Alan 20-3

Hadley Centre for Climate Change
    181
health care 15, 17, 128, 146-7, 155,
    172-3, 214, 216, 219, 229-30, 238,
    243
*Healthy Work: Stress, Productivity, and
    the Reconstruction of Working Life*
    (Karasek and Theorell) 150
Hey Kid, Buy This! (Leonhart and
    Kerwin) 166
History of Economic Analysis
    (Schumpeter) 12
Hobson, John 112, 115
housing 57, 101, 218, 220, 229, 237-9
human capital 28, 38-9, 221, 238

industrial reserve army 72, 120
industrial sabotage 98-103, 192
inequality 17, 19, 22, 34, 57, 78, 95,
    103, 134, 142, 189, 266
inflation 125, 191, 222-3, 225, 227-
    8, 235
infrastructure ix, 27, 37-8, 127, 162,
    174-6
innovation 30, 32, 38-9, 44-5, 67-8,
    101, 192-3, 203, 250-1
Instinct of Workmanship (Veblen) 104,
    238
integration 220-1
International Monetary Fund (IMF)

129-30, 183
*Internationalization of Cooperatives,
    the: The Case of the Mondragón
    Cooperative Corporation* (Errasti)
    258, 265
Internationalization of Mondragón, The
    (Clamp) 265
invention 28, 29, 32, 38, 44, 45, 47,
    48; endogenous invention 29-32,
    38-9; exogenous invention 29-30,
    32, 38, 47, 276
invisible hand 41-3, 45, 48, 60, 86

job training 237

Keynes, John Maynard ix, 7, 11,
    17, 19, 21, 23, 40, 76, 77, 105-
    32, 161, 194, 196, 214, 243, 275,
    278-81, 283; and Bretton Woods
    107, 130; and economic methodol-
    ogy 122-3; and employment 119-
    21; and U.S. economy policy since
    123-9
Kong, Delores 151-2

Labor and Monopoly Capital
    (Braverman) 203, 211
labor theory of value 39-41, 49, 64-5
laissez-faire 25, 36, 39, 42-3, 48, 119,
    125-6, 129, 130, 169, 200, 233,
    278
leakages from the flow of income 116-
    8, 195-6
leisure class 84, 88-91, 104
Leonhardt, David 21
limited laissez-faire 25-6, 37, 40-3, 47-
    8, 275
liquidity trap 118-9
lumpenproletariat 74

mainstream economics vii, ix, 1-4, 8,
    10-12, 15-17, 19, 22, 41, 73, 76,
    86, 93, 104, 107, 131, 161-62,